New York Nouveau

Post 45 Loren Glass and Kate Marshall, Editors
Post•45 Group, Editorial Committee

New York Nouveau
How Postwar French Literature
Became American

Sara Kippur

Stanford University Press
Stanford, California

Stanford University Press
Stanford, California

© 2025 by Sara Kippur. All rights reserved.

No part of this book may be reproduced or transmitted in any form or by any means, electronic or mechanical, including photocopying and recording, or in any information storage or retrieval system, without the prior written permission of Stanford University Press.

Library of Congress Cataloging-in-Publication Data
Names: Kippur, Sara, author.
Title: New York nouveau : how postwar French literature became American / Sara Kippur.
Other titles: Post 45.
Description: Stanford, California : Stanford University Press, 2025. | Series: Post·45 | Includes bibliographical references and index.
Identifiers: LCCN 2024055059 (print) | LCCN 2024055060 (ebook) | ISBN 9781503642614 (cloth) | ISBN 9781503643086 (paperback) | ISBN 9781503643093 (ebook)
Subjects: LCSH: French literature—Publishing—New York (State)—New York—History. | French literature—Translations into English—History and criticism. | French literature—Appreciation—United States—History. | French literature—20th century—History and criticism.
Classification: LCC PQ143.U6 K57 2025 (print) | LCC PQ143.U6 (ebook) | DDC 840.9/3273—dc23/eng/20250129
LC record available at https://lccn.loc.gov/2024055059
LC ebook record available at https://lccn.loc.gov/2024055060

Cover design: Ann Weinstock

The authorized representative in the EU for product safety and compliance is: Mare Nostrum Group B.V. | Mauritskade 21D | 1091 GC Amsterdam | The Netherlands | Email address: gpsr@mare-nostrum.co.uk | KVK chamber of commerce number: 96249843

To my father

Contents

	Acknowledgments	ix
	Introduction	
	Projects for a Revolution in New York	1
	A New Literary History	
1	New York's New Writers	21
	Francophone Women and American Publishing in the 1940s	
2	Commissioned for the Screen	62
	French Avant-Garde Literature for American TV	
3	When France's New Novel Met the American Textbook	102
	French and the College Classroom	
4	Oulipian New York	129
	On Transatlantic Translators and Intimate Potentialities	
	Conclusion	
	New York and the Twenty-First-Century Global Francophone Novel	154
	Notes	167
	Index	203

Acknowledgments

GIVEN THAT THIS BOOK AIMS, among other things, to give credit to unsung collaborators and editors, it would hardly feel right to publish this one without doing my very best to recognize all the institutions, colleagues, and friends who offered me their support, advice, wisdom, and expertise.

Most of the research and writing I did for this book took place while I was on the faculty at Trinity College in Hartford. Trinity's generous institutional support, including a Charles A. Dana Research Associate Professorship and a Mid-Career Faculty Research Grant, enabled me to conduct archival research abroad and to devote invaluable time to writing. My colleagues in the Department of Language & Culture Studies were supportive interlocutors, many of whom read drafts of my work, asked engaged questions when I presented material in progress, and were patient and supportive as I learned the ropes as department chair. Thank you to all of my former LACS colleagues, especially Diana Aldrete, Carol Any, Julia Assaiante, Doyle Calhoun, Dario del Puppo, Martina di Florio, Jason Doerre, the late Johannes Evelein, Kifah Hanna, Rosario Hubert, Karen Humphreys, Anne Lambright, Priscilla Meléndez, and Blase Provitola. My thanks go to other Trinity colleagues, including Kathleen Kete for helping me to brainstorm the book project at different phases, to Chris Hager, Beth Notar, and David Rosen for their excellent feedback on drafts of my work, and to Sonia Cardenas for unwavering support from the Dean of Faculty's office.

I am grateful to all the archivists, librarians, and individuals who facilitated my access to archival materials. My thanks to Nicole Westerdahl and Amy McDonald at the Special Collections Research Center at Syracuse University; to Jocelyn K. Wilk and Michelle Margolis Chesner at Columbia University libraries; to Hélène Favard and Paul Ruellan of the Institut Mémoires de l'édition contemporaine; to Anne-Lise Depoil at the Bibliothèque Nationale de France at Richelieu; to Claire Lesage at the Bibliothèque de l'Arsenal in Paris; and to John Pollack of the Kislak Center for Special Collections at the University of Pennsylvania. I am especially grateful to Yvone Lenard and the late Wayne Rowe for their enthusiasm for my research project and for sharing documents and personal memories with me. I extend my gratitude as well to all of the estates and individuals who responded to my queries and graciously allowed me to include material in this book, including Catherine Benamou, Valerie Borchardt, Beverly Charpentier, James Fry, Irène Lindon, Catherine Robbe-Grillet, Jeannette Seaver, and Sylvia Richardson and Marianne Saluden of the Indivision Richardson Saluden, rights holders for Georges Perec.

Generous fellowships and grants provided me with the time, resources, and contacts to make crucial progress on my book. As a fellow at Wellesley's Suzy Newhouse Center for the Humanities in 2020–2021, I benefited immensely from the intellectual community of my cohort, especially at a time when in-person meetings weren't often possible. Thank you to Eve Zimmerman and Lauren Cote for coordinating a productive series of exchanges; to Codruța Morari for serving as a supremely thoughtful and astute respondent for one of my papers; to Larry Rosenwald, reader extraordinaire; and to my community of Zoom writing partners—Veronika Fuechtner, Irene Mata, and Mary Kate McGowan—who have kept me accountable to my writing progress, then and now. As a 2024 fellow at the Camargo Foundation in Cassis, France, I was lucky to finish this book in one of the most beautiful places on earth. Thank you to Julie Chénot, Zoé le Voyer, Sofia Malizia, and all the other staff at Camargo for providing the space for writing and reflection, and to my fellow residents and new friends—Gaven Dianda, Merve Fezjula, Rebecka Rutledge Fisher, Adèle Haenel, Stephanie Heit, Petra Kuppers, Tricia Postle,

VK Preston, Lara Tabet, and Eleanor Verrette—who cheered me on with their friendship and were always down to party.

I want to thank everyone who assisted me at various phases of my research and gave me opportunities to workshop portions of the manuscript in progress. Thank you to Wellesley's Maison Française, to Marc Bizer at the University of Texas, Austin, and to Peter Connor of the Barnard Center for Translation Studies at Reid Hall in Paris for their invitations to present my work. Engaged questions from colleagues and students always pushed my thinking further, and I appreciated having the chance to share my ideas at invited talks, as well as at several MLA, ACLA, and SHARP conferences. I could not have asked for more diligent and helpful undergraduate research assistants as I wrote this book. Seth Browner, Megan Caljouw, and Melani Norsigian at Trinity all helped me sift through a wealth of correspondence and other archival documents, and Julia Calventus and Suzana DeRosa-Farag at Wellesley located, organized, and synthesized old newspaper clippings. I very much appreciate the value placed on faculty-student collaboration at liberal arts colleges, and for as much as these students helped me, I also hope to have shared with them the exciting potential of literary research.

Many academic colleagues have provided encouragement and expertise as I developed this book. Thank you to my biography reading group and to my colleagues on the PMLA editorial board for their sustained interest in my work. Thank you to Julie Elsky for discussing all the ins and outs of French archives and permissions; to Alice Kaplan for introducing me to Yvone Lenard's work; and to Susan Suleiman, who has remained my closest ally and mentor even after graduate school. And thank you to my new colleagues in French, Francophone, and Italian Studies at Wellesley College—Daniela Bartalesi-Graf, Hélène Bilis, Jennifer Carr, Vinni Datta, Marie-Cécile Ganne-Schiermeier, Scott Gunther, Flavia Laviosa, Michelle Lee, and Sergio Parussa—whose generosity in welcoming me into their department has been astonishing.

For permission to republish portions of this book, I gratefully acknowledge the *Los Angeles Review of Books*, *Modern Language Notes*, and *PMLA*. Portions of Chapter 2 first appeared in "Reading Translation Otherwise: TV, Translation, and Lost Texts," *MLN* 136, no. 4 (September 2021): 886–906 (copyright © 2021 Johns Hopkins University Press) and in the May 2023 issue of *PMLA* (vol. 138, no. 3), published by the Modern Language Association of America and reprinted with permission. Parts of Chapter 3 and the Conclusion originally appeared in the May 2020 issue of *PMLA* (vol. 135, no. 3), published by the Modern Language Association of America, and in the *Los Angeles Review of Books* on February 2, 2018.

I hoped this book would find a home in Stanford University Press's Post45 series, and it's a thrill to have that aspiration realized. Thank you to Loren Glass and Kate Marshall, editors for Post45, for seeing that my book could fit in their series. I'm especially grateful to my editor Erica Wetter, who shepherded this project with thoughtfulness, enthusiasm, and transparency. Thank you to Caroline McKusick and Natalie Gabriela Rovero for keeping me organized and on task, to Jennifer Gordon for meticulous copyedits, and to the design and production team for their creative vision and beautiful work. I'm extremely thankful to the two anonymous readers whose thorough reports and spot-on suggestions made this a better book.

To my dear friends: thank you all for your patience, love, brilliance, and support. I could not have finished this book without you in my corner. Vanessa Bartram, Julia Boorstin, Greg Cohen, Laure Cohen, Kyra Fries, Tim Fries, Kerry-Ann Grant, Idit Klein, Jordan Namerow, Audrey Plonk, Michal Shein, Zandy Smith, and Julie Walsh saw me through to the finish line with enthusiastic questions, helpful brainstorming, and coffee breaks. Michael Grubb, Kevin Masse, Avi Patt, and Ivy Patt generously hosted me when I was commuting and always made me feel like I had a home away from home. Nicole Dudukovic and Brice Kuhl made me feel like my literary work has relevance even for scientists, and that my books will always have a place on their coffee table. I'm so grateful to Lida Maxwell for our Friday morning writing sessions and lunches, which always left me feeling smarter and more accomplished than I actually am. Lia Brozgal and Loren Wolfe have been my best readers, my fiercest advocates, and my most reliable sources for all advice, fashion included.

The support of my family, Kippurs and Lamberts both, allowed me to make progress on this book even in challenging times. Thank you to my sister Sabrina and to all my in-laws for their words of encouragement. My mother, Susan Kippur, became an avid reader of Marguerite Duras ever since my undergraduate days and always read with gusto any books I recommended to her; I am forever grateful for our deep, sustained conversations about literature.

This book is dedicated to my father, Stephen Kippur, whose career trajectory, from French history to New York publishing, could be said to have inspired it. His love of books, work ethic, and commitment to detailed research helped to make me the scholar I am today.

Josh Lambert read every single word of this book more times than seems reasonable to expect of any human. I am profoundly lucky to share a life and home with the most brilliant, generous, and insightful person I know. Thank you, Josh, for always being willing to workshop an idea, large or small, and for inspiring me to do my best work. Asher and Noemi, you are probably too young to remember a time when I was *not* working on this book. I am grateful for your perceptive questions, for your eagerness to understand what I'm working on, for your patient and loving support, and for our heated (and often hilarious) debates about book titles. This book might not be as exciting as a Broadway musical, but I hope you'll pick it up one day to learn about another side of New York cultural life.

Introduction
Projects for a Revolution in New York
A New Literary History

WHEN MARGUERITE DURAS published her novel *Le Ravissement de Lol V. Stein* (*The Ravishing of Lol Stein*) in 1964, Jacques Lacan famously hailed it as a work of extraordinary psychoanalytic acumen.[1] In the decades that followed, the novel became one of the "classics" of twentieth-century French literature. After selling over 9,000 copies in its first year in France, *The Ravishing of Lol Stein* went on to be translated into twenty languages and was taught in classrooms around the globe.[2] It has since inspired an extensive body of international scholarship that, following Lacan, emphasizes Duras's brilliant demonstration of the mechanisms of psychoanalysis, as well as her pressing interrogation of female subjectivity, trauma, and desire.[3] As Duras poignantly put it in an interview late in life, her Lol novel was poised to outlive its author by a hundred years.[4]

This is the narrative about Duras and *The Ravishing* that almost any scholar of twentieth-century French literature will know. Yet there is another side of *The Ravishing* that became apparent to me only when I happened upon some of its archival traces. In 2014, I was conducting research in the Grove Press special collections at Syracuse University for a very different project (one in which I was looking at books that had been recommended for the international literary Formentor Prize), when I came across some of Duras's personal papers that caught my attention. A letter from her American literary agent, Georges Borchardt, suggested that Duras had shown drafts of *The Ravishing* to Grove editors Barney Rosset and Richard Seaver well before the release of the French publication.[5]

In an effort to learn more about this pre-history of the novel, I visited the

Institut de Mémoires d'édition contemporaine (IMEC) in France, a historic, renovated abbey in Normandy where most of Duras's papers are housed, alongside an extensive collection of publishing archives and manuscripts by other influential writers and artists of the twentieth century. Scattered within Duras's massive folders of drafts and papers, we can see the cardstock paper on which she composed the French version of *The Ravishing* by hand. The pages are thick and heavy—almost like manila folders—and each one of them is stamped with the name of a different American publisher: MACMILLAN, RANDOM HOUSE, APPLETON-CENTURY-CROFTS, SCRIBNER, RINEHART & CO., PUTNAM, and so on. Most of the stamps reference big American trade publishers such as these, though some include more vague titles like "university presses miscellaneous," as if someone were compiling a list of possible venues for publication. When Duras was drafting the novel in 1962 and 1963, she had yet to set foot in the United States, nor had she been published in translation by any of the presses listed. A handful of her books had been translated into English and published by Grove—*The Square* (1959), *Moderato Cantabile* (1960), *Hiroshima mon amour* (1961), *Ten-Thirty on a Summer Night* (1962)— but Grove's name did not figure among the stamped markings. How and why did Duras come to write on these particular pages? What could it mean that a mid-century novelist firmly rooted in the world of French letters—a person who had just won the inaugural *Prix de Mai* literary prize in France and was referred to in the 1960s as "the leading woman novelist of France today, with Simone de Beauvoir"—drafted an entire French novel on manuscript pages that all invoke the American publishing industry?[6]

This book makes the broader case that material details such as these are not just incidental. Duras's manuscript indexes synecdochically a more capacious literary history about the role of American publishing in French literature of the postwar period. As this book will contend, some of the major literary movements that we associate with postwar French literature intersected in meaningful and transformative ways with the American publishing world. French writers were at the vanguard of postwar literary innovation, from the experimental minimalism of the New Novel, to the literary games of the Oulipo, to the existential angst in theater of the absurd. While many of the writers associated with these literary endeavors may have written primarily (though not exclusively) in French, they worked closely with American editors and translators, published actively with American presses, and often theorized transatlantic connections within the body of literary works themselves. Like the incongruous, fascinating manuscript pages that have been ignored in Duras scholarship (a subject that will be treated in more detail in Chapter 2), the prevailing critical tendency has been to overlook just how dramatically the New York publishing scene has shaped twentieth- and twenty-first-century French letters.

New York Nouveau aims to acknowledge, challenge, and rethink the relationship between French literary experimentalism and New York publishing in the postwar decades. My starting point, as the title of this Introduction makes plain, is Alain Robbe-Grillet's 1970 novel *Projet pour une révolution à New York*, a book that critics in France bemoaned as having very little to do either with revolutions *or* with New York. Where, they asked, was the spirit of social, cultural, and political revolt so present in the global imaginary since 1968? And what exactly was Robbe-Grillet's version of New York, where most of the action took place in apartments that could be anywhere, and with so few reference points that actually anchored the plot in the streets or neighborhoods of New York? In a full-page spread that *Le Monde* devoted to the novel in October 1970, reviews were decidedly mixed, but all critics agreed that Robbe-Grillet's New York bore little resemblance to the actual city. Its lack of local color gave it, for Jacqueline Piatier, the "seedy look of an imaginary or even symbolic city."[7] For the writer Pierre Bourgeade, this was an unforgivable version of New York, which "looked like New York as much as a building resembles a bowl of corn flakes."[8]

New York *was* indeed still a myth for Robbe-Grillet. When he started drafting *Projet pour une révolution à New York* in 1969, he had not yet started a teaching gig at NYU that would bring him to live in Manhattan every other year from 1972 to 1991. Given his relative unfamiliarity with New York, it is easy to forgive some of the casual mistakes he makes that any New Yorker would recognize, as in a reference to a subway at the "Madison Avenue station."[9] (There were not then, and are not now, any subways on Madison Avenue in New York.) The novel takes us on subways and down alleyways and into apartment buildings, where, as readers are accustomed to doing in most Robbe-Grillet novels, we shift between different narrative perspectives, much of which centers in this book around abandoned girls, lascivious men, and acts of violence. With its nonchalant depictions of sexual assault, where women are bound and trapped in a world of male fantasies, the book feels fairly unreadable—and certainly unteachable—today. In the years after it was published, though, the novel was widely read and reviewed, and feminist critics did important work to unpack its sado-erotic violence as deeply tied to masculine ideas of authorship.[10] Robbe-Grillet's novel still, however, begs an unanswered question: what exactly *did* New York mean to the French literary avant-garde in the 1960s and 1970s?

This book reclaims both the revolutionary spirit and the situatedness of New York as meaningful and relevant for postwar French literary history. Just as New York remains elusive in Robbe-Grillet's novel, literary criticism has not sufficiently accounted for the fact that the city presented new and unusual opportunities for twentieth-century French fiction beginning during World War II. I take Robbe-Grillet's title as a challenge to discover alternative histories of French literary and cultural productions that come into view when we attend to New York as a real and tangible site of inquiry. By this I'm referring less to New York as fictional setting—although that can matter—than to the city as a cultural locus for writers, editors, translators, and teachers of the postwar period to articulate edgy and experimental literary ideas through new publishing initiatives in French. Shifting the center of gravity from Paris to New York does not just suggest a re-historicization of Pascale Casanova's tentative observation that Paris was losing its literary dominance to anglophone city centers only at the end of the twentieth century.[11] It also brings into view unknown voices and literary figures, many of them women, whose contributions have not received proper credit, but who helped to foster a sense of new possibilities for twentieth-century writing in French. These untold histories, stitched together here through research in special collections and personal archives on both sides of the Atlantic, in Syracuse and Caen and Los Angeles and Philadelphia, as well as more obvious publishing centers like New York and Paris, served as the primary motivations for writing this book.

While *New York Nouveau* attends closely to writers who belong to what remains for many readers the canon of twentieth-century experimental French fiction—in addition to Marguerite Duras and Alain Robbe-Grillet, writers like Samuel Beckett, Eugène Ionesco, and Georges Perec—its critical methodology works to amplify the voices and labor of those who have been less visible, though no less relevant. One of the primary interventions of this book is to show how collaborations between French writers and American cultural agents with close ties to the publishing industry shaped works and literary movements that we have come to see as foundational in a French literary canon. By tracing the origin stories of a selection of projects, and by seeing how they were generated through collaboration and exchange—even in cases when only one person's name earns recognition on the cover page—this book contributes to the dismantling of rigid notions of canonicity, authorship, and national literature.

In what follows, I unpack the theoretical frameworks signaled in both the book and the Introduction's titles, from the idea of French literature's Americanness, to notions of literary revolution and experimentation, to the centrality of New York as a publishing center. These sections show how *New York Nouveau* intervenes methodologically to place scholarship on Franco-American cultural exchange into critical dialogue with important recent work in the fields of translation, book history, and cultural studies that, through attention to manuscripts and publishing realia, recover the impactful role of less studied figures. The experimental French literature of the mid-twentieth century that still inspires artists all over the world is no less French for being ineluctably connected to New York. In recognizing this, we gain a more nuanced sense of the global dynamics that undergirded French literature of the last century.

French Literature, Born in the U.S.A.

As every student of American history and *Hamilton* viewer knows well, France and the United States have a long, storied, and deeply enmeshed past as modern nations. From Thomas Jefferson's oft-cited quip that "every man has two countries, his own and France," to the Marquis de Lafayette's similarly expressed sentiment—"My heart has always been truly convinced that in serving the cause of America, I am fighting for the interests of France"—the late eighteenth-century revolutionary histories established a firm political and ideological connection between the two countries.[12] This sense of shared affinity extended from politics to literature and culture, and readers on both sides of the Atlantic were eager to learn more about the other nation.

In the salon culture of eighteenth-century Paris, the French-born American immigrant J. Hector St. John de Crèvecoeur became a celebrity figure when he published *Letters from an American Farmer* (1782), a volume of fictional correspondence about American society after the Revolution. French readers without a strong working knowledge of English were keen to hear a Frenchman's firsthand account of American cultural life, however fictional it was, and with the help of the *salonnière* Madame d'Houdetot and her literary circle, Crèvecoeur published a French translation of his *Letters* to much acclaim.[13] The early nineteenth century would see other such cultural ambassadors who traveled to the United States and reported back to French readers about their impressions of American culture and politics, from François-René de Chateaubriand's *Voyage en Amérique* (1826) to Alexis de Tocqueville's *Démocratie en Amérique* (1835). The formation in the mid-nineteenth century of an international book market for translation facilitated literary and cultural exchange across languages, especially in the wake of the 1885 Berne Convention that established regulations around copyright and authorized translations. By the end of World War I, "exporting French books abroad became one of the missions of French foreign policy," as Gisèle Sapiro has shown.[14] As American readers gravitated towards French writers like Alexandre Dumas, Honoré de Balzac, and Jules Verne, who were among the most widely translated and popular novelists worldwide in the nineteenth and twentieth centuries, readers in France witnessed an astounding rise in translations in the interwar period, particularly of American novelists like Dos Passos and Faulkner.[15] In the expansion of the publishing market after World War II, and in our current era of globalization, the number of translations between French and English has soared astronomically.

As this very brief and schematic sketch affirms, there are plenty of compelling reasons why scholars have attended to the history of Franco-American literary and cultural exchange. The extensive bibliography among intellectual historians and political theorists about shifting transatlantic sentiments and popular perceptions, particularly in the wake of Vichy and Cold War–era Americanization, is too vast to cite exhaustively.[16] Meanwhile, the old and enduring trope of "Americans in Paris" across cultural media—from Gershwin's 1928 eponymous musical rhapsody to Ta-Nehisi Coates's piercing essay on race and fear in *Between the World and Me* (2015), with hundreds of other examples in-between—continues to resonate, testifying to the historical reality and sustained idea that Paris offered a mecca for Americans seeking artistic, cultural, and personal freedom. The sheer number of recent books with "Americans in Paris" in the title speaks volumes to its staying power as a cultural symbol.[17] Literary scholars, journalists, and cultural historians have explored in great detail both the creative possibilities that Paris afforded American writers and intellectuals across the twentieth century, as well as, from a reverse angle, how the U.S. has figured in the French literary and cultural imaginary.[18] This line of thinking has led to a wealth of scholarship centered closely on questions of representation, intertextuality, and aesthetic influence between France and the United States. From Claude-Edmonde Magny's foundational *L'Âge du roman américain* (1948) through William Cloonan's more recent *Frères ennemis* (2018), scholars have attended to the ways that French writers have borrowed and adapted literary techniques from their American counterparts, and vice versa.[19]

This book harnesses this critical energy for Franco-American literary exchange and channels it through a close attention to publishing histories. Through a carefully curated set of examples, I show how literary texts written in French in the second half of the twentieth century were conceived and created with a keen eye to American publication. In some cases, this meant a rare opportunity for new francophone writers to encounter editors in New York willing to take a chance on them by publishing their first novels with American presses—in French no less. In other cases, this involved commissioned, collaborative projects that persuaded well-established French writers to try out new media forms expressly for American audiences. In still other cases French writers adopted formal and conceptual techniques that made their works seem strategically suitable for a U.S. translation market, in what Rebecca Walkowitz has called a kind of "born translated" novel characteristic of twenty-first-century global literature.[20] In all cases, we see how French literary production and experimentation were deeply imbricated in, and shaped by, U.S. cultural networks.

This overarching phenomenon that I am proposing, by which French literature "became" American, does not signal a definitive or categorical switch from one cultural positioning to another. It indicates rather the various processes and mechanisms through which postwar French literature emerged and shifted as a result of American cultural figures and contacts. These shifts began in the 1940s and accelerated in the wake of the Second World War, when massive changes in the American university and publishing industries gave French writers new opportunities to participate in literary and cultural projects in the United States. Transatlantic collaborations between writers and other cultural figures energized new avenues for French literature by expressly targeting a U.S.-based audience, and the projects that emerged from these encounters challenged the boundaries and assumptions about French cultural productions of those periods. A behind-the-scenes look at the conversations, ideas, and collaborative drafts that fueled such works offers a new way of understanding these transformative transatlantic exchanges. Tracing a cross-cultural narrative of these literary projects—one that programmatically attends to their material and genetic histories—shows us that even those works that seem most avant-garde, most unconcerned with commercial viability, were anchored in American publishing and university networks that aimed to attract large audiences. In other words, the centrifugal force of the American literary field had a lot to say about what French works were created, and even which ones became commercial successes back in France.

Throughout this book, I insist on the multidirectional nature of these networks, tracing narratives from France to the United States and back again. While most of the French-language projects that I discuss were published, aired, or distributed *in* the U.S., their creation had reverberations back in France too—whether that was through their eventual adaptation for a French readership, in their reception histories, or in the ways that they shifted the direction and nature of French writers' subsequent works. This critical perspective adopts a "French global" disciplinary approach, as articulated by Christie McDonald and Susan Suleiman, and builds on recent scholarship attentive specifically to the ways that American institutions have interacted with and promoted French culture.[21] François Cusset's *French Theory* has been especially important in this regard, showing how the category of "French theory" was born on American university campuses in the 1960s and 1970s, a product of "creative misunderstandings" that took place when French philosophical thought was translated—both literally and culturally—into an American context.[22] Cusset dates the precise "birth" of French theory to a 1966 Johns Hopkins conference that gathered together some of France's most prominent thinkers—Roland Barthes, Jacques Derrida, and Jacques Lacan among them—who began to develop what would later be known as poststructuralism. The invention of French theory as a unified construct involved a process of "uprooting and reassembling," whereby ideas and texts by Derrida, Michel Foucault, Jean-François Lyotard, and other French philosophers came into contact with editorial, linguistic, and pedagogical norms in the U.S. that pushed towards legibility, quotability, and comprehensive paratexts aiming to clarify material.[23] A rigorous philosophical discipline in France became a far more amorphous (and less sophisticated) category called "theory" in America, a cultural mistranslation and rebranding that not only decontextualized and distorted the meaning of highly complicated texts, but was mobilized in the American academy, as Cusset details, for various ideological and political ends that further disconnected the source material from its application in a U.S. context.[24]

We should understand the rise of French theory as one prong in a larger operation through which American cultural institutions reshaped French literary and cultural productions. *New York Nouveau* in that respect develops Cusset's work in two important ways: first, through a comparative literary practice that, echoing David Damrosch's "mode of reading" world literature across cultures, attends both to the circulation of texts in a U.S. context and to its cross-cultural aftereffects in France; and second, by establishing a literary pre-history that contextualizes the conditions in which French theory emerged.[25] Literary texts largely fall outside the scope of *French Theory*—with the exception of moments when Cusset suggests that some French writers are read in the U.S. as illustrations of French theory—but they reveal important parallels with and precursors to the rise of French theory in the United States. As we'll see, American publishing houses and universities during World War II and in the postwar period initiated opportunities, well before the Johns Hopkins conference, that were essential for opening up a space for French theorists and writers alike. A publishing landscape in which French literature held particular cultural capital, and in which American editors and professors cultivated a curious readership, allowed for the invention not just of "theory" as a category but of innovative literary endeavors.

In this focus on literary collaboration, *New York Nouveau* participates in a growing body of scholarship attentive to the instrumental role of editors, publishers, and other cultural agents—"committed mediators," as Gisèle

Sapiro calls them—in the literary marketplace.[26] Book historians and sociologists have long reminded us of the institutional conditions that enable and foster literary production, while literary scholars have increasingly attended to the ways that editors and agents shape reading practices.[27] Jordan S. Carroll credits editors at City Lights Books, Grove Press, *Playboy*, and elsewhere with sparking America's sexual revolution, and Loren Glass dials in on Barney Rosset and Richard Seaver at Grove as "siphon[ing]" European cultural capital to New York and, through cheap paperback editions, inspiring university students and mainstream readers to read avant-garde writers and playwrights in translation.[28] Meanwhile, Mark McGurl's groundbreaking work *The Program Era* does not just show how creative writing programs "transformed the conditions under which American literature is produced"; it also offers compelling case studies of celebrated editors whose developmental edits and attentiveness to market demands transformed the literary legacy of American writers.[29] The recent scholarship of Dan Sinykin, Laura McGrath, Kinohi Nishikawa, and other literary scholars continues to demonstrate the critical relevance and instrumental role of editors, literary agencies, and publishing houses in shaping literary taste in the U.S., particularly in the postwar period.[30]

This book widens the lens to show how editors and other cultural agents in the U.S. played pivotal roles in reshaping French literature, too. Alice Kaplan credits the publisher Blanche Knopf's strategic marketing strategy of Albert Camus's *The Stranger* in 1946 as the reason why existentialist thought became wildly popular, particularly among American students.[31] The idea that committed mediators—in the form of literary agencies, rights agents, scouts, and translators—could function as taste-shapers informs many recent works about Franco-American cultural exchange, from Cécile Cottenet's *Literary Agents in the Transatlantic Book Trade: American Fiction, French Rights, and the Hoffman Agency* (2017), to Laurence Cossu-Beaumont's *Deux agents littéraires dans le siècle américain: William et Jenny Bradley, passeurs culturels transatlantiques* (2023), to Laura Claridge's *The Lady with the Borzoi: Blanche Knopf, Literary Tastemaker Extraordinaire* (2016).[32]

New York Nouveau follows in this scholarly lineage, but as a cultural history firmly grounded in literary studies, it situates close textual readings alongside archival documents to show how the conditions of production informed writing practices themselves. This book looks particularly at projects that originated in a U.S. context by virtue of cultural contacts. By considering a writer's manuscripts, editorial notes, and correspondence, we can see just how much the "work of revision," to borrow Hannah Sullivan's phrase about modernist anglophone writers, was a collective enterprise that informed publishing practices in the second half of the twentieth century.[33] Through collaborations with U.S.-based partners, French-speaking writers devised innovative projects, often in ways that transformed their subsequent literary practices. The sheer volume, financial power, and cultural capital of the U.S. publishing industry were enormous draws for writers abroad, and this laid the groundwork for greater aesthetic experimentation. American publishing opportunities led many francophone writers to pursue new and unprecedented projects that could not have existed otherwise, or in any other cultural context. The work of this book is to illuminate how these projects came to exist, from the germ of an idea, across unpublished and translated drafts, through to a finished project that circulated across languages and cultures.

Writing the *Nouveau*: Between (Literary) Revolutions and Commercialism

The opportunity for francophone writers to develop and publish works in the U.S. prompted various literary, political, and social innovations. The case studies throughout this book aim to capture the revolutionary spirit and stakes of these opportunities—whether that was in the emergence of a new class of women writers that altered who and what could get published, in the liberatory potential of addressing a new audience that freed up writers to explore questions of race and gender for the first time in their works, or in the expansion of new media, particularly in the realm of television, that could invigorate literary modes in new ways. In that sense, the revolutionary projects that we will encounter have different aims and outcomes but cohere in their impulse to chafe at conventions and challenge formal and social codes.

Many of the literary figures discussed in this book self-identified as experimental writers and translators who adhered to avant-garde literary movements with distinct principles for breaking with conventions. Georges Perec was one of the earliest members of the Oulipo group, an interdisciplinary mix of writers, mathematicians, and pataphysicians, who sought to liberate language through imposed formal constraints. The "great mission" of the Oulipo, as François Le Lionnais articulated it when co-founding the group in 1960, was "to open new possibilities unknown to older writers."[34] The Oulipo members followed through on that aim with seemingly impossible literary challenges, yielding such formally inventive books in French as Perec's *La disparition* (*A Void*), a 300-page novel written as a lipogrammatic experiment without the letter "e"—a book that nonetheless manages to remain entirely coherent while brilliantly complex.

Alain Robbe-Grillet, another example, professed himself the leader of the "Nouveau Roman" or "New Novel," a literary movement that began in the 1950s and that captured the literary energies of dozens of other novelists. In his foundational manifesto, Robbe-Grillet took aim at literary critics and writers who instrumentalized literature as political action and privileged realist modes or conventionalized storytelling; his vision for a renewed "art for art's sake" model involved a radical destruction of characters, narrative, and temporality that one finds across New Novelists' works.[35] Meanwhile, as innovators of what became known as the "theater of the absurd," Eugène Ionesco and Samuel Beckett revolutionized mid-century drama in plays that subverted theatrical conventions around language and communication and exposed the incomprehensibility of human behavior.[36] All of these movements sprouted up in France in the second half of the twentieth century, and despite important aesthetic differences, overlapped in their self-conscious attempt to radically destabilize the boundaries of form and the limits of meaning.

One of the main dynamics that I explore is how this experimental drive, with its emphasis on aesthetic innovation, intersected with commercial pressures to produce works that might appeal directly to American audiences—a dynamic that recalls Pierre Bourdieu's discussion of the literary field as a perpetual source of tension between "art-as-commodity" and "art-as-pure-signification."[37] In taking on commissions from U.S. publishers and academics, French writers walked a tightrope between maintaining rigid aesthetic principles and acceding to market demands. By exploring this tricky balance for postwar French writers, *New York Nouveau* contributes to contemporary debates, particularly in Anglo-American scholarship, about the interconnections between commercialism and literariness. Merve Emre's *Paraliterary* suggests that postwar American institutions—government bodies, universities, publishers, and so on—were all in some ways responsible for producing reading practices organized around ideals of public communication, cultural diplomacy, and international relations.[38] The risk of literature, as Emre shows throughout, is its inability to remain independent from market forces and escape the push to commercialize it as a product.[39]

Lawrence Rainey dated this dynamic even earlier, as intrinsic to the modernist literary project. Countering a prevalent critical tendency to see modernism as contemptuous of mass culture, Rainey posits that "modernism, among other things, is a strategy whereby the work of art invites and solicits its commodification."[40] Rainey sees Anglo-American modernism and commodity culture as "fraternal rivals," whereby publishing institutions and literary patronage—think of Sylvia Beach and Adrienne Monnier's *Shakespeare & Co.*, as one example—serve as reminders that works by James Joyce, Ezra Pound, and others were deeply embedded in capitalist practices.[41] The creation of limited editions, the practice of collecting, and the commitment to investing publishing resources in avant-garde writers prove, for Rainey, just how much modernism was imbricated with commercialism right from the start.

This argument aligns quite closely with Andreas Huyssen's general point that both modernism and postmodernism operate dynamically and dialectically with mass culture, both in the United States and Europe. His assessment of Theodor Adorno's engagement with U.S. culture offers an instructive parallel: where Adorno's experiences in the U.S. convinced him that American cultural institutions, and their prioritization of the profit motive, were ultimately antithetical to the production of real art, Huyssen recognized a more synergistic interplay between cultural forces. As he put it, "The possibilities for experimental meshing and mixing of mass culture and modernism seemed promising and produced some of the most successful and ambitious art and literature of the 1970s."[42] Huyssen saw American culture as a laboratory for exploring the ways that commercial pressures and high art necessarily came into contact—not inevitably as oppositional forces, but as dynamic and fluid. His case studies draw largely from German film, television, and the theater, but offer productive comparisons for postwar French cultural works in the United States. As many of the chapters in this book contend through different lenses, it is precisely by addressing head-on the tension between commercialism and experimentalism that French writers uncovered new literary forms and methods.

This perspective offers a counterpoint to Kristin Ross's *Fast Cars, Clean Bodies*, which takes as its object of inquiry the cultural landscape of France and the U.S. in the 1950s and early 1960s and examines the ways that French writers grappled with the threat of rapid Americanization in the postwar era. Ross demonstrates how the parallel historical realities of American cultural hegemony and decolonization worked in tandem to produce and enforce racial exclusions and capitalist modernization, and she takes to task those writers and intellectuals whose works seemed to deny historical contingencies, and who prized evenness, timelessness, hygiene, smoothness, and related tropes at the expense of all that might have been uncomfortable or "other." This is why Ross so vehemently critiqued the projects of the New Novel, the Annales school, and structuralism as hiding "under the auspices of scientific rigor rather than those of history" and as "complicitous with the workings of capitalist modernization, in part because of its avant-gardist refusal or dismantling of historical narrative."[43]

Ross makes a case for turning to artists and writers that embrace historicity and realist modes—people like Georges Perec (his earlier texts, at least), Simone de Beauvoir, or Jacques Tati—as a way of learning about the lived experiences of people at a critical moment when American culture loomed so large in the French imaginary and made direct and tangible changes in everyday life in France. Ross reads through objects themselves—refrigerators, cars, televisions—whose textual and cinematic presence testify to the reality of Americanization in France. Objects signal the values that accompanied the U.S. push towards capitalist modernization: a tendency to efface messiness and prize hygiene, a willingness to gloss over ambiguity, a steadfast denial of historical and structural inequities. Ross reads the New Novel, in that context, as derivative of both decolonization and the postwar American mindset: Robbe-Grillet's focus on surface over metaphor—what Ross calls his "cleansing of literary language"—aligns with the cultural prizing of hygiene and cleanliness (think of American kitchens and advertisements for cleaning products) over the "dirtiness" of a rising immigrant population.[44]

In this forceful and sharp condemnation of mid-century novelists, Ross nonetheless misses an opportunity to see behind the surface of things: that is, experimental literary movements like the New Novel, with their resistance to realist modes, nonetheless reveal, both textually and paratextually, anxieties about commercial culture and modernization that complicate how we read and integrate those texts. Ross is absolutely right to point out the connection between novels in the 1950s and 1960s and their alignment with capitalist forces, without fully reconciling how realism as a genre is perhaps maximally capturable by commercial interests. The publishing and genetic histories of many texts by Robbe-Grillet, Beckett, Duras, Ionesco, and others demonstrate, in fascinating ways, how experimental writing negotiated underlying ambivalences about the conditions of their production, and in so doing offered responses of their own to the challenges for avant-garde writers of working within and against market dictates. *New York Nouveau* brings to light these stories and shows how the fact of writing for a U.S. reading public enabled French writers to reaffirm the value of experimental, non-realist literary works.

In one of the only references to "revolution" in Robbe-Grillet's *Projet*, one of the characters makes this casual response in defense of a text he had written to report a crime:

> "This time I must say you're the one who's exaggerating! Especially since no one has ever claimed that the narrative was being made by an American. Don't forget that it is always foreigners who prepare the revolution. Now where was I?"

> "Cette fois-là, je trouve que c'est vous qui exagérez! D'autant plus que personne n'a jamais prétendu que le récit était fait par un Américain. N'oubliez pas que ce sont toujours les étrangers qui préparent la révolution. Où en étais-je?"[45]

Robbe-Grillet was notorious for moments like this of metanarrative reflection, and though a crime report is not the same thing as a novel—except, perhaps, in Robbe-Grillet's unconventional literary universe—the character almost winks knowingly at this dynamic of literary revolution and foreign publication that I have been outlining. The revolutionary nature of the literary projects in this book takes various forms, but, as we will see, all speak to the ways that a "foreigner" might be particularly well-positioned to spark innovation *and* meet commercial demands.

On New York and the Literary Projects It Spawned

New York City has long held considerable sway in the French cultural imaginary. Paul Morand praised "the great city" in 1930 as "the sole refuge from intolerance," a place that has the electric energy of most modern cities, but "New York is at least madness that is worthwhile."[46] In her *America Day by Day*, Simone de Beauvoir waxed lyrical as she described her delight in walking through legendary places like Broadway and Times Square: "New York is here; everything is real. Truth bursts in the blue sky, in the soft damp air, more triumphant than the night's unreliable charms."[47] Meanwhile, her companion Jean-Paul Sartre, who had traveled to the U.S. a year earlier, saw in the topography of Manhattan a physical embodiment of the puzzling American paradox between individualism and conformism.

> Seen flat on the ground from the point of length and width, New York is the most conformist city in the world. From Washington Square north, there is not a single oblique or curving street. . . . These are the avenues, which are intersected by hundreds of smaller furrows rigorously perpendicular to them. . . . But if you look up, everything changes. Seen in its height, New York is the triumph of individualism. The tops of the buildings defy all the rules of town planning.[48]

If for Sartre the topography of New York reflected the spatial equivalent of Americans' "freedom in conformism," for Nathalie Sarraute it was an opportunity to see the world anew. As she described it in a private letter to her husband Raymond Sarraute in 1964, "everything is fabulous. The view from the top of the Empire State Building was in this respect the great shock of a lifetime. I learned from it the beauty of architectural art of the future, and I saw the most beautiful sight in the world."[49] A year later, Hélène Cixous would travel to New York as a Fulbright Scholar, but for decades would be unable to write about those places that haunted and enchanted her—"les endroits à envoûtement de Manhattan"—as if the acronym of the place itself, NY, the French negation N'Y—not there—long served as an injunction against the act of writing about it.[50]

Jean Baudrillard, Michel Butor, Louis-Ferdinand Céline, Saint-John Perse, Léopold Sédar Senghor, Georges Simenon—the list could go on and on of francophone novelists, poets, and intellectuals who have memorialized New York. In their works, New York figures as a setting for real or fictional experiences, a place, as Jean-Philippe Mathy has shown, at once revered and reviled in the French literary imagination.[51] My interest in New York stems less from these descriptions than from the city as a locus of significant institutional change that gave French writers greater access to new literary opportunities. The rapid expansion of trade publishing, the growth of the college textbook business, the rise of television: these were all burgeoning industries in the postwar period that were centered squarely in New York City. As the cases that I highlight throughout this book show, New York became a critical site where French writers came into contact with book publishers, television producers, professors, students, and translators—all of whom changed the direction of French literature in meaningful ways.

Each chapter in this book centers on a different literary or cultural project, extending from World War II and the immediate postwar period through the early twenty-first century. In all cases, we find instances of cross-cultural collaborations that yielded innovative works across genres, including novels, television, textbooks, and films. The first chapter anchors this study during the Second World War, when publishing in France was severely hampered by paper shortages and political censorship. All of a sudden, the New York publishing industry saw an opportunity for expansion and global influence—and not just for English-language books. As this chapter shows, French editors capitalized on this moment to pave the way for new literary works, particularly by women for whom French was not their native tongue. While most literary histories of French exiles during the period have centered on established literary men who made New York their temporary home—writers such as André Breton, André Maurois, or Jacques Maritain—this chapter uncovers the voices of lesser-known, first-time women writers who envisioned themselves as cultural mediators at a moment of political turmoil and crisis. I attend most closely to one of these women, Consuelo de Saint Exupéry, a native of El Salvador and wife of the famed pilot, whose 1945 novel *Oppède*—about an artists' community in southern France—offers a counterpoint to masculinist historical narratives and, in so doing, imagines a new space for women writers and artists. As a literary project, *Oppède* and other books of the period show how the New York publishing industry was in a financial and cultural position to take risks and expand opportunities for writers at a pivotal historical moment.

As New York became the center of the expanding television industry in the 1950s, writers and editors began experimenting with new connections between text and screen. The second chapter explores Grove Press's experimental television projects in the early 1960s that relied on French writers to develop new screenplay ideas. One such screenplay was Marguerite Duras's early version of *The Ravishing of Lol Stein*, the one written on thick paper marked with American publishers' logos, which she wrote first for television before converting it into the novel we know today. That project, along with other screenplays developed by Samuel Beckett, Eugène Ionesco, and Alain Robbe-Grillet, were commissioned by Grove's emergent subsidiary, "Evergreen Theater, Inc.," to air on Dick Powell's hit network TV show, *Four Star Playhouse*. This chapter examines the curious intersection between avant-gardist and popular cultural forms and argues that New York's television opportunities transformed the literary projects of many of France's most innovative writers and playwrights of the time. In its methodological approach, this chapter also makes a case for reading aesthetically radical works somewhat against the grain, as documents that can self-consciously grapple with their referentiality and rootedness in New York and that issue commentaries on race, gender, and other social concerns of the mid-twentieth century. Many of these screenplays have never been seen or read before; translated into English and abandoned in Grove's archives after funding dried up, none except Beckett's *Film* ever reached the production phase. Read collectively, the screenplays offer a fascinating set of responses for how French experimentalism adapted and responded to changing visual technologies.

The third chapter turns to another influential cultural phenomenon anchored in New York: the wildly successful market for college textbooks in the wake of the GI Bill and subsequent baby boom. Between the late 1950s and early 1990s, college textbook publishing expanded from an $84 million industry, to one that grossed $2 billion annually.[52] This growth of the college market meant not only that original and translated works of French literature could be pitched and sold to American college students; it also curiously catalyzed original works of French fiction by avant-garde writers. This chapter demonstrates that American college students of beginner and intermediate French language had a hand in making the French *nouveau roman* (New Novel) more commercially viable as a genre. Looking first at Ionesco's beginner-language textbook *Mise en train*, which he co-authored in 1969 with Michel Benamou, I take a deep dive into the making and marketing of *Le rendez-vous*, an intermediate French-language textbook co-written by Yvone Lenard, a textbook author and instructor of French in the U.S., and Alain Robbe-Grillet, once he *was* finally living and teaching in New York. The chapter recovers Lenard's story and integral role in shaping the project, after her name was removed from the cover when Robbe-Grillet published the book in France. What was most *nouveau* about this project was how the invisible labor of a woman—one who had her finger on the pulse of American students and trends in language pedagogy—could lead to the commercial success of the New Novel on both sides of the Atlantic.

Chapter 4 sustains a reflection on experimental literary practices but shifts the focus from editors and professors to translators. It makes the case that the Oulipo, the literary group established in 1960 and that remains active today, can help us understand how the experimentalism of French literary productions in the postwar decades was predicated on intimate social practices between French writers and American cultural figures, particularly translators. An acronym for Ouvroir de Littérature Potentielle (Workshop for Potential Literature), the Oulipo thrives on the idea of "potentiality"—what is habitually understood in terms of the possibility of expanding the boundaries of literary practices through imposed formal constraints, much like in Perec's lipogram. This chapter proposes a rethinking of Oulipian ideas through what I term "intimate potentialities," a concept I trace through Georges Perec's mutual translations with his close friend and fellow Oulipian, the American writer Harry Mathews. The chapter weaves together their archival documents about translation and the textual and audiovisual project *Récits d'Ellis Island* (1980), a film Perec made and wrote with Robert Bober, and whose American version was translated by Mathews. The quintessential gateway to America, Ellis Island drew Perec's interest as a relic in ruins, and he traveled to New York City several times in the late 1970s to tour the site and conduct interviews with immigrants who had made New York their home. The chapter reads the two-part film, with its auditory and visual traces of Perec, as a model of intimate potentialities that Perec and Mathews had been developing together throughout the 1970s. Though less obviously formally innovative than some of Perec's other works, *Récits d'Ellis Island* registers an idea of translation as crucially embedded in the Oulipian project—a point that I emphasize through Perec's private journals from that period, through his and Mathews's correspondence and shared practice of translation, and through comparative readings of a more recent New York–centered Oulipian text, Hervé Le Tellier's Goncourt-winning novel, *L'anomalie* (2020).

Across all of these chapters, we see instances of how literary experimentalism drew energy from collaboration and cross-cultural exchange over the second half of the twentieth century. These case studies are exemplary of a spirit of transatlantic partnership and of a literary ecosystem in which writers benefited from close contacts in the American university and publishing worlds. To be clear, this phenomenon far exceeds the set of examples I trace in this book. As in any curatorial process, my case studies cannot be exhaustive, but they point to other examples that could be understood within a new framework that recognizes just how much French letters in the second half of the twentieth century were entangled with U.S. publishers, translators, and university networks.[53] This broader tendency, as I develop in the Conclusion, has led in the early years of the twenty-first century to a number of contemporary francophone novels that obsessively probe the stakes of global publishing and its rootedness in New York.

The Conclusion takes stock of this wider trend and looks closely at several prizewinning international bestsellers of recent years that point to New York publishing and university networks as an enduring material, symbolic, and aesthetic influence on French fiction. To what extent should we be concerned that the global francophone novel of the twenty-first century has become so thoroughly American that it has lost its critical edge? The Conclusion takes up this question and shows how the revised literary history proposed in this book equips us to be more informed readers of the present and future.

New York's New Writers
Francophone Women and American Publishing in the 1940s

> Well now, a French book, published in America at this time ... what type of readers would be interested in that kind of book? Will it reach a large audience?
>
> —PAULE D'ONCIN, *Plympton House* (1943)[1]

AS THE REALITY OF THE COVID-19 pandemic set in, my research plans in 2020 shifted from archive visits to extensive interlibrary loan requests. I was, at that time, in the earliest phases of research for this chapter, which had the general scope of examining the role of New York–based cultural institutions (publishing houses, magazines, newspapers, radio shows, etc.) in representing French literature during World War II. But without access to publishing archives or personal papers, I shifted course and ordered any French literary works I could find on WorldCat that had been published in the early 1940s. I was astonished to discover just how many books—hundreds!—had been originally written in French and published in New York City between 1940 and 1945, and I set out to read all of them.

One book whose author had caught my attention turned out to be particularly hard to track down. That book, titled *Oppède*, was by Consuelo de Saint Exupéry—wife and widow to Antoine, the famed pilot and author of *The Little Prince*—and it had been published by Brentano's Books in New York in 1945. Every time I ordered the book, though, despite carefully specifying the publication details, I was sent an alternate version: sometimes the reprint that Gallimard issued in 1947, sometimes the English translation, *Kingdom of the Rocks*, released by Random House in 1946, but not the original French version from Brentano's. It took nearly six months to get ahold of the 1945 version, but the wait for the copy sent to me was well worth it. I opened the package to discover an old book whose delicate spine and fraying pages suggested that it should have been housed in special collections rather than in circulation from Western Connecticut State College's library. The inside of the book confirmed that impression even more: the personal dedication note from Consuelo on the title page revealed that this copy had been a gift to Varian Fry. As I carefully leafed through the book, I had firsthand access to Fry's reading experience of *Oppède*, with his handwritten commentaries and notations in the margins throughout.

Consuelo de Saint Exupéry's novel exuberantly narrates the daily travails of members of an artists' community that was, in fact, established in the town of Oppède, outside of Marseille, in late 1940 and that welcomed artists, writers, and foreigners in need of safety who sought to continue their artistic and cultural pursuits during the early years of the war. The material paratexts of this edition were illuminating: while Consuelo's signed dedication implicitly recognized Fry's pivotal role in helping her secure safe passage to the United States in 1942 through his work for the Emergency Rescue Committee ("To Varian Fry, this book waiting for doors to be opened for it, with my friendship"; "À Varian Fry, ce livre qui attend qu'on lui ouvre la porte, avec mon amitié," Figure 1), his notes throughout emphatically challenge her memory and the factual accuracy of the events she narrates.

The jarring discrepancy between Consuelo de Saint Exupéry's appreciation for Fry and his private dismissal of her work in marginal notes indexes what I have come to understand as a stunning and pervasive erasure of francophone women's writing during the war period. Literary histories of French publishing during the war tend to fall into two categories. On the one hand, they rightly emphasize the dramatic reduction in French books, a result of Vichy censorship, repressive pressures, and supply shortages, and that led, in France, to clandestine publishing networks.[2] On the other hand, they recognize the works of writers in exile whose geographical displacement in cities like New York, Mexico City, Montreal, Rio de Janeiro, or Buenos Aires enabled them to continue writing and publishing with relative security.[3] While historically sound, the predominance of these two narratives about French wartime publications—what we could call the "book shortage" or "famed writers in exile" frameworks—has nonetheless obscured an alternative strand

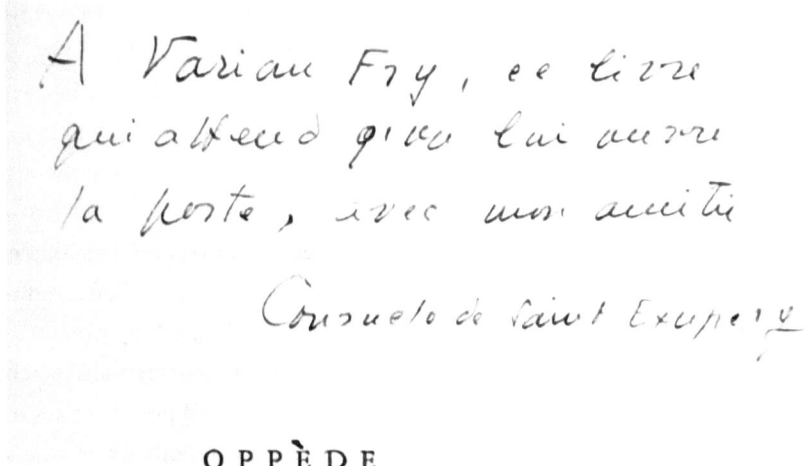

OPPÈDE

Figure 1: Consuelo de Saint Exupéry's *Oppède* (1945), signed copy for Varian Fry, illustration by Consuelo de Saint Exupéry

of this literary history: namely, the remarkable number of French books published in New York in the early 1940s by first-time women writers. The publishing record encourages us to take a closer look at who and what was being published in French during the war, and why so many of these books, despite the financial and cultural investment of publishers, have largely been forgotten. As this chapter will suggest, Fry's private engagement with Saint Exupéry's novel is indicative of what Joanna Russ has identified as a widespread tendency throughout the anglophone publishing world to "suppress women's writing," a perspective that may help to explain the erasure of these works from our collective memory.[4]

A closer look at the women publishing in French in the early 1940s reveals a number of shared characteristics between them. Many of these writers, including Consuelo de Saint Exupéry (1901–1979), who was born and raised in El Salvador, were native speakers of languages other than French. This included many American-born anglophone authors, such as Tryphosa Bates-Batcheller (1876–1952), a concert singer from Massachusetts, who wrote several books in English in the early twentieth century before authoring two books in French during the war; Florence Conrad (1918–2012), a francophile and philanthropist who organized the Rochambelles unit of all-women ambulance volunteers that assisted on the Western Front; Margaret Hughes (1894–1980), a volunteer in a German P.O.W. camp who kept detailed notes about her experiences during the early years of the war; and Helen Mackay (1876–1961), an American-born poet who eventually settled in France and wrote mainly in French. All of these women published books with Brentano's in the 1940s in which they testify to their personal involvement in various wartime initiatives. Their books function in that sense as historical documents about France in the Second World War and the possibilities for French-speaking women to participate in the war effort. At the same time, many of these texts also reach beyond historical events and experiment with fictional and poetic modes of storytelling. In so doing, they imagine new, idealized visions for women's roles that seem to exceed social contingencies.

This outpouring of women's voices in wartime books could not have emerged without a broader network of publishers, journalists, and translators who paved the way for francophone writing in New York. To trace this literary history and understand the stakes of a diversifying set of publishing opportunities in New York, this chapter begins with the context of French wartime publishing, when material, social, and political constraints determined who and what could be printed. It then turns to the literary market in New York, both to demonstrate how American publishers sought to attract an audience of avid readers during the 1940s, and to challenge widely held perceptions that French publishing in New York mainly served to sustain established writers in exile who needed a temporary venue for their work. This broader framework helps to situate my focus on presses and editors, most notably Robert Tenger at Brentano's Books, whose literary vision and support of francophone women writers have gone unacknowledged in histories of wartime publishing.

By spotlighting several of these texts, with particular emphasis on Consuelo de Saint Exupéry's *Oppède*, this chapter suggests that American publishing houses offered a space for francophone women writers to reimagine themselves in the wake of war. If American book publishers learned during the war that they could "shape the minds" of readers through their editorial choices, as John Hench has argued, then Tenger's list demonstrates a profoundly innovative commitment to seeing women as foundational in rebuilding a sense of community after the war.[5] Expanding upon Hench's exploration of the political stakes of wartime publishing, this chapter shows how French-language books positioned women writers as figures of cultural diplomacy. This precedent and model lay the groundwork for the next several decades, during which the U.S. publishing industry did not just support French-language writers on publishing lists but intervened in critical ways to shape new and experimental forms of writing in the second half of the twentieth century.

Wartime Publishing in France

The chances of succeeding as a woman writer in France before World War II were slim. As Susan Suleiman put it describing Irène Némirovsky's exceptionally unusual rise to literary fame in the 1930s: "While French publishers were always on the lookout for new talent and were starting to exploit the publicity methods familiar today ... their eye for such promotion almost never fell on a woman."[6] A woman in France had never won the Prix Goncourt—or for that matter, the right to vote—until 1944, when Charles de Gaulle's provisional government granted women's suffrage, and 1945, when Elsa Triolet's novel *Le premier accroc coûte deux cent francs* was awarded the coveted literary prize.[7]

While there were exceptions like Némirovsky, Triolet, and most notably Colette, women who sought to publish literary works in France in the first half of the twentieth century needed to contend with rampant prejudices about the quality of women's writing. Scholars like Jennifer Milligan and Angela Kershaw have called attention to the misogyny that permeated the French publishing industry in the interwar years.[8] It was not uncommon, for instance, to see women's writing described as "having a bad reputation," as revered writer and critic Paul Nizan put it in his 1937 article "Littérature féminine," attributing such a reputation to writing that had "a lot of emotion; an invincible taste for lyrical chattering; loose ideas, passions, and style; [and] a tendency to disclose the adventures of one's private life with a shamelessness rarely found with men."[9] Nizan voiced these ideas with exceptions like Edith Thomas and Henriette Valet in mind, whose works held the promise of greater "modesty" and "force," but his words nonetheless bespoke a masculine literary tradition, in which the markers for literary achievement could be determined by adherence to values established by and for men. It is telling, for instance, that when in 1934 the journal *Toute l'édition* published a list of the 100 best books of all time, it included only one authored by a woman: Madame de Sévigné's *Lettres*.¹⁰

In one sense, the Occupation in France altered the tendencies of the publishing industry from the interwar period. Repressive new measures and German-imposed censorship vastly reshaped the publishing landscape in the early years of the war, both in terms of the personnel authorized to publish books and the content of the books themselves. The establishment of the *Propaganda-Abteilung* under German leadership expressly censored Jewish affiliations, political dissent, and anti-German sentiment in all realms of cultural life, and the infamous "Bernard" and "Otto" lists of 1940 enabled the seizure and censorship of hundreds of thousands of books.[11]

Publishers responded to the increasingly repressive measures in varying ways, as Gisèle Sapiro has extensively detailed, with presses like Grasset, Denoël, and Gallimard (under Pierre Drieu la Rochelle's new leadership) more willing to collaborate with the German occupier. Regardless of the political stance of a press, *any* book printed or reprinted during the Occupation needed to secure a "publication visa" to authenticate its strict adherence to newly articulated goals of moral unity and national defense.[12] Censorship oriented new reading practices, as Jacques Cantier has shown; bookstores and publishers alike were mobilized to promote books that glorified German culture, that expressed pro-Vichy and pro-Pétain sentiment, and that exemplified moral rectitude.[13] Strangely enough, book culture boomed in the early years of the Occupation. Readers were just as eager to read about current events and the recent *défaite* as they were to distract themselves with adventure novels and police thrillers that could pull them away from the reality of daily life.[14] What Cantier has called a national "soif de lecture" ("thirst for reading") defined the early years of the war, revealing a fascinating paradox by which a collective surge in reading went hand in hand with a reduction in the subject matter and variety of books in circulation.[15]

One factor that remained largely *consistent* in French book publishing between the interwar and wartime years was the number and role of women in the literary field. Gallimard's illustrious council of readers who evaluated manuscript submissions remained exclusively male; even as the council underwent other changes during the war—such as the removal of Jews or the inclusion of a younger generation of writers like Albert Camus and Maurice

Blanchot—it remained closed to women.[16] Most national book prizes (the Goncourt, the Renaudot, the Prix de l'Académie française) continued to be awarded throughout the war, and Cantier interprets the temporary wartime suspension of the all-female jury for the Prix Femina as an explanation for why "committees only awarded prizes to male writers. The powerful and original women's voices that were emerging then—Simone de Beauvoir, Marguerite Duras, Dominique Rolin, Maria le Hardouin—remained outside of the award system" ("les jurys n'ont distingué que des hommes écrivains. Les voix féminines puissantes et originales qui s'affirment alors—Simone de Beauvoir, Marguerite Duras, Dominique Rolin, Maria Le Hardouin—restent à l'écart des récompenses").[17] While Cantier might say more to lament this purported acceptance of gender bias in all-male juries—the Femina jury, for instance, has since its inception in 1904 awarded books in fairly equal measure to both men and women—his observation supports the writer Edith Thomas's pointed description of France in 1943 as fundamentally "a Gallic nation and thus misogynous" ("un pays gaulois et donc misogyne").[18]

While largely marginalized from publishing in wartime France, a few literary women—including Thomas—were able to break through the barriers and publish, in some cases for the first time, even if their books did not earn the recognition that comes with literary prizes. Both Simone de Beauvoir and Marguerite Duras published their debut novels during the Occupation—Beauvoir's *L'Invitée* with Gallimard (1943) and Duras's *Les impudents* with Plon (1943). The Russian émigré and Jewish writer Elsa Triolet was, in a fabulous irony, one of the collaborationist publisher Denoël's three bestselling authors in the early 1940s, alongside the antisemitic writers Lucien Rebatet and Louis-Ferdinand Céline; how her books *Mille regrets* and *Le Cheval blanc* managed to slip past the collaborationist authorities until 1943—when the French Gestapo ordered her arrest and Triolet escaped to the free zone with her fellow communist sympathizer and husband Louis Aragon—remains a mystery.[19]

At the same time as these mainstream French publishing houses were continuing to publish books despite limited means and resources, the clandestine publisher Éditions de Minuit emerged as the literary voice of the Resistance, in no small part due to the labor of several women. Founded by the writers Pierre de Lescure and Jean Bruller (better known under his pseudonym

Vercors, author of *Le silence de la mer*), the Éditions de Minuit published over forty books between 1942 and 1944, all of which had the express goal of "affirming the resistance of the French spirit against Nazi control" ("affirmer la résistance de l'esprit français à l'emprise nazie").[20] Yvonne Paraf, a childhood friend of Vercors later known under her *nom de guerre* Mme Desvignes, was a crucial founding member who printed Minuit books from her home, traveled between the Occupied and free zones to transport information (between Jean Paulhan, Paul Benda, and others), and both acquired and translated Steinbeck's novel *The Moon Is Down* for the Minuit imprint (*Nuits noires*, 1944). As Jacques Debû-Bridel detailed in 1945, in his firsthand account of the press, Mme Desvignes and other women had an integral role in the production and distribution of underground literary works; as unsuspicious "elegant and seductive young Parisians" ("jeunes Parisiennes élégantes et pimpantes"), women could circulate freely by metro or bike, delivering books across the city, and they could help in the creation and binding of books from the privacy of their homes.[21] Among the Minuit books published during the Occupation, two were by women, both of whom were active members of the French Resistance and previously published authors: Triolet's *Les Amants d'Avignon* in 1943, which would become one of the stories incorporated in her Goncourt-winning book *Le premier accroc coûte deux cents francs*, and Thomas's *Contes d'Auxois* about the daily travails of ordinary citizens living in occupied France, published pseudonymously in 1944.[22] Perhaps unsurprisingly given their largely marginalized roles, it was through concealed identities, by looking unsuspicious and working in enclosed and private spaces, that women could most easily participate in literary production in wartime France.

John Hench's study shows how a massive shift in global publishing took place during World War II that aligned the book industry with the American war effort, empowering publishers to promote the idea of "books as weapons." The Éditions de Minuit, in France, does not figure in his book, but it proclaimed such a goal explicitly: "More than ever, all clandestine publications must become combat weapons" ("Plus que jamais, toutes les publications clandestines doivent devenir des armes de combat").[23] In France, such an endeavor could happen only on a small scale, given the limited access to supplies and dangers of publication. American publishers, however, swooped in to capitalize on this opportunity, seeing potential to expand their global reach by compensating for a shrinkage in European publishing output. Echoing the publisher W. W. Norton, President Roosevelt put into circulation the idea that "books are weapons in the war of ideas," and American government officials and publishers worked closely to circulate books that could counter Nazi propaganda and win over readers across the globe.[24] Such an effort worked financially and politically, Hench shows, both because it implemented more frugal models of publishing and because it motivated book publishers to see themselves as mission-critical in the business of shaping minds.[25] American publishers experimented with producing books in other global languages, primarily French and German, that could ideally not just reach foreign audiences but influence their political positions. The U.S. government provided funds for book translations, helped to establish Overseas Editions, Inc. for disseminating books internationally, and especially supported those books that telegraphed themes of Americans as "well-informed, well-intentioned, progressive, and not standardized."[26] The close collaboration between U.S. military efforts and U.S. publishers represented an astonishing moment of cultural diplomacy where books took center stage as a powerful political tool, and where publishers could reasonably position themselves as key players in a new world order.

This is the context in which to understand the emergence of new francophone publishing ventures in New York during the war. Publishers were not just motivated to support the literary projects of writers in exile or reach the growing francophone communities of readers in New York; they were instrumental cultural diplomats, empowered politically and financially to publish books with a visionary scope. The next section takes a closer look at this critical moment in which New York offered new possibilities for French-language publishers in the war years and how it ultimately allowed one publishing house in particular to center the voices of francophone women whose stories were largely absent in wartime France.

Book Publishing in the 1940s: Why New York?

In many ways, New York was a natural home for francophone book publishing at the dawn of World War II. Though virtually no original books in French had been published before on U.S. soil, New York was awash in French literature, with a substantial body of readers eager to consume works in French. One index of that readership, at the beginning of 1938, was the *New York Times*'s commissioning of Charles Cestre, a French professor of American literature at the Sorbonne, to write a column first called "The Literary Scene in Paris," and meaningfully changed to "The Literary Scene in France" shortly after the June 1940 armistice that put the capital city into the hands of the German forces. The columns—over fifty in all—appeared every two to three weeks, from March 1938 until June 1941, and offered American readers a snapshot of the latest releases and trends in French literature coming out of presses like Plon, Denoël, or Albin Michel. Cestre sometimes reviewed a single title alone but more often discussed several books at once, attentive both to their literary quality and to their contemporary political and social relevance, particularly as the realities of war began to sink in. "If the war lasts," Cestre mused in a review on January 21, 1940, "there is little probability that a large quantity of war literature will be issued."[27] For Cestre, war was transient, while literature—"concerned with permanent reality"—was transcendent, and readers, he said, should expect "the renown of French literature" to be maintained "even in a troubled world." Cestre's belle-lettrist claims might seem simplistic and naïve today, but the mere existence of his frequent columns, along with their tone, tell us something about his audience of American readers: this was a group sufficiently interested and well-versed in the vagaries of French literature as to merit a bi-monthly *New York Times* column about works that, for the most part, were not readily accessible on U.S. soil, let alone available in English translation.

Cestre's columns abruptly came to an end on June 28, 1941, and in its place arrived a new column, "New Books in French in America," by the journalist and translator Katherine Woods. Her first piece in August of that year surveyed recent books published by the new Éditions de la Maison Française, founded by Isaac Molho and Vitalis Crespin in New York during the war, and Brentano's Books, whose origins dated back to the nineteenth century. These two presses, along with another publisher to emerge in New York in the war, Éditions Didier, published hundreds of original works in French during World War II.[28] The shift from Cestre's to Woods's columns marked a practical publishing reality: the center of French publishing during the war period had shifted from France to New York, where an avid group of readers—Americans and French exiles alike—eagerly awaited access to the latest books in French.[29] New York, in that sense, siphoned the cultural prestige of French letters and became the de facto replacement for Paris at a time when France could not maintain its pre-war publishing agenda.

That publishing history—in which, for a few brief years, New York served as a global center for original literary works in French—provides critical context for situating the emergence of new francophone writers in the war. In the face of a rapid decline in book imports, publishers were presented with a singular opportunity to respond to a market of over 350,000 native French speakers in the U.S. around 1940.[30] That audience, combined with publishing incentives from the U.S. government to prepare books to send abroad to France and North Africa that could boost America's image in the eyes of French readers, fueled dramatic growth in the French-language publishing industry.[31]

The combination of those twin factors—the local and the global francophone literary communities—complicates a common narrative that French-language publishing primarily was by and for a select group of French literati in exile in New York. Historians and literary scholars have carefully detailed the critical interventions of French exiles living in New York during the war period, whose cultural productions sustained their sense of intellectual continuity and community.[32] From André Breton's Surrealist magazine *VVV*, to Claude Lévi-Strauss's early structuralist writings, to literary works by Jacques Maritain, André Maurois, Denis de Rougemont, and Antoine de Saint Exupéry, New York was awash in celebrated authors and intellectuals who had fled France and found temporary refuge in the United States. Colin Nettelbeck calls them "standard authors of the exile"—those who, unable to continue publishing in Vichy France, actively pursued their writing careers and found (and in some cases, founded) American magazines and publishing houses willing to support their literary endeavors in French.[33] The same was true for publishers, such as the Franco-Jewish émigré Jacques Schiffrin, another New York exile who worked tirelessly during the war to continue publishing books by his close friend André Gide, and who eventually became a major publisher of French works at the new Pantheon Press.[34] The historical record that captures this moment of French wartime publishing in New York sustains what we could call a masculine literary history of this period—one that centers the distinguished, Gallimard-associated literary celebrity figures who made New York a temporary home during the war, for varying reasons related to their politics and religion.

Attending to this largely masculine literary history has for the most part enabled scholars to show that important intellectual work was taking place in New York among French exiles. The emergence of what Emmanuelle Loyer calls "French political literature of exile" ("littérature politique française de l'exil") demonstrated how New York–based writers and intellectuals articulated their political positions about Vichy, de Gaulle, Pétain, and *la défaite* across cultural media.[35] By establishing the Éditions de la Maison Française in 1941, Molho and Crespin had the express goal of publishing books by well-known writers and journalists who actively engaged with France's political upheaval; from André Maurois and Saint Exupéry ("known for being close to Vichy"; "réputés proches de Vichy") to anti-Pétainists like Jacques Maritain, to Henri de Kérillis ("fiercely Gaullist before becoming as fiercely anti-Gaullist"; "furieusement gaulliste avant de devenir tout aussi furieusement antigaulliste"), the press remained committed to publishing works across the political spectrum.[36]

In differentiating the Éditions de la Maison Française (EMF) from the two other French-language presses in New York, Loyer notes the relative paucity of Didier's overall number of books (roughly 20 in all, versus 120 at EMF) and the fact that Brentano's books were comparatively "prestigious" but "geared towards a more limited public" ("prestigieux" but "destinés à un public plus limité").[37] All of the examples of books that Loyer cites are by male authors (Pierre Mendès France at Didier; and at Brentano's, André Breton, Saint-John Perse, André Maurois, Maurice Dekobra, Pierre Lazareff, Denis de Rougemont, Philippe Barrès, and Alexandre Koyré), with the single exception of Rachel Bespaloff's *De l'Iliade* (Brentano's, 1943), a scholarly work by a Jewish Ukrainian French philosopher. It makes financial and political sense that presses—and especially new presses—would publish books by well-known writers and intellectuals, and that scholars would subsequently attend most closely to those works. At the same time, this sampling of titles perpetuates the impression that the only, or only important, francophone publications happening during the war were by fairly established figures, which does not bear out in fact. As Antoine Bon's bibliographic data of the period shows, hundreds of French-language books were published in the Americas between 1940 and 1944, in city centers ranging from New York to Montreal to Rio de Janeiro to Buenos Aires, and many of them were contemporary literary works by lesser-known writers.[38] Bon's list is certainly not exhaustive—and it does not account for books published in early 1945—but it does offer a glimpse into the *new* francophone writers that came into view during the war.

In parallel, then, with a group of writers who had already gained literary renown in France but who could temporarily not be published there (Breton, Maritain, Maurois, etc.) emerged another set of writers who owed their literary existence in the French language to the American publishing scene. Though many of these writers remain unknown today, their collective emergence helpfully underscores a dynamic shift in publishing culture that would extend beyond the war years. The financial support for French literature gave publishers the freedom to experiment and encouraged the discovery of new voices and texts. This commitment to experimentation—and to publishing a diverse, unconventional, and unusual set of voices in the literary sphere—augured a turn in the following decades towards other unprecedented and innovative publishing practices.

Brentano's Books: Robert Tenger and New Women Writers

Brentano's Books, as I have been suggesting, was the key player in this story of new writers. Their willingness to take greater publishing risks owed at least in part to their longer history of publishing a wide range of books. Originally established as an independent bookstore, Brentano's had a long and complicated past. Its founder, the Austrian immigrant August Brentano, arrived in New York in 1851 "with no money and no friends, but he had energy and imagination."[39] Brentano had worked in the newspaper business in Europe, and his idea was to sell international periodicals and books from abroad in America. He founded the first Brentano's location in Manhattan in 1853—originally just a little newsstand on the corner of Broadway and Houston that he dubbed Brentano's Literary Emporium—and the family business grew rapidly over the next few decades, with multiple locations in New York, as well as branches in Chicago, Washington, DC, Philadelphia, Boston, Pittsburgh, Cleveland, London, and Paris.

Brentano's billed itself as an international institution, and the stores were a natural home to exile communities looking for fellowship and camaraderie, as well as for news and reading material in languages other than English. Brentano's recognized its place in the market as a site of linguistic exchange, and in the late nineteenth century began a publishing branch of the business, with books largely devoted to instructional texts about language and culture for travelers and students. Dictionaries, phrase books, grammar manuals, and tourist guides dominated their publishing list in the early years of the twentieth century, with a select number of works translated from foreign languages including French, German, and Italian. They also published literary, theatrical, and political works, in English, by notable writers including George Bernard Shaw, Eugène Brieux, and Margaret Sanger. Their willingness to take on risky projects—such as printing Sanger's controversial texts on birth control, including *Woman and the New Race* (1920) and *What Every Boy and Girl Should Know* (1927)—reflected both the company's progressive, cosmopolitan ethos and its financial solvency. On the eve of the Great Depression, Brentano's reported to the American Bookseller Association annual earnings of over 3 million dollars.[40] But between the devastating economic downturn, and a perhaps over-zealous expansion of their chain, Brentano's was forced to file bankruptcy in 1933. Members of the Brentano family stayed connected to branches of the bookstore that remained open in cities like New York and Chicago even after the company was acquired by external parties, but the publishing wing of the company stuttered to a halt.

That changed with the start of World War II. All of a sudden, in late 1940, the Brentano's publishing business picked up again—but this time, the vast majority of the books were not in English but in French. Between 1940 and 1945, Brentano's published nearly 200 books in French under the editorial direction of Robert Tenger, a lawyer-turned-publisher who left France at the start of the war. Some of the books were reprints of classics, such as Victor Hugo's *Poésies choisies* or Arthur Rimbaud's *Oeuvres complètes*. Several other books were written by the coterie of recognized writers, journalists, and intellectuals living in exile in New York—such as André Maurois, Pierre Lazareff, and Denis de Rougemont, as referenced earlier. The 1942 publication of Rougemont's *La part du diable*, for instance, was reportedly such a celebratory event among the exile community that Marcel Duchamp, André Breton, and Kurt Seligmann created an elaborate Surrealist window display at Brentano's to commemorate it.[41] Yet the most surprising feature of Brentano's list was the remarkable number of books published in French that were written by women largely unknown in the literary community, many of whom were publishing books for the first time and, in many cases, not in their native tongue.

The publication of these women writers marked a diversification of French authorship, through which women from different linguistic and cultural backgrounds made a case for themselves as cross-cultural mediators in a changing political landscape. In fictional and non-fictional texts alike, the Brentano's list relied on a slate of new voices eager to express their affiliations with France. One of Brentano's earliest wartime texts, Margaret Hughes's memoir *Les lauriers sont coupés* (1941), recounts an American woman's involvement as a volunteer during France's "phony war." Hughes was forty-six years old when the war broke out and when she decided to leave New York City and join a volunteer war relief unit in France. She kept nearly daily journal entries from April to September 1940 that detailed the political intensity of France's defeat as Hughes and fellow volunteers of the *American Friends of France* worked to evacuate cities under German attack. The memoir that she published the following year maintains the journal structure in straightforward, unadorned prose. Despite modest aims—"*I deliver these notes to readers as I wrote them.... They are full of imperfections, the faithful report of an American woman*" ("*Je livre ces notes au public telles que je les ai écrites.... Elles sont avec toutes leurs imperfections, le compte-rendu fidèle d'une Américaine*")—Hughes offered a valuable record of history in the making.[42]

Hughes foregrounds her status as a non-native French speaker who writes with "imperfections," and the book, while competently written, does indeed carry the trace of her foreign voice in its slightly clunky prose style, what one reader has called "persistently flawed" on the level of "sentence structure and articulation."[43] Note, as one example, the heavy syntax in this phrase:

> Our plan consisted, since we had just learned that it was the Blois bridge that had blown up provoking the great explosion that had awakened me, in surrendering in order to go south to Herbaux, Tours, and Chinon, and then Niort in Deux-Sèvres where there is the Morgan bank.
>
> Notre plan a consisté, puisque nous venions d'apprendre que c'était le pont de Blois qui avait sauté en provoquant l'explosion formidable qui m'avait réveillée, à nous rendre pour aller au sud, à Herbaux, Tours et Chinon, puis Niort dans les Deux-Sèvres où se trouve la banque Morgan.[44]

The veracity of Hughes's eyewitness testimony is conveyed through her unedited French, written on the spot and in real time. In maintaining her written style in French, clunkiness and all, the book makes a case for linguistic fidelity as a marker of historical accuracy. Hughes would later be recognized and decorated by the French government for her service to France, and *Les lauriers sont coupés* remains the only book she wrote and record of that service.[45] Hughes's diary-memoir succeeded in documenting an American's contributions to the war effort, and the proceeds from book sales were reportedly donated to *American Friends of France* to help French war prisoners.[46]

For Brentano's purposes, a writer like Hughes represented a cultural bridge between France and the U.S., and a year after the publication of *Les lauriers sont coupés,* she prefaced another firsthand account of occupied France, this time by a pseudonymous French author publishing under the name Louis le François.[47] Hughes's avant-propos to *J'ai faim! . . . Journal d'un Français en France depuis l'armistice* (1942) emphasizes her cultural awareness. The preface begins rhetorically by establishing Hughes's presence in wartime France—"Towards the end of July, one month after the Armistice, we started to see them [Nazi soldiers] in the streets ("Vers la fin du mois de Juillet, un mois après l'Armistice, on commençait à les voir dans les rues").[48] It is from the vantage point of her firsthand knowledge—the "on" of which she is part—that Hughes can emphatically insist on the veracity of the account, despite not knowing the author's identity:

> It's clearly a true story, since it's full of details that a mind could not imagine or guess. It's certainly not a story written by someone who, safely in America, imagines what a life in Europe under Nazism might look like.
>
> C'est manifestement une histoire vraie, car elle est pleine de détails que l'esprit ne peut pas imaginer ou deviner. Ce n'est certainement pas une histoire écrite par une personne qui, bien à l'abri en Amérique, imagine à quoi peut ressembler la vie dans une Europe soumise aux Nazis.[49]

Hughes's literary stamp of approval formalized her role as a cultural go-between who could speak to the political urgencies of the moment and authenticate a book's truth value.

Like *Les lauriers sont coupés,* other books in the Brentano's series, while varied in scope and style, similarly relate American women's perspectives on a changing France. Hailing mainly from wealthy families, with resources at their disposal to travel and live abroad, these women writers present themselves as adept cultural go-betweens who have the expertise, knowledge, and connections necessary to communicate an idea of France to readers in the United States. The New England socialite Tryphosa Bates-Batcheller authored two French books for Brentano's during the war: one a biography of the Polish queen Marie de Gonzague, *L'Âme d'une reine* (1942), the other a personal account of life in Paris during the Occupation, *La France au soleil et à l'ombre* (1944). Both books emphasize in their paratexts Bates-Batcheller's prominent social network. It is, for instance, thanks to Eleanor Roosevelt that *La France au soleil et à l'ombre* came to be: "I was invited to the White House by First Lady Roosevelt. She encouraged me to put into a permanent form an account of my meetings and experiences, and she gave me her full approval" ("Je fus invitée à la Maison Blanche par Madame Roosevelt. Elle m'encouragea beaucoup à mettre sous forme permanente mes conférences et le récit de mes expériences et me donna toute son approbation").[50] The book's dedication to President and Eleanor Roosevelt bolsters Bates-Batcheller's claims to cultural mediation, as if to index the authority of her literary project and its ultimate claim that "a renewed and glorious France" ("une France renaissante et glorieuse") will rise out of historical tragedy.[51]

We find a similar tendency in Florence Conrad's *Camarades de combat* (1942), a vibrant tale of volunteering during the war by another well-to-do American who had lived in France. Conrad recounts her experience of being taken prisoner by the Germans and of earning accolades for her heroism, including from Maréchal Pétain. The book gushes with praise for France ("la plus intelligente et adulte des nations"; "the most intelligent and mature of nations" and "un pays que j'aime"; "a country that I love") and attempts to understand and contextualize its stunning defeat.[52] In a purported exchange with Pétain, narrated in the book, Conrad references the diverging political positions between France and the United States, and Pétain in turn reportedly asks her to represent him kindly to Roosevelt ("Ne manquez pas de remercier le Président de ma part"; "Don't forget to thank the President for me").[53]

The exchange reads as politically ambitious and likely fictional, especially given Conrad's wartime role as an ambulance driver in the Second Armored Division: it seems improbable that Pétain would have taken the time to speak frankly with an American volunteer fighting to liberate France. What the book demonstrates, however, and what connects it to so many other books on Tenger's list, is how Conrad presents herself narratively as a privileged cultural diplomat. She plans to leave France and make it her mission to tell Americans—her "compatriotes"—what she has seen and to testify that "the French soldier has done his best" ("le soldat français a fait de son mieux").[54] Hence the implicit rationale for the book, whose aim is simultaneously one of historical documentation, self-promotion, and cultural propaganda. As a material object, the book also represented a stunning product: it included sixteen illustrations by the famed muralist Jean Pagès, whose drawings lined the walls of New York's fanciest French restaurants. In that sense, the book, like many others in the series, reflected Brentano's investment in book design: one of Brentano's main publishing objectives, as Tenger indicated in a 1945 article for *Pour la Victoire*, was "to give the books an agreeable and attractive appearance" ("donner aux livres une forme plaisante et attrayante").[55] The illustrations did not significantly alter the list price—at $2 a copy, Conrad's book was only modestly more expensive than Brentano's standard $1.50 for non-illustrated books—but they underscore the press's material and aesthetic investment in their titles.

In constructing his Brentano's list, Robert Tenger balanced new or obscure literary voices with a careful eye to paratexts that could bolster attention to his books. In most cases, the subject matter and the paratextual framing of the books cohered to suggest the power of cross-cultural exchange in Franco-American relations. Two books by Helen Mackay, for instance—*La France que j'aime* (1942) and *Sainte terre de France* (1944)—offer poetic and fragmented accounts of the author's memories of wartime France, with titles that put on display the writer's francophilia.[56] Unlike many of the women writers that Tenger supported, Helen Gansevoort Edwards Mackay, an expat from New York who lived much of her adult life in France, had published books before, in both English and French, and had even purportedly won awards for two of them: *Patte Blanche* (Plon, 1929, *Prix des portiques*) and *La Croix païenne: contes d'Irlande* (Plon, 1933, recognized by the Académie française).[57] In a recent attempt to rescue Mackay from literary oblivion, Margaret Higonnet argues for reading the little-known author's English-language poetry and prose sketches from World War I (*London, One November*, 1916, and *Journal of*

Small Things, 1917) as rhetorically inventive, indicative of her ability "to shape a female mode of modernist war literature."[58]

Mackay's narrative style shines through in her later writings, too, in fragmented and evocative descriptions of her wartime experiences. Mackay had volunteered as a nurse in both world wars, and *La France que j'aime* recounts her experiences at Les Invalides upon France's defeat in 1940, in a lucid narration that confronts the sadness of what she calls "la ruine d'un monde" ("the ruins of a world").[59] In his preface to the edition, Antoine de Saint Exupéry praises the lyrical tone of the book, noting that it was written "as if one were remembering a friend" ("comme on se souviendrait d'un ami").[60] His approbation served to legitimate the book's literary merit—though a published author and wife of a wealthy real estate developer, Helen Mackay was not well-known as a writer—and it exemplified the ways in which Tenger attended to connecting women writers on his list with the French literary establishment of New York. The paratextual connection between Saint Exupéry and Mackay enacted the kind of cross-linguistic friendship that was the subject of her books: in both *La France que j'aime* and *Sainte terre de France*, Mackay casts an American woman's gaze on France to remind readers of the two countries' close cultural ties. "I came to see you because it gives me pleasure to chat with French people" ("Je viens vous voir parce que ça me fait plaisir de causer avec des Français"), tells Mackay, in *Sainte terre de France,* to one of the wounded French soldiers in the hospital where she volunteers. "Well, me too! It's a pleasure. I don't speak English" ("Eh bien! Moi aussi, ça me fait plaisir. Je ne parle pas l'anglais"), the wounded man replies, signaling their solidarity and solidifying her position as a cultural and linguistic translator.[61]

This message—and paratextual performance—of cross-cultural alliance presents a literary throughline across Brentano's francophone list. Bolstered by the U.S. publishing mission, Tenger would have been motivated to find books that could contribute to the war effort, and particularly the U.S.'s aim of stockpiling French books that could be exported as soon as 1943 and be readily available to readers upon France's liberation, whenever that might be. "The highest priority," as Hench writes, "was to secure books to be used in France and Belgium, nearest the planned invasion landings. The Office of War Information (OWI) asked the French-language publishers that had established operations in New York before or after the fall of France to recommend titles 'they feel valuable in the way of showing democracy in action and as an example of American thought and writing.'"[62] Tenger does not figure in Hench's book—and Brentano's Books receives only a few passing references[63]—but it is easy to imagine that the aspiration to provide books for the war effort offered a compelling publishing incentive. For a book to be selected for stockpiling, it needed to be approved by a series of review boards and independent advisory committees. Given that one member of the committee, Joseph Margolies, was an employee of Brentano's bookstore, it seems certain that Tenger would have been well-aware of the program.[64] To demonstrate "American thought in action," the selected books needed to "serve as propaganda," even if they were not expressly written as such.[65] Publishers raced to propose books that would serve the cause, and while none of Tenger's books were ever selected for the program, his publishing commitments aligned closely with the U.S. war efforts.[66] It is important not to overstate this point: a book like Hughes's *Les lauriers sont coupés* (1941) pre-dated the ramping up of the U.S. publishing agenda in 1943. But we can read the common threads across Tenger's list as an indicator of a publishing vision that would have resonated with the U.S. war effort: that women, and particularly American-born francophones, were particularly well-poised to speak on behalf of Franco-American relations, and to make a case for themselves as key cultural diplomats in a new world order.

The editors' notes and prefaces to many of the Brentano's editions give us a clearer sense of the audience and aims that the press had in mind. The paratexts suggest that Tenger—unlike the editors at presses like the *Éditions de la Maison française*—was invested less in the French exile community than in reaching American readers of French and in fortifying Franco-American relations for readers in the U.S. and abroad.[67] As an older and established literary institution, with a history of publishing guidebooks and dictionaries, Brentano's was well-positioned to reach a wider audience of American readers, even language learners. For instance, in publishing *La garde montante* (1944), a firsthand account of the fall of Paris by Françoise Perrier and Claude Lebel, two French students who went on to study at Columbia, Robert Tenger argued for the necessity of a glossary to accompany the work:

> The Editor, mindful of the fact that the work is published in the United States, asked the authors to complete it by adding a list of helpful expressions for students. The asterisk sign * tells readers to look at the list in the back of the book.

> L'Éditeur, se rappelant que l'ouvrage est publié aux États-Unis, a demandé aux auteurs de le compléter en ajoutant un lexique des expressions étudiantesques. Le signe * renvoie le lecteur à ce lexique placé à la fin du livre.[68]

The pedagogical apparatus clarifies Tenger's expectation that non-native French speakers would be interested in reading the book as an exercise in cultural and linguistic edification. Such an aim was similarly at stake in Marcelle Dorval's *Le Coeur sur la Main/The Heart on the Sleeve* (1943), a bilingual phrase book illustrated by Jean Carlu, in which colloquial expressions are rendered in both literal and idiomatic translations. Thus an expression like "couper un cheveu en quatre" is shown as both "To cut a hair in four parts" and as "to split hairs" (literally "fendre des cheveux")—a visualization of translation that underscores both the humor of errors and the complexity of productive and meaningful interchange. Cross-linguistic ties were intrinsic, then, both for the writers on Tenger's list and the anticipated readership he had in mind.

Across multiple editors' notes included at the beginning of Brentano's wartime books, Tenger signaled Franco-American reciprocity as a beacon of hope. "One can serve a country by one's acts and one's words" ("On peut servir un pays par des actes et par des mots"), Tenger wrote for Helen Mackay's *Sainte terre de France*, and he went on to explain how, especially as an American writing in her non-native French, Mackay, "through the expression of her love for France, contributes to the healing of its wounds" ("par l'expression de son amour pour la France contribue à la guérison de ses plaies").[69] This idea that cultural cohesion offered a critical step towards postwar recovery—that an American book could have the power to cure a French wound—illustrated the concept undergirding Brentano's wartime publishing mission. The gendered dimension of that curative ideal was clear: books embodied an idea of healing, a literary extension of the wartime volunteer work in which many of these women participated and later described, realistically or imaginatively, in their published works.

Tenger's editorial choices diverged dramatically from his contemporaries; while his French-speaking colleagues in New York remained committed to authors of the past, Tenger envisioned a new literary order that centered the voices and experiences of women as political, linguistic, and cultural healers. From a contemporary progressive standpoint, Tenger did not take as many risks as one might have hoped in his selection of diverse authorship; after all, most of the women he published had some form of cultural capital, financial or otherwise. But the laser-sharp focus and continuity across his list exemplifies a clear editorial vision, an enactment of Brentano's mission articulated in 1945 "to neglect nothing that might help maintain an attachment to French culture, the love of France abroad, and the friendship of this continent for France" ("ne rien négliger de ce qui pourrait être utile pour entretenir l'attachement à la culture française, l'amour de la France à l'étranger et l'amitié de ce Continent pour la France").[70] Their publishing enterprise made a case for literature as a pragmatic and symbolic tool during a period of war, a mechanism not just for registering a political reality, but for modeling cross-cultural communication. By reaching beyond the French exile community and by prioritizing women's voices, Brentano's took critical steps to diversify the francophone literary sphere. What united their collection of writers was a commitment not to literary prestige but to new models of international cooperation.

We might understand Brentano's francophone wartime books, then, in the context of what Merve Emre has identified as a set of reading practices thriving in the postwar era that put "pressure on ordinary citizens to communicate with one another in the constitution of an internationally minded public sphere."[71] The overwhelming production of "paraliterary" texts—pamphlets, personal diaries by government officials, speeches, diplomatic treatises—signaled a national project focused on international communication, where literature could serve a "communicative and public value in a rapidly internationalizing world."[72] From the invention of study abroad programs as a mechanism of cultural ambassadorship, to the new Fulbright scholarship that framed cultural diplomacy through discourses of feeling and love, postwar readers, Emre shows, were taught to approach reading as a form of cross-cultural communication.[73] With Tenger's editorial vision, we see the engine of this mode of reading at work even earlier, during the war itself. If books could function pragmatically as cultural tools for cultural communication, then with Tenger's list, we see how women strategically positioned themselves in this shifting world order.

Tenger's publishing vision was nonetheless misaligned with certain realities of the literary world. Readers were all too willing to misread a book by a woman writer, to cast it aside as historically inaccurate or indulgently eccentric. The privileged insight we have into the reception of Consuelo de Saint Exupéry's *Oppède*, by way of Varian Fry's notations, serves as an instructive guide in this final section. Through *Oppède,* we can see how, with the encouragement of her editor, a woman could turn to literary modes to imagine and assert her place in a rapidly changing world. From her vantage point of wartime New York, Consuelo de Saint Exupéry wrote directly into a literary context in which ideas of rebuilding and cross-cultural negotiation had become transparent publishing priorities. While her experiences and imagination lent themselves well to that mission, the reception and (mis)translations of her novel after its 1945 publication offer an indelible example of the possibilities and limits of francophone authorship in the postwar United States.

Oppède: Consuelo de Saint Exupéry Meets Varian Fry

As German troops descended on Paris in June 1940, Consuelo de Saint Exupéry knew she had to get out of the city as soon as she could. She had been married to Antoine de Saint Exupéry for nearly a decade (he was her third husband; she had been divorced and widowed before), and while he flew to Algeria on June 20 to join his military unit, she found temporary refuge in the southwest city of Pau, near the Pyrenees in the free zone, before making her way to Oppède, a small village on the outskirts of Marseille, where she would reside until late 1941. Historically the village of Oppède had been known for its medieval fortress built at the beginning of the thirteenth century, but in the wake of the Armistice, it became an artists' colony and haven for Jews, other marginalized groups, and resistance fighters in need of community and safety.

It is not hard to imagine why the ancient ruins of Oppède, with its towering, hilltop position and its labyrinthine topography, would become an ideal spot to escape from the war. But Oppède was not just a place to hide; its founders saw it as a site for creative and pedagogical exchange. A Russian-born American photographer for *Harper's Bazaar*, Alexey Brodovitch, had bought the old oil mill of Oppède, and his brother Georges, alongside fellow artist friends—many of whom had met as students at the École des Beaux-Arts in Paris—saw an opportunity to embark upon a collective restoration of the site.[74] In their "Manifeste du Groupe d'Oppède," written in August 1940, the group articulated their shared mission of rebuilding through various artistic media, with the goal of "harmony," "enthusiasm," "passion," and "beauty."[75] Artists of all kinds—painters, sculptors, architects, musicians, writers—heard about the community through word of mouth, and many spent weeks, months, even years there. The renowned architect Bernard Zehrfuss became the de facto organizer of the group, and it was likely by way of his invitation that Consuelo, whom he had met when she was studying sculpture at Beaux-Arts in Paris, found herself in Oppède.[76]

The book that she would go on to write and publish in New York in 1945 provides a glimpse into the daily lives and interactions of wartime Oppède and is currently the *only* published book about that period and place in history. Apart from a few articles and an unpublished master's thesis, virtually no scholarship exists on Oppède's wartime history; in that sense, *Oppède*, the book, functions as a valuable historical record of an unaffiliated francophone community who mobilized themselves through restorative art practices.[77] At the same time, though, the book's factual accuracy should not be overestimated. The first-person narrator "Dolorès" likely derives her name either from Consuelo's eponymous younger sister, or is in reference to Miguel Hidalgo's famous "cry of Dolores" ("Grito de Dolores") to rally Mexicans in favor of independence and equality—in either event, a mark of the book's status as a fictionalized object.[78] Many of the characters and events draw inspiration from real life—such as the architect and patron of Oppède, a certain Bernard from Alsace who wins the Prix de Rome, who surely represents Bernard Zehrfuss; or the American man Consuelo meets in Marseille ("Mr. Fryan") who works to rescue European intellectuals and gain them safe passage to the U.S. *Oppède* navigates a fine line between fact and fiction, but through its name changes and exuberant, fanciful storytelling, calls attention to itself as a work of literary fiction in the style of a *roman à clef*.

Oppède takes place over a full year and follows, in four sections organized by season, the lives and adventures of Dolorès, Bernard, and others as they build the community of Oppède. After spending several days at the Villa Air-Bel in Marseille—where, in real life, such famed figures as André Breton, Marcel Duchamp, Max Ernst, and Serge Victor congregated before obtaining exit visas—Dolorès announces her plan to join friends from Beaux-Arts en route to Oppède. In novelistic fashion, she depicts herself as the motivational force that compelled others to go to Oppède as well. "If you stay in the city, I'll stay too. If you go up to Oppède, I'll go" ("Si vous restez en ville je reste aussi. Si vous montez à Oppède, j'y monte"), the Bernard character tells Dolorès.[79] Though improbable as a real-life interaction, their exchange reflects the spirited tone of the book—Dolorès is frequently depicted as an energizing, inspirational figure—and sets the stage for their romantic tension. Dolorès will contemplate running away with Bernard, who expresses his love for her in the closing chapters, but she will ultimately choose her fiancé in New York. That Dolorès remains unmarried in the diegetic world of Oppède—in contrast to Consuelo, who had been married to Antoine for almost ten years by the outbreak of war—further signals the fictionalization of her character. The Dolorès and Bernard love story serves as a sporadic backdrop to the main day-to-day dilemmas: how to find enough food, paper, ink, and other supplies; how to gain trust among the eclectic mix of artists and with the local villagers; or how to navigate conflict when some members attempt to set up a rival "école de musique" near their architecture school.

As a writer, Consuelo is a masterful storyteller, who relishes dramatic dialogues and complicated interpersonal dynamics. Each chapter centers on an isolated conflict or character—a village wedding, a German masquerading as a Frenchman—and depicts up close the heightened emotions and stakes surrounding the events. In one scene before arriving in Oppède, Dolorès wins over the affection of a young girl named Conchita who is prone to torturing frogs. Dolorès reflects on the stakes of accepting a gift Conchita has offered her:

> Speaking with children is a dangerous battle. You win or you lose, and if you lose, there's no going back. If I had hurt Conchita that day, she would have continued jabbing frogs and poking their eyes out while singing the most joyous songs. . . . If I accepted her gift of beautiful shoes, it was a signed pact between us. . . . I was too overwhelmed to respond.

> Parler avec les enfants, c'est une bataille dangereuse. On gagne ou on perd, et si on a perdu c'est sans appel. Si j'avais blessé Conchita ce jour-là, elle aurait continué à piquer les grenouilles, à leur crever les yeux en chantant ses chansons les plus gaies. . . . Si j'acceptais ses beaux souliers, c'était un pacte conclu entre elle et moi. . . . J'étais trop émue pour répondre.[80]

Dolorès and the other characters frequently find themselves overcome by feelings, caught in situations with high emotional stakes that dramatize the intensity of human encounters. At another point later in the novel, when Dolorès goes on her first mission to collect food for the group, a local woman named la mère Leval reluctantly offers her some cherries and reacts with suspicion when Dolorès chooses to save them for the community's children, rather than eat them on the spot: "Her loud husky voice scared me," Dolorès reports. "'For children! You're dragging children up there! . . . They're all crazy!' . . . And she walked towards her house muttering about how these Parisians should just go back home" ("Sa voix rauque et sonore m'effraya. . . . 'Aux enfants! Traînez des enfants là-haut! . . . Ils sont tous fous!' . . . Et elle s'en fut vers la maison en grommelant que ces Parisiens n'avaient qu'à retourner chez eux").[81] Moments later, la mère Leval sheds a tear recalling that her eldest son is being held as a German war prisoner. Characters in the novel flash between wildly different moods, as if to underscore the palpable energy and passions at the heart of the Oppède project.

What unifies the book, across the varying plot points, is a depiction of Oppède as a utopian space. Before arriving at Oppède, Dolorès hears talk of it as an "old utopia for socialist communities" ("vieille utopie des communautés socialistes"), and she summons others to join her on this pilgrimage to an artistic mecca: "If you still have the strength to create something, to make ruins come to life, let's all go there instead of keeping ourselves busy doing nothing here!" ("Si vous avez encore la force de créer quelque chose, de faire fleurir des ruines, allons-y tous au lieu de nous ronger les os ici à ne rien faire ensemble!").[82] The description of her ascent only confirms her impression of Oppède as a quasi-mystical, sacred spot: "I was entering a new country, and my heart was beating fast. I felt that anyone coming to Oppède must be touched by grace, or by fire" ("J'entrais dans un pays nouveau, mon coeur battait. Je sentais que celui qui arrive à Oppède doit être touché par la grâce, ou par le feu").[83] Women, students, Jews, and Arabs gravitate towards this land of possibility, where all are welcome, where no one needs to show their papers, and where everyone can contribute to the well-being and growth of the community. "In this new earthquake of an invasion," Dolorès tells us, "I understood that we needed to create solid things that last" ("Dans ce nouveau tremblement de terre de l'invasion, j'ai compris qu'il fallait créer des choses solides et qui se perpétuent").[84]

In this commitment to construction and restoration, Dolorès posits an idea of collective art as both political contestation and national redemption. At Oppède, at least in the world of the novel, she earns the title of "head of propaganda" ("chef de propagande"), the leading figure to advocate publicly for the value and possibilities of their mission. It is thanks to Dolorès's critical intervention with the mayor that they are granted full rights to build at Oppède. At the mayor's office, all employees are mesmerized by Dolorès's foreign accent, her fabulous tales of exile, and her compelling narrative about Oppède's artists. The mayor is in fact so persuaded by her vision and how it would be meaningful to his son, an aspiring architect who was captured as a prisoner of war, that he breaks down in tears: "Our country is in ruins, like your town. But if your courage and faith succeed in having new life burst out of the debris, there is still hope for France" ("Notre patrie, elle est en ruines, comme votre ville. Mais si votre courage et votre foi arrivent à faire surgir de ces décombres une vie nouvelle, il y a encore de l'espoir pour la France").[85] In the narrative universe of *Oppède*, Dolorès legitimates the group's legal right to the village and offers the promise of rescuing France from its ruins.

It's not hard to imagine readers balking at the scene's hyperbolic staging and the narrator's excessive self-importance. Surely such scenes, like Florence Conrad's depiction of an intimate conversation with Pétain, did not take place *exactly like that*. Consuelo's recourse to hyperbole and self-aggrandizement is an instructive reminder of *Oppède*'s status as fiction—a novel that certainly draws from historical circumstances and relies on first-person experiences to do so, but that veers self-consciously and playfully into whimsical flights of fancy and wish fulfillment. Such would have been appealing for Tenger's editorial vision: *Oppède* modeled the idea that women writers could position themselves as intermediary figures—often dramatic ones at that—whose foreignness and communication skills were keys to their success. If Consuelo's literary power of persuasion through *Oppède* was any bit as effective as Dolorès's storytelling, then it too could serve a redemptive purpose. As outsiders to a community and a language, writers like Consuelo de Saint Exupéry, Mackay, Conrad, and others offered to Tenger a coherent editorial vision founded on female agency and cross-cultural reciprocity. Their books offered a space to imagine their own positionality as beneficial and politically useful, often in ways that would have been unimaginable outside the world of fiction. Published in their non-native French in New York, such books indexed an ideal of reciprocity, a belief—or at a minimum, a hope—that literature could have a redemptive force and offer an alternative to the threatening political realities.

Brentano's material investment in a book like *Oppède* is worth noting, especially given wartime paper shortages. The 1945 edition includes a total of nineteen illustrations, almost all of which are paintings by the author. Consuelo's abstract images included two depictions of the village of Oppède, but mainly represented the women, mothers, and children that she describes in the book (Figures 2–4). In sharp contrast to these paintings is a single photograph, taken at Oppède in 1941, of six men carrying a large piece of wood towards a construction site (Figure 5). We see the men from behind, discernible only by their short hair and workers' clothes. While the photograph serves as the single visual reminder of the novel's historical indexicality, the paintings shift the focus elsewhere: to mothers running around frantically in search of their kids; to images of Dolorès's friends, including Jeanne and Attine; to a self-portrait of a feverish Dolorès who imagines that she herself has turned into stone. All of the paintings, accompanied by textual markers to indicate what passages and people they are depicting, give physical form to women's lives, characters who escape the historical record of the single photograph.

Consuelo's abstract style stands in sharp relief against the single photograph, as if to insist upon the imaginative creation of a world of women that her book endeavors to represent. As the men march in unison, their faces invisible and their bodies joined by the collective labor of rebuilding, her female characters are individuated, supple, figurative, their faces visible in abstraction. The non-referentiality of the images gives a visual rendering of Consuelo's fictional project: just as it would be absurd to look at her self-portrait (Figure 4) and accuse it of not bearing enough resemblance to the painter, so too would it be a mistake to read her novel solely for its historical precision. The abstract paintings, like the genre of fiction, encourage imagination and figurative idealization. The figures in her images belong to what she calls in the novel "we, the women" ("nous les femmes"), the growing community of women who participate in "women's work" ("travaux féminins") and keep Oppède running; it is Pivoulon, Dolorès's close friend and head cook for the group, who "became at that time the most important figure in our group" ("devint à cette époque le personnage le plus important de notre groupe").[86]

Figure 2: "Mothers Running Everywhere," illustration by
Consuelo de Saint Exupéry, in *Oppède* (1945)

Figure 3: "Jeanne and Attine," illustration by Consuelo
de Saint Exupéry, in *Oppède* (1945)

Figure 4: "How I Turned into Stone," self-portrait by Consuelo de Saint Exupéry, in *Oppède* (1945)

Figure 5: "The Group at Work," photograph dated 1941, in *Oppède* (1945)

As Dolorès states it simply early in the novel: "We need women in Oppède" ("On a besoin de femmes, à Oppède").[87]

The narrative that Consuelo offers the reader, then, centers the experiences of women, whose labor sustained the existence of Oppède, and whose stories deserved textual and visual representation. The book elaborates a space for Consuelo to imagine women's positionality—a striking assertion of proto-feminist reclamation and female agency, especially for a woman who lived in her husband's shadow. The extensive Saint Exupéry correspondence, recently published by Gallimard, reveals the degree to which Consuelo constantly fought to carve out a space for her artistic projects in the face of her husband's criticism. She served as his muse and writing coach, giving him the time and motivation to keep creating—"I will take care of my dear husband," she writes to him in the third person, talking of their future, "I want him to work on his ideas, to build an eternal work; I want to be proud of him" ("Je m'occuperai de mon homme chéri. Je veux qu'il travaille ses idées, qu'il construise une oeuvre éternelle, je veux être fière de lui").[88] He, meanwhile, reproaches her for her talentless abstract art: "When I see you keep filling up pages, I know it's going nowhere" ("Quand je vous vois multiplier les pages successives, je sais que ça ne va nulle part").[89] He begs her to stop spending time with intellectuals like André Breton, and instead, to "learn to take care of a geranium or a bunny. That is what's hard. That is what builds bonds. That is what makes money" ("Apprenez à soigner un géranium ou un lapin. Ça, c'est difficile. Ça, ça crée des liens. Ça, c'est payant").[90] Her letters from 1944 reveal her joy about diving into her art and writing projects, enthusiasm for which she repeatedly finds herself apologizing: "I'm telling you too much about my painting, I'm sorry"; "I asked you to write a preface [for *Oppède*] in a moment of thoughtlessness. Like children asking for a star from the sky" ("Je vous parle trop de ma peinture, pardon"; "Je vous ai demandé une préface [pour *Oppède*] dans un moment d'irréflexion. Comme les enfants demandent une étoile au ciel").[91] Her self-disparagement and shame seem unsurprising in the face of his belittlement of her artistic efforts. Consuelo started writing the manuscript of *Oppède* only once Antoine had left New York to rejoin the war effort. It's perhaps not too much to say that just as characters in the novel flee fascist persecution to build a female-centered utopia, Consuelo herself needed space and distance from an overbearing husband to find room for her creativity and writerly voice.

Around the same time as Consuelo was writing *Oppède,* she was also privately working on her memoirs. These included a series of intimate, personal reflections composed in 1945 and that she appears not to have shared with anyone—so much so that the manuscript was discovered by chance in her belongings in 1999, twenty years after her death. *Mémoires de la rose* (*The Tale of the Rose: The Love Story Behind "The Little Prince"*) was released to great fanfare in France in 2000, at a time when the country was celebrating the 100-year anniversary of Antoine's birth. To the disgruntlement of his heirs, the book gives pride of place to Consuelo as the inspiration for *The Little Prince* and shows Antoine to be somewhat of a maniacal egotist, who broke plans with Consuelo, left her stranded and alone, and changed their address without informing her—even as she maintained an absolute devotion to him. She is frequently sad and depressed, prone to fevers and illness. The one time where she describes herself as totally blissful is in Oppède. There, "the old utopian ideal of fraternal, monastic, or socialist communities was taking root in me."[92] She adopted an alternate identity there—"I decided to call myself Dolorès"— and she learned both the value of kinship ("with my friends at Oppède I had experienced a state of honest intimacy, a different way of thinking") and the possibilities of rebuilding as an activist strategy "to resist defeat and the terrible blows being dealt to civilization."[93] Consuelo describes her vocation there as one of resistance and subterfuge (they steal German supplies), where collective action and reconstruction function as acts of defiance. It's noteworthy that, in contrast to the deference she shows towards her husband in their letters, in Oppède, as she describes it in her memoir, she takes action, displays initiative, and works tirelessly over the course of her year-long stay. Consuelo's private reflections confirm the sense that *Oppède,* as a novel, seized a space for reimagining the social order. It's not that men or love ceased to exist in the world of the novel, but Consuelo actively rejects them; she describes Bernard's warm feelings towards Dolorès, who ultimately refuses his advances—an act that radically undermines the centrality of a man's love in fiction. Her focus on her and other women's embodied experiences suggests how powerfully *Oppède* registered a desire for female agency as part of the village's utopian vision.

The manifesto and news reports about Oppède that circulated in the early years of the war romanticize a vision of masculine camaraderie at the core of the group's mission. To succeed, according to the *Manifeste du Groupe d'Oppède*, "it is essential that men learn to get to know each other, to form groups and to work together" ("il faut que les hommes apprennent à se connaître, à se grouper, à travailler ensemble").[94] The potential for reading "les hommes" here as a universal collective is undermined in the manifesto's subsequent call to welcome new members: "This Center is intended for young men eager to gear themselves towards an artistic, technical, or artisanal profession" ("Ce Centre est destiné à recevoir les jeunes hommes désirant s'orienter vers une profession artistique, technique ou artisanale").[95]

The popular press similarly insists on Oppède as a fundamentally male space. One journalist for a Marseille-based newspaper wrote about the secretary-general of youth in Provence, a certain Monsieur Magnan, who, hearing about the "groupe d'Oppède," is eager to learn more about them:

> He wants to meet these young men who live in a nearly abandoned village, who start their days gathering firewood, who continue their studies while lending a hand, and who eat food prepared by one of their wives.
>
> Il désire connaître ces jeunes hommes qui vivent dans un village quasi abandonné, commencent leurs journées par la corvée de bois, continuent leurs études tout en louant leurs bras, et mangent la cuisine que prépare la femme de l'un d'eux.[96]

Cast in a supporting role, women are sidelined to the margins, despite historical records affirming the presence of many women artists in Oppède: the designer and dressmaker Jeanne Violet; the gallerist Nina Einstein-Auproux; the artist and illustrator Yliane Rémy-Labaudt; the painter and engraver Madeleine Rollinat; the pianist Adrienne Serres.[97] Consuelo de Saint Exupéry's novel reasserts the presence of women as creators against their radical exclusion in official and popular documentation.

One could argue that for Tenger, publishing the illustrated book *Oppède* in part reflected his commitment to the ideals held by the group of Oppède: notably, that art (and here, literature too) could imagine a way out of political and social distress. Tenger took this a step further—in all likelihood, unbeknownst to him—by centering the perspective of a woman artist. In his editor's note that accompanies the publication, Tenger describes the book as an enactment of a promise: "When Consuelo de Saint Exupéry left [France] in 1942 to meet back up with her friends in the U.S., she made a promise to her friends to tell the story of the group of Oppède. This book, where the unreal seems to blend with the real, is the fulfillment of that promise" ("Lorsque Consuelo de Saint Exupéry partit en 1942 pour rejoindre ses amis aux États-Unis, elle fit serment à ses amis de raconter l'histoire du groupe d'Oppède. Ce livre, où l'irréel semble se mélanger au réel, est l'accomplissement de sa promesse").[98] The book indexes an ideal of art as redemptive, but where—and this goes unstated in his remarks—a woman can imagine herself as critical to the future of a nation and of international cooperation.

It is notable that Tenger's 1945 version of *Oppède* bears the traces of this ideal more than any subsequent version. In both the English translation in 1946, and the republished French edition that Gallimard released in 1947, erasures and dishonest translations have given a misguided impression of the book to readers. Within a year of the Brentano's edition in New York, Random House released the English version of *Oppède* as *Kingdom of the Rocks: Memories of Oppède* and entrusted Katherine Woods, the first English translator of *The Little Prince*, with the translation. The book's new lyrical title gave it a novelistic touch, but its subtitle squarely signaled the genre as memoir. Woods's brazen revision of novel into memoir insisted that the audience view the author and protagonist as the same person, renaming the latter Consuelo. "Consuelo! It *is* you! Here in Marseille!" cries out the first character to use her name, an insistence on identity recognition rather than geographical displacement ("Vous, Dolorès, à Marseille?" in the French), that mimics the translator's own move to stamp an identity of the writer behind the tale.[99]

The Random House records do not make clear whether it was the translator or publisher who made the decision to change the main character's name, but in either case, the Random House edition emphatically rewrote Consuelo's novel. The English translation was pitched to readers as a straightforward "personal narrative," eliminating fictional ambiguity, or what Tenger called the "irréel." Early drafts of the jacket copy described the book in relation to Antoine's work ("It is a book that, without striving to do so, in many ways will enchant the large audience that cherished the lyric mysticism of M. de Saint-Exupéry"), a passage that gets struck out and replaced instead, in the final version, with one that insists on the veracity of the tale: "It is a human book, a true story of the loves and jealousies of stubborn individualists who attempt to build a creative life in a brave new world."[100] Many of the early chapters of the book are entirely removed in English, as were all illustrations, and passages are rewritten such that the main character (now Consuelo) is proclaimed married to Antoine. Meanwhile, the 1947 Gallimard edition retained the French text in its entirety, including Tenger's editorial note, while eliminating the illustrations. To date, almost all French copies of *Oppède* in circulation bear the Gallimard imprint, which means that readers who have been fortunate enough to read the novel have likely not ever seen Consuelo's accompanying paintings. With the decision to remove the illustrations and to pitch the book as a memoir, the 1946 and 1947 versions constrained, in different ways, an understanding of *Oppède* as an articulation of female agency, a fictionalized space where a woman could paint herself into the story.

Early readers of the 1945 version *did* register *Oppède*'s status as fiction. "*Oppède* is a novel based on facts," wrote one reviewer of the Brentano's edition, praising it as "a complex and beautiful novel [that] is at times vigorously realistic in tone and again evanescent like a dream."[101] Reviewers of *Kingdom of the Rocks* unanimously found the book difficult to classify, describing it as "a strange exalted sort of book," as having descriptions that, while "sharply realistic . . . seem to have an unearthly shimmer, as though they were ready to dissolve into the unreal and the surreal."[102] None of the English-language reviews called the book a novel—quite understandably, given its stated genre—and they attributed this indeterminate status of the book to a perception of Consuelo's own personal instability: "One senses the author's own lack of balance—she acknowledges to having lived in a realm of fantasy," says a reviewer for *Kirkus*; or, as a writer for the *Weekly Book Review* put it, "The book itself defies definition or classification for the reason that Madame de St-Exupéry, widow of the French aviator and writer, defies classification. From her pages, she emerges as a highly sensitive woman, lost in memories and dreams."[103]

This kind of critical reception, in which a reviewer comments on an author's "lack of balance" and "sensitivity" rather than the book's substance or literary merit, aligns closely with what Joanna Russ has described as the pervasive "suppression of women's writing" across the anglophone publishing world. Russ enumerates various techniques through which critics and reviewers over the centuries have denied and denigrated women's writing, from prohibiting publication of their books; to refusing them agency over their works (an assumption that women could not possibly have written them); to devaluing their perspective or the content of the books they write; to miscategorizing the genre of their books; to isolating women socially post-publication; and so on. The reviews of *Kingdom of the Rocks* and the Random House translation are complicit in multiple modes of suppression; we see in the book reviews what Russ calls a "pollution of agency," an attempt to delegitimate a writer by insisting that there is something "wrong" or "hysterical" or "abnormal" about her as a person.[104] Russ would likely have condemned Random House's repackaging of the novel as memoir as a case of "false categorizing" that is particularly widespread among women and minority writers; such a move—which she traces in critics' insistence that "[James] Baldwin (they said) was *not a novelist*"—has the "virulent" effect of moving "art object X from the category of 'serious art' to the category of 'not serious.'"[105] Translators, publishers, and reviewers participated collectively (and unthinkingly) in a network of choices and rhetorical strategies that would have longstanding effects on how (and whether) we read a novel like *Oppède*.

Varian Fry's personal copy of *Oppède* offers a privileged insight into this misreading in action—a misreading that was not a result of the Random House translation (Fry's notations are on the original Brentano's French version), but of a male reader's gaze on a text. Fry met Consuelo in Marseille, and they were later neighbors on the East Side of Manhattan—where many French ex-pats lived during the war—who occasionally saw each other in the laundromat or over dinner.[106] One can imagine Consuelo handing Fry a copy of her book at his apartment or at a restaurant, the personal dedication a sign of gratitude for his help in securing her safe passage from France to New York.

Fry read *Oppède* with a pencil in hand and with an eye towards error. When Dolorès describes meeting "Mr. Fryan" for the first time at the Cintra café in Marseille ("On me présenta un étranger qui portait de grosses lunettes et s'appelait Mr. Fryan"), Fry notes in the margins that it was "not at the Cintra" (p. 34 of Fry's copy of the book). The margins are riddled with markings of "X" and "?" to signal when something seemed factually inaccurate to Fry (Figure 6a): the description of the pianos and décor at the Villa Air-Bel; the location of Dolorès's guest room there; a reference to a friend,

Octave, who Dolorès guesses may have spent the night at the Cintra; a mention of the length of a journey from the train station. Each of these are underlined, with an accompanying marginal notation affirming a discrepancy with reality. On the blank pages at the back of the book (Figure 6b), Fry records additional reactions and correctives to these mistakes: "P. 18—There is no Promenade des Anglais at Marseille"; "p. 34—I first met C. at Air-Bel, not at Cintra"; "p. 36—Ten minutes, not a half hour from train station." Fry read with the gaze of a witness and a historian—of a person who *had* been there and could thus assess the accuracy of any description. He finds her fanciful account of a break-in at the American consul's house "ridiculous," and it seems to be around this point in the book when the notations disappear, and he abandoned reading altogether. "What's the point," one can imagine Fry asking, as he put the book aside, "of reading a story about this time and place that's not historically accurate?"

Fry's reading notes suggest how even a person who cared so much about art that he had risked his life to save those of artists and intellectuals could not read a woman's novel as fiction. Even in the French edition, with a narrator's invented name and identity, and an editor's note testifying to the book's blending of genres, readers and publishers were eager to judge it on the merits and failures of its truth claims. There is something brutally ironic in the fact that *The Little Prince*, the most globally successful and translated French book of all time, is cherished for its fanciful and imaginative account of an aviator who misses his home and partner—a fiction rooted in Antoine de Saint Exupéry's personal story that includes many invented details—while Consuelo is casually denied a reading that took seriously her own novel based on her wartime experiences.[107] This irony is especially cruel given that recent scholarship makes plain Consuelo's role as the inspiration for the Little Prince's "rose." As Esther Allen writes in the preface to the English translation of *The Tale of the Rose*, no longer could Consuelo be "airbrushed out of the picture," but must instead be recognized as the impetus for *The Little Prince*'s creation, the reason why the prince longs to return to his rose after his lengthy travels away.[108]

Fry's private undermining of Consuelo's novel aligns with publishing practices that limited a woman's ability to write fiction or be read as a novelist. As Russ puts it well: "To read the visionary's blazes of illumination as

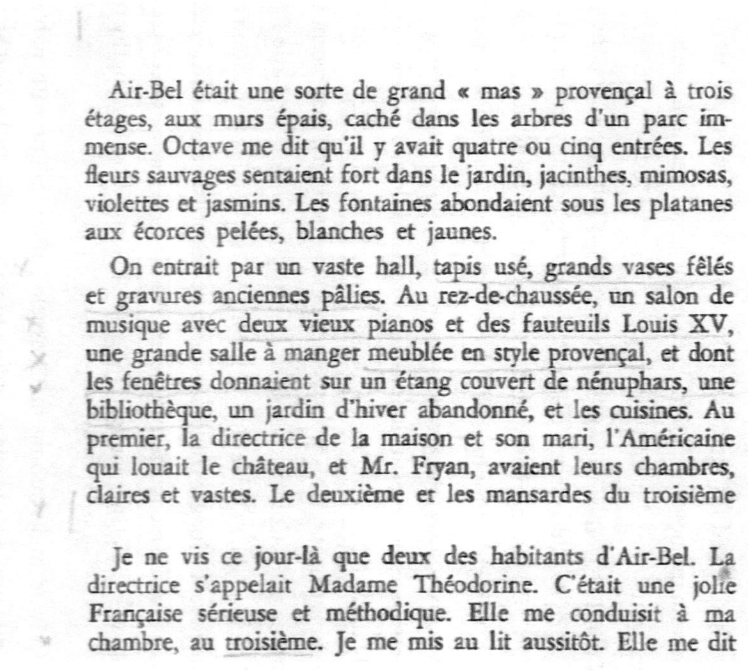

Air-Bel était une sorte de grand « mas » provençal à trois étages, aux murs épais, caché dans les arbres d'un parc immense. Octave me dit qu'il y avait quatre ou cinq entrées. Les fleurs sauvages sentaient fort dans le jardin, jacinthes, mimosas, violettes et jasmins. Les fontaines abondaient sous les platanes aux écorces pelées, blanches et jaunes.

On entrait par un vaste hall, tapis usé, grands vases fêlés et gravures anciennes pâlies. Au rez-de-chaussée, un salon de musique avec deux vieux pianos et des fauteuils Louis XV, une grande salle à manger meublée en style provençal, et dont les fenêtres donnaient sur un étang couvert de nénuphars, une bibliothèque, un jardin d'hiver abandonné, et les cuisines. Au premier, la directrice de la maison et son mari, l'Américaine qui louait le château, et Mr. Fryan, avaient leurs chambres, claires et vastes. Le deuxième et les mansardes du troisième

Je ne vis ce jour-là que deux des habitants d'Air-Bel. La directrice s'appelait Madame Théodorine. C'était une jolie Française sérieuse et méthodique. Elle me conduisit à ma chambre, au troisième. Je me mis au lit aussitôt. Elle me dit

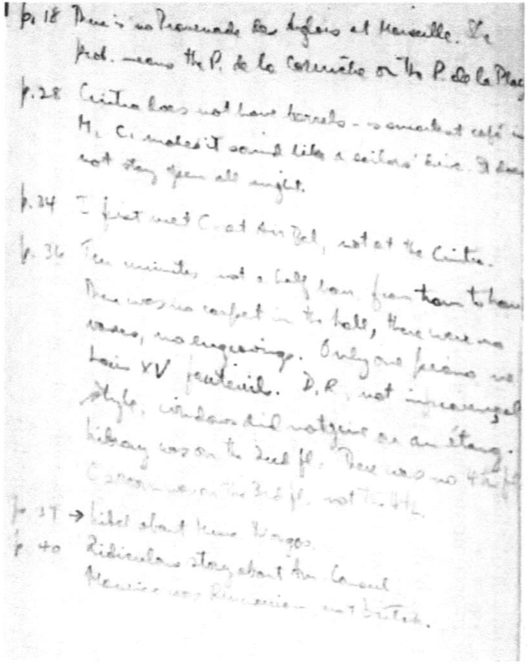

Figures 6a and 6b: Varian Fry's annotated copy of *Oppède*

faulty structure, fantasy as if it were failed realism, to read subversion as if it were nothing but its surface, is automatically to condemn minority writing, among which is the writing of women."[109] Random House, in their efforts to brand the book as memoir, insisted on Consuelo's status as a married woman and engaged in a thoroughgoing erasure of multiple chapters and passages in which "Mr. Fryan" appears as a character. In so doing, the English version anticipated potential challenges to the veracity of the text—precisely those challenges that Fry's marginal notes reveal, in service to the recategorization of the book's genre. Neither Fry nor Random House saw in the book a woman's creative struggle to find her place in a world that privileged men, husbands, and the cultural elite. Instead, they bent the novel into a new shape that all but ensured its failure.

Consuelo's *Oppède* faced suppression at every stage: from the refusal to acknowledge the role of women artists in the community in the wartime press, all the way through to the novel's publication history and reception. The fact that literary historians have ignored works like Consuelo's that collectively form a broader network of francophone women writers publishing during the war, seeking to make a space for themselves and their writing, signals just how successful that suppression was. Tenger's publishing list at Brentano's made an implicit argument for francophone women's narratives at a time of international political unrest. Their stories showed the ways in which women could participate in acts of cultural diplomacy and enact a vision of themselves as critical to a new political order. Tenger's editorial decisions no doubt reflected a moment of book culture in the U.S., as Hench has described it, when publishers sought out and promoted books to foster a particular message or agenda. Yet less than pro-American propaganda, the books he published by Consuelo de Saint Exupéry and her contemporaries posited an ideal of hope and community, a belief both that women could intervene as mediating figures across cultures and that publishing in one's non-native French could enact that commitment. By attending to these French books published in New York during the war, we can perceive that aspirational gesture, that hope of cracking open a space for a women-centric visions of cultural collaboration, rooted not in weapons and military action, but in diplomacy, collective art practices, and the novel itself.

In the immediate aftermath of the war, one sensed the potential force and possibilities of Tenger's literary achievement, albeit not in the most obvious of places. In a short essay for *Publishers Weekly*, "Market for French Books Maintained in America," Charles Peignot, a French publisher specializing in print technologies and typeface, discusses his visit to New York in 1945 and praised a few editors, including Tenger, for their publishing leadership during the war. "The main reason for my trip here is to re-establish contact with our American friends and to learn from them of the technical progress that has been made in printing during the war." But, Peignot adds, "I also came over to study the most favorable means for the establishing of a useful cooperation between the editors in France and in the United States . . . [and] to find out what should be done in order that books may circulate freely between our two countries and in that way fulfill their function as vehicles for culture and civilization."[110] Peignot had understood Tenger's literary vision of cultural reciprocity and wanted to extend it into the postwar era. In looking at technology and typeface—in focusing on the surface of things, rather than what was underneath and inside the books themselves—he missed a key piece of that innovation.

Peignot, like so many critics since, might have instead given some of Tenger's books a read. In one, a French-language novel from 1943 called *Plympton House*, written by an unknown and previously unpublished writer named Paule d'Oncin and cited in this chapter's epigraph, a young French woman (Geneviève) comes to the United States as a student and stays on when the war breaks out. She has an unhappy marriage and divorce with an American man, and in the closing section of the novel, sets out to write a fictional book based on her experiences. In picking up her pen to write a novel, Geneviève can tell one of the characters directly "all that she did not have the courage to tell him" ("tout ce qu'elle n'avait pas eu le courage de lui dire"), an opportunity to live an idealized version of herself not possible in reality.[111] Unsure of the quality of her manuscript, she reaches out to a well-known French writer (a fictional character named Maurice Vincent), who reads her novel and assures her of its literary merit. "So . . . do you think . . .", she asks him tentatively, "that an editor might accept it?" ("Alors . . . vous croyez que . . . qu'un éditeur pourrait l'accepter?"). Vincent's rhetorical musings give voice to Geneviève's concerns about being published as a first-time woman writer:

"An editor will consider the question from a commercial point of view, as is his job, right? He needs to live. Well now, a French book, published in America at this time . . . what type of readers might this kind of book interest? Will it reach a large audience?"

"L'éditeur, lui, envisagera la question au point de vue commercial, c'est son métier, n'est-ce pas? Il faut bien qu'il vive. Or, un livre français, publié en Amérique, en ce moment . . . quelle classe de lecteurs ce genre de livre pourra-t-il intéresser? Atteindra-t-il le grand public?"[112]

Vincent encourages her to send the complete manuscript to Albert Millet, a famed (and fictional) New York editor, who responds favorably to Geneviève's book, which she publishes as *Parsons House*.

The *mise en abyme* structure of Paule d'Oncin's novel articulates clearly what a woman in 1943 might have been thinking about her chances of publishing a first novel in French in New York. The odds might have been stacked against her—the commercial viability of such a book might not be self-evident—but editors *were* willing to take a chance on her, precisely because (as Oncin intuited but her character Vincent did not), favorable market conditions allowed them to publish books with a very distinct aim, aside from commercialism. The pages of a novel registered awareness of the inner workings of the U.S. publishing industry at a critical moment of change and innovation: a prominent New York press might take on an unconventional literary project, in French, by a first-time writer, and in so doing, reveal how market and social conditions—in this case, the wartime support for French-language publishing and the urgent need for Franco-American cooperation—could itself spur innovation. These publishing practices would continue to evolve in fascinating ways in the 1950s and 60s, as new media expanded the possibilities for literature and offered renewed possibilities for Franco-American cultural exchange.

Commissioned for the Screen
French Avant-Garde Literature
for American TV

> Found texts thrust us into the opposite of the irreversible: no longer
> absence, destruction, or loss, but rather a supplement of presence . . .
> the newly recovered arrival gives us the joy of receiving the old as new.
> —JUDITH SCHLANGER, *Présence des oeuvres perdues*[1]

IN LATE 1962, BARNEY ROSSET, publisher and owner of Grove Press, approached several prominent writers in Grove's stable with a proposal: would they be interested in writing an original screenplay for American television audiences? Grove had never before ventured into the motion picture industry, but Rosset, hoping to capitalize on the expanding television market of early 1960s America, saw a potential role for his coterie of international avant-garde writers who had brought Grove renown and success in the U.S. All of the writers Rosset asked were European, and most wrote in French—Samuel Beckett, Marguerite Duras, Jean Genet, Eugène Ionesco, and Alain Robbe-Grillet, in addition to Ingeborg Bachmann, Günter Grass, and Harold Pinter—and with the exception of Bachmann, Genet, and Grass, all accepted and submitted original works for production. In the end, only Beckett's *Film* was produced and distributed, while the other screenplays gathered dust in the files of publishers' archives.

It is, in large part, my discovery of these unproduced screenplays that motivates this chapter. While some scholars in France have been aware, for example, that an early screenplay version of Marguerite Duras's *Le Ravissement de Lol V. Stein*, pre-dating the novel, might have existed, it was long deemed a "*script perdu*," a lost script absent from Duras's archival collection in France aside from a brief synopsis of its plot.[2] Though Duras's screenplay, like Ionesco's "The Hard-Boiled Egg" and Robbe-Grillet's *Frank's Return,* were never filmed, for reasons that will be discussed, Grove took the television project seriously, translating all the scripts into English to prepare them for production. These texts constitute early examples of what Rebecca L. Walkowitz has called "born-translated literature," in that translation was a crucial and fundamental "condition of [their] production."[3] As commissioned works, the screenplays were created for a translation market, conceived and written with an eye to their reception by television viewers in the United States. Reading these screenplays alongside a host of manuscripts, letters, and other documents that I have pieced together from archives on both sides of the Atlantic tells an extraordinary story about how the opportunity to write for an American audience shaped the writing of some of France's most celebrated mid-century writers. In that sense, the scripts offer a rare opportunity both to consider new materials absent from official Pléiade editions and other scholarly records, and also to apprehend a dynamic moment in Franco-American literary history in the early 1960s when French writers were asked to think seriously about American TV.

That writers such as Beckett, Duras, Ionesco, or Robbe-Grillet would have even agreed to such a project was not inevitable. Years later, Rosset recalled the vehemence with which Genet categorically refused to submit a screenplay:

> Fred Jordan [a Grove editor] and I met with Jean Genet at the Ritz Hotel in London. Genet was then and later a Grove author, but that did not keep him from angrily (though with a wonderfully comic effect) dismissing our proposal. Using the room's TV set as a prop, Genet explained to us—or at least to himself—that the little people on the screen were not really there. He proved this by walking to the back of the set. Where were they? He wanted "real actors."[4]

Genet's reaction was emblematic of the widespread skepticism about television as a medium that circulated in postwar Europe. His indictment of TV's artificiality recalled Theodor Adorno's 1954 essay "Television and the Patterns of Mass Culture" and its critique of the "sham" embedded in modern mass media.[5] It was commonplace for intellectuals in France in the 1950s to see television "as a creeping symptom of a mass modernity that had yet to arrive."[6] France was slow to integrate television into daily life, in large part on ideological grounds that rejected commercial culture.[7] By the 1950s, television had yet to occupy a central role in the French middle-class home, as it did in the United States; in 1953, only 60,000 homes in France boasted a television set—well below the 28 million in the U.S. in the same year—and not until 1961 did the network grid reach all of mainland France.[8] When Rosset met with Genet in London to try out his idea, the French television broadcast system included only a single nationally run channel: *Radiodiffusion-Télévision Française* (RTF). France was on the eve of a television expansion. In 1964, RTF would become ORTF (*Office de Radiodiffusion-Télévision Française*) and a second channel would be created, leading to a wider array of programming. But in late 1962, when French novelists were considering Rosset's offer, one can imagine that the idea of writing for television could be as much a source of distrust and concern—as it was for Genet—as it could have also been, for others, an appealing opportunity, both economically and aesthetically, to participate in a new technology still in nascent form in France.

What, then, did it mean for a French writer to take on such a project? What do their scripts reveal about their engagement with television as a new medium and their expectations of American audiences? In what ways did their writing for the American TV industry—even if most of the projects went ultimately unrealized—impact their subsequent literary and cultural productions? Before turning to the screenplays themselves, this chapter first considers these questions in light of comparative developments in American and French television culture of the 1950s and early 60s, dialing in on the context for Grove's Evergreen Theater project, the respective differences in programming in the U.S. and France, and the opportunities available for avant-garde authors to present works on television.

Evergreen Theater, the Avant-Garde, and Postwar TV

When Rosset launched Evergreen Theater, Inc. in 1963, his aim was to expand Grove's role in making innovative modernist writers from Europe known to an American public. Loren Glass's in-depth study of Grove has shown how the press, with its strong commitment to publishing avant-garde literature in translation, successfully "siphoned cultural capital from Paris to New York in the 1950s and 1960s."[9] Evergreen Theater followed on the heels of Grove's *Evergreen Review*, a journal founded in 1957 to publish essays on contemporary literature and, increasingly over time, on modern cinema as well. With Evergreen Theater, Rosset expressly sought, as publicized in the company's press release, "to originate and produce motion pictures by prominent contemporary European writers and playwrights."[10] Rosset had good reason to believe that the television industry would be interested in such projects: as early as 1960, CBS asked him about the possibility of obtaining television rights for a Beckett play.[11] By the time the company was formally launched, Rosset had already received confirmation from Beckett, Duras, and Ionesco that they would contribute screenplays and had secured a funder for the project: the actor and TV entrepreneur Dick Powell.[12]

Powell's untimely death in 1963 both complicated production plans and makes our access to this history incomplete, but it is nonetheless worthwhile to reconstruct what would have been appealing to Powell and his company, *Four Star Productions*, in agreeing to fund the Evergreen project. Powell had gained a name for himself in Hollywood—first as a musical actor in Busby Berkeley films of the 1930s, and later for his starring role in crime dramas like *Murder, My Sweet* (1944).[13] When Hollywood started to shift into TV production in the 1950s, Powell saw an opportunity both to invest in a new market as a producer and to gain independence from major film studios like Warner Brothers and Paramount. With the help of industry friends, he secured financial backing to open *Four Star Productions* in 1952; by 1956, when distribution companies bought the rights to his anthology series *Four Star Playhouse*—named for the four actors, including Powell, who would alternate starring roles in the biweekly series—Powell had become a millionaire.[14] The episodes of *Four Star*, as well as Powell's later venture *The Dick Powell Theatre*, ranged in tone and type, from light comedy to film noir to family drama, but they all figured within the expansion of the "telefilm series," the genre that Christopher Anderson has shown to have dominated American prime-time television since its inception in the 1950s with famous series like *Alfred Hitchcock Presents*.[15] *Four Star Productions* not only became "the fastest rising company in telefilm production," but it innovated by seeking to empower writers to oversee the entire process, from composing original screenplays to managing production.[16] Most of the writers Powell hired worked within the Hollywood industry—writers like Aaron Spelling or Blake Edwards who would become immensely successful—and Powell showed an interest in adapting literary works for the screen. The concept for *Dick Powell's Zane Grey Theatre*, produced by *Four Star Productions* and aired from 1956–1961, was originally based on the eponymous writer of western novels. The commercially successful American novelist Zane Grey was stylistically quite different from the French avant-garde writers that *Four Star* agreed to help produce, but the *Evergreen* project reflected nonetheless Powell's commitment to place writers at the center of the TV film process.

In 1962, when Rosset first approached him, Powell was riding high from his recent Emmy successes. The first season of the *Dick Powell Show* had been nominated for outstanding drama series, and though it ended up losing in that category, one of its episodes, "The Price of Tomatoes" won an Emmy for Peter Falk's performance in a leading role. As was customary in many playhouse series of its time, the episode was functionally a short telefilm, unrelated in content to other installments in the series, here narrating the story of a truck driver (Falk) who helps an undocumented immigrant crossing the southern border to birth a child in the United States. Episodes of playhouse series varied in length from thirty to sixty minutes, but they were all conceived as original screenplays for a TV audience. The commercial success of these short films made exclusively for TV gave producers like Powell the freedom to experiment with different kinds of narratives and the knowledge that they drew on a steady base of viewers interested in original filmed productions. Indeed, so popular had filmed productions become that by 1962, they represented three quarters of all programming on the three major networks—CBS, ABC, and NBC—supplanting the popular live television of a decade earlier.[17]

In that context, while one might imagine that short films by experimental European writers would constitute a significant departure from mainstream American telefilms, the leap that *Four Star Productions* was willing to take might not be as great as one would expect. In *TV by Design*, Lynn Spigel has shown just how crucially American TV, since its inception, was engaged with modern art and ideas of the avant-garde. Countering conventional narratives of television as a lowbrow, popular medium, Spigel highlights countless examples of commercials, shows, and design campaigns in the 1950s and 60s that explicitly emulated the style of the avant-garde, from CBS's Surrealist eye logo, to commercials modeled on Alain Resnais's *Last Year at Marienbad*, to made-for-TV art films.[18] By the early 1960s, not only were international art films increasingly featured on network TV, but many network series had begun to develop an "artier, cinematic feel" indebted to *film noir* and the New Wave.[19] Rosset's vision of original art films by European directors to air on television, then, evolved within a historical context where viewers could be expected to have at least some basic familiarity with certain avant-garde tropes.

By contrast, French television of the same period was at a much more rudimentary stage, technologically and aesthetically. Even with only a single national channel in operation before 1964, television in France did not yet have non-stop programming.[20] The reluctance in France to adapt to new technologies reflected a certain ambivalence about the new visual medium, as Jérôme Bourdon has argued: on the one hand, those at the helm of French television in the early 1960s fully rejected the logic of commercialism that seemed crucial to the American and British television enterprise, while they simultaneously struggled to articulate an alternative vision.[21] Most of French television served a pedagogical function—modeling RTF's guiding motto to "educate, inform, and entertain"—and were filmed "en direct," including adaptations of classical theater, cooking shows, and lessons in French history, as seen for instance in the ever popular *La Caméra explore le temps*, the historical anthology series that led the ratings from 1957 to 1966.[22]

Telefilms had not yet gained a footing in France, as they would later in the 60s, and when films were featured on television, they typically aired long after their cinematic release. That French television would favor rereleases and theatrical adaptations of classic plays makes sense economically: the conditions were simply not conducive to original production without strong financial backing, and even with the creation of the *Service de la recherche*, charged with bringing original artistic content to television, financial woes abounded.[23] Bourdon tells of a moment in 1963 when Albert Ollivier, then director of the RTF, who was hoping to expand the television medium to include original cinematic production, invited Jean-Luc Godard, François Truffaut, and Louis Malle to his office. "*Come work with any scripts that you'd like*" ("*Venez travailler avec les textes que vous voulez*"), he told them, before realizing that the offer was unfeasible given the drastic budget and pay differences between TV and film.[24] French cinematographers and writers alike might have seen their works aired or performed on television—as was the case, for example, in November 1962, when Ionesco authorized a production of *Les Chaises*, or in January 1963, when Beckett granted permission to Robert Pinget to adapt for

French TV his radio play *All That Fall* as *Tous ceux qui tombent* (while Beckett himself did not participate in the production). In all such cases, television borrowed from other media to display products translated or adapted in a new visual form, rather than providing a compelling opportunity for original writing itself.

This state of French television in the early 1960s helps to explain why writers like Beckett, Duras, Ionesco, and Robbe-Grillet might have been drawn to Barney Rosset's proposal. The American television industry certainly had the financial capital to invest in original avant-garde writing—in ways that were not feasible in France—and it promised a broad audience increasingly familiar with, and receptive to, arty and cinematic forms. Moreover, on a political level, the situation in France prohibited certain writers from participating in television at all: any signatory of the 1960 "Manifesto of the 121" denouncing France's military involvement in the Algerian War for Independence (1954–62)—which included Duras and Robbe-Grillet, among many other writers and intellectuals—were sanctioned by General de Gaulle, who barred them from appearing on TV and radio.[25] With television deployed as a blatant instrument of government control, writers would have sensibly been wary of it.

This helps to explain why ambivalence about television as a medium is a palpable subtext in the manuscripts each writer submitted to Grove. The scripts presented these writers with an opportunity to intervene in a rapidly expanding medium through a topic of their choosing and to question television as a form. Such a dynamic is, of course, a hallmark of the avant-garde project, relying, as it historically has, on art practices to issue an ideological critique of cultural and social institutions.[26] In taking seriously as cultural productions scripts that never reached fruition, I follow Jean-Louis Jeannelle's call, in *Films sans images*, to treat "invisible cinema"—scripts that never get made, or remain unfinished, or lack the funding to get produced or diffused—as an ontologically meaningful category of literary objects in which the "surviving traces" testify to a work's "creative dynamic" ("une dynamique de création telle qu'en attestent toutes les traces subsistantes").[27] What we see across the Evergreen screenplays—whether produced in the case of Beckett or not, for all the others—are varying degrees of fascination, skepticism, and anxiety about shifting audiovisual technologies. Attending to these scripts, and following the traces that they leave, enable a wider lens through which to understand each writer's literary and cultural project.

The New Wave for the Small Screen: Beckett and Robbe-Grillet

It made perfect sense, at the beginning of the 1960s, for writers in France to be thinking about visual media. The concurrent explosion of the New Novel (*nouveau roman*) and the New Wave (*nouvelle vague*) in the late 1950s had the effect both of bringing writers and filmmakers into closer contact and of making filmmakers out of writers. This coincidence between the two movements was certainly not coincidental, as Lynn Higgins has argued, and accounts for the "shared *écriture*" between novelists and filmmakers, whose characteristic techniques—"repetition, circularity, return, refusal (or inability) to achieve closure, spiraling in on themselves, gaps, holes, blank spaces, aporias of all kinds, jumps and cuts, proliferating *mises en abyme* and figures of infinite regress"—reshaped literary and cinematic works of that period.[28]

When presented with the Evergreen proposal, Robbe-Grillet and Beckett came equipped with vastly different film experiences. Robbe-Grillet had just made *L'année dernière à Marienbad* with Alain Resnais in 1961, a film that met with immediate acclaim and would become a cult classic. In writing the screenplay, Robbe-Grillet had sought to embody the perspective of the filmmaker, "to conceive [the story] in images, with all that entails in the precision not just of gestures and setting, but of the position and movement of the cameras, as well as the sequence of film shots" ("concevoir [l'histoire] en images, avec tout ce que cela comporte de précisions non seulement sur les gestes et les décors, mais sur la position et le mouvement des appareils, ainsi que sur la succession des plans au montage").[29] Beckett, meanwhile, had no prior experience with the screen. "The film thing has me petrified with fright," he wrote in March 1963 to the American theater director Alan Schneider after meeting with Rosset in Paris.[30]

Though a novice at filmmaking, Beckett admired contemporary French cinema, and Resnais's work in particular. In 1958, there had been talk of Resnais adapting Beckett's BBC radio play *All That Fall*, an idea that appealed to Beckett: "Talk also of a film (Alain Resnais) of the French *All That Fall*. I have not yet given the green light for this, but so admire Resnais that I probably shall."³¹ Though it is not clear why that plan fell through, and why Michel Mitrani, and not Resnais, ultimately directed *Tous ceux qui tombent* in French in 1963, Beckett seems to have forever associated Resnais with the project—so much so that in the French version, the main character Maddy Rooney is renamed Mme Resnais.³² Resnais remained an elusive presence for Beckett's early engagements with the screen: in 1964, as the production of *Film* was underway on the streets of New York City, Resnais made a stand-out appearance on the set amongst the "hordes of onlookers" who had come to observe Beckett on his first (and last) visit to the United States.³³

The fact that Resnais returns as a frequent, if but symbolic, reference point for Beckett helps to situate *Film*, alongside Robbe-Grillet's screenplay, as efforts to grapple with New Wave cinema techniques for the small screen. Both *Film* and *Frank's Return* activate a sense of the camera as itself one of the films' protagonists—an idea that, by 1963, would not have been foreign to *nouvelle vague* cinema—except they did so particularly through a reflection on the camera's invasiveness into private life. In reading *Film*, a production over which much ink has already been spilled, alongside *Frank's Return*—heretofore absent from any scholarly criticism—we gain insight into a cultural moment in which two renowned *auteurs* investigated how the camera interacts with its subject and encroaches on the domestic sphere.

As its title portends, *Film* would be the only cinematic work that Beckett would ever write and produce. Working within the constraint of a thirty-minute film, Beckett sought to explore the limits of the Irish philosopher Bishop Berkeley's claim that "esse est percipi" or "to be is to be perceived." Turning Berkeley's claim back on itself, Beckett asked in *Film* whether "the man who desires to cease to be must cease to be perceived."³⁴ The man in question—played in the film by Buster Keaton—effectively has two roles, each one representing the elements of individual self-perception: he is both the subject of the gaze (denoted in the script as "E," for eye) and its object ("O"). While E has a clear power of perception, O's gaze is rendered as fuzzy, an effect that required two cameras to achieve. The screenplay directions were largely conceptual in scope, with diagrams that detailed precise camera angles for every shot. At its core was what Beckett called the "angle of immunity": so long as O was perceived by E from behind, at an angle of less than forty-five degrees, all was well. But if E's angle of vision ever exceeded forty-five degrees,

O would experience intense anguish—the anguish of being perceived—that would be immediately perceptible to the viewer. It is only in the final moments of the film that O catches E—the camera—in the act of viewing him directly, and the film closes on this moment of self-perception.

The critical discourse on *Film* has been largely shaped by Gilles Deleuze, who deemed it "the greatest Irish film" ever made.[35] For Deleuze, *Film* makes the claim that it is only in death that one becomes imperceptible, but that death, for Beckett, is never finite and is always moving towards another idea of spirit. Deleuze analyzes the three "scenes" of *Film*—the first, as the man nervously ascends a staircase, hovering close to the wall; next, the barren interior room where he encounters photographs, animals, and a series of miscellaneous objects; and the last, where he is seated in a rocking chair, dozing (and whose momentary immobility evokes death), only to be shocked awake by the camera's gaze—and proposes that each scene corresponds to the three critical layers of cinematic "image-movement": action, perception, and affection. Beckett's "originality" for Deleuze was in disaggregating symbolically and sequentially each of these layers, representing the action of stairway ascent through a medium shot, the perception of objects through an establishing shot, and the affect of self-perception through a close-up.[36] By teasing apart these dimensions of the cinematic image through "complex technical means," Beckett epitomizes in Deleuze's terms "an important tendency of the so-called experimental cinema [that] consists in recreating this acentred plane of pure movement-images in order to establish it there."[37]

Though Deleuze could not have anchored his analysis of cinematic images in Robbe-Grillet's unproduced *Frank's Return*, he might very well have identified a similar effect, had the film ever been made. Robbe-Grillet's script is written as a series of prescriptive camera angles—635 shots in all—with clear and precise directives about what must be included in the frame and how each shot should be filmed.[38] Set in a port city somewhere on the coast of Brazil, the narrative revolves around Frank's return to this hometown and his desire to win back Marie-Esmeralda from a rival, Grant. There are a series of other minor characters, but most of the "plot"—to the extent that there ever is one in a work by Robbe-Grillet—centers on the confrontation between the two men, in scenes that jump, double back, and undercut any notion of linear time. We are given to understand that Frank and Grant echo each other beyond just their love interest: "Although his stature, his clothes, even his face greatly resemble Frank's, we now see that it [Grant] cannot be Frank," the script reads, as Grant faces his rival head-on, positioned behind the camera (Shot 24). Frank and Grant are repeatedly depicted as visual doubles, filmed in identical camera shots (e.g., Shot 25) or walking with a similar gait (Shot 527). The confusion between them suggests a splitting not entirely different from E and O, in this case through frequent reverse shots that emphasize the subject-object divide in perception. Frank and Grant almost never occupy the camera at the same time, and in the rare moments when they do, they are presented in profile, mirror images, preparing for battle against each other. Elsewhere Deleuze had associated Robbe-Grillet's cinematography with "l'image-temps" ("time-image")—as distinct from "l'image-mouvement" ("movement-image")—particularly in *L'année dernière à Marienbad*'s collapsing of past and present, and of reality and fantasy.[39] While one might reasonably contest Deleuze's conceptual opposition between *Film* and *Marienbad*—Beckett certainly had Robbe-Grillet's film in mind when E, like the character A in *Marienbad*, confronts photographic images of himself in the past[40]—what seems clear is that both *Frank's Return* and *Film* turn on a shared concern for angle of vision and for the character's gaze, embodied by the camera, that prompts all action and (self-) perception.

Film and *Frank's Return* align, in that sense, in their shared depiction of the camera as a menacing object whose presence brings with it the threat of violence. In Robbe-Grillet, this violence is overt: as Frank imagines confronting Grant over Marie-Esmeralda, he "slowly raises his right hand to the pocket of his jacket (as though to grasp a revolver inside)" (Shot 25), a foreshadowing of the eventual, accidental murder of the wrong person, Marie-Esmeralda (Shots 619–620). The film does not resolve whether she is killed by Frank or Grant in their face-off—given their explicit doubling, it ultimately doesn't matter—but what *is* clear is just how much the violence is provoked by, and directed at, the camera itself. As shots ring, "Grant brandish[es] his sawed-off shotgun at the camera (that is, toward Frank)" (Shots 601–603). Throughout the screenplay, different characters exhibit heightened anxiety as they notice Frank, positioned as he is with the camera: one character stares at the camera with an "anxious expression" as he recognizes Frank (Shots 33–34); another, Marie-Esmeralda, looks at Frank/the camera with "wide, trusting, alarmed eyes" that turn "frightened" (Shots 50, 59); and Grant is described as having "a kind of set grin as if provoking his invisible adversary (where the camera is)" (Shot 156). As a physical embodiment of the camera, Frank evokes in those who see him the fear of being perceived, the sense that his mere presence can incite violence.

In *Film*, meanwhile, the potential of violence lurks in the character's risk of self-perception. Consistent with Beckett's plays and novels, *Film* counterbalances the tragedy of existence with comedic effect: while O exhibits visceral anxiety if the angle of immunity is ever breached, he also engages humorously with the objects in his midst—such as in one slapstick scene where he repeatedly tries and fails to usher a cat and dog out of the apartment. The character's goal is to rid himself of all objects that might register perception of him—animals, a mirror and religious iconography on the wall (both of which he covers), or old family photographs that he rips up—but the one subject that he cannot evade is that of E / the camera.

The reverse shot that closes the film, in which O is abruptly rendered conscious of E's gaze, dramatizes the thrust of all that has led to that moment, what Beckett called in his notes the "unbearable quality of E's scrutiny."[41] The critic Graley Herren has interpreted the closing scene as emblematic of how *Film* is "foredoomed philosophically [and] cinematically" in its very conception, for try as O might to achieve imperceptibility by destroying objects, or evading E's gaze, his position as the main object of the *audience*'s gaze, of "*being on film*" throughout, contravenes from the outset the film's premise.[42] Herren is right to point out *Film*'s indictment of the spectator, aligned as the audience is in E's "predatory perception" by which we "participate by proxy in stalking O."[43] At the same time, we might read this less as a conceptual cinematic oversight on Beckett's part than as an effective mode of engaging the inescapability of the gaze. *Film* is indeed a film about watching, and spectators are reminded with each shot of their problematic complicity in that dynamic. Even when O is momentarily off-screen, as Colin Gardner shows, the objects of E's / the camera's / our gaze—such as a man-and-woman couple outdoors, or an elderly flower-seller in the apartment stairwell—are presented as victims in clear distress, tortured by whomever, and whatever, is watching them.[44] Whether outside on the street, or locked inside a solitary apartment, spectators are made to understand themselves as invaders of public and private space.

In the denouement of *Frank's Return*, we confront a mob of characters, some previously seen, others unnamed faces, but all of whom constitute "Grant's allies in the crowd" (Shot 582–584). Robbe-Grillet presents many of them in consecutive shots, such as these: "Another spectator in the front row of the crowd: Joe, the owner of the bar. Another spectator: John. All these characters must be in identical positions and all must be equally motionless" (Shots 579, 580). As Frank and Grant face off in battle, "men are converging" on all sides (Shot 590), in a gesture that appears to be a direct assault on the camera. In sequence, one character at a time "advances toward the camera..." and "pass[es] into extreme close-up" as the "music grows shrill and irritating" (Shots 595–599). The intensity of the moment culminates in Grant's three gunshots that, as cited earlier, take aim at Frank and the camera (Shots 601–603). Frank retaliates, shooting blindly at the crowd, none of whom appear injured (Shots 616–618). In the final camera shot, Frank is seen backing away from the crowd and departing on his boat, with Marie-Esmeralda's dead body by his side (Shots 622–626, 635). The crowd has not succeeded in saving Marie-Esmeralda, but their collective assault, with Frank's boat disappearing into the distance, manages in the end to chase the camera away.

It will surprise exactly no one that Robbe-Grillet and Beckett would both explore the idea of spectatorship through the medium of film, given New Wave cinema's formal preoccupation with reflexivity. The title and tenor of *Film* makes this point abundantly clear, as other Beckett scholars have noted.[45] Yet it matters, too, that both *Film* and *Frank's Return* were commissioned and conceived for TV, and we can locate traces of that particular visual medium in their shared thematization of a threatening spectatorship that yields both violence and fright. Both works nod to early Surrealist cinema—and Beckett surely had Luis Buñuel's *Un chien andalou* (1929) in mind as he worked on drafts of *Film*, whose working title was "The Eye"[46]—while they insist most emphatically on the camera's invasion into the domestic and private sphere. Nowhere is safe, even within the confines and security of a private home. Frank's presence disrupts the rhythms of everyday life, and characters hide indoors, as Frank tries to breach the boundaries of private space ("He's going to try the door again," announces a woman off-screen, trying to withdraw inside her home, as Frank "begins moving, again approaching the door of the house," Shot 189). Beckett's *Film* takes us from the outside in—from a street scene, shot near Brooklyn's Fulton fish market, much of which was cut for the final version[47]—to a bare room, staged from the exterior street shots of a New York City brick building (Figure 7) to the stairway ascent.

We (with E) watch O as he approaches the quintessential New York City apartment door, signaled by the large central peephole (Figure 8). Might Beckett and Robbe-Grillet both have been evoking, in these chosen settings, and in characteristic reflexive fashion, the invasion of the screen into domestic life, conforming to what Lynn Spigel has identified as common tropes about the "prying eye" of television in the postwar period?[48] The scripts seem to suggest so, and Beckett's papers make clear that this was, for him, a distinctly "TV project."[49] *Film* rightly belongs in cinema history, given its premier at the Venice Film Festival in 1965 and subsequent distribution, but in its conception and narrative focus, as with the unproduced Robbe-Grillet script, it posed questions that engaged directly and specifically with the nature of the small screen.

This ontological reflection on television as a medium goes a long way in explaining Beckett's subsequent productions. What began for Beckett as a tentative ambivalence about television as a medium turned into a full-fledged exploration of its technical potential. Though Beckett would make no other film, he went on to create many more works for television audiences: among them, *Oh Joe* (1966) and *Quad I* and *Quad II* (1981), all of which aired first in Germany and then on the BBC; *Not I*, a play staged first in New York by Alan Schneider and then adapted for American television (1977); *Ghost Trio* and . . . *but the clouds* . . . (BBC, 1977); and *Nacht und Träume* (Germany's SDR, 1982).[50] His final TV project, *What Where* (1986), took years to make and ultimately aired in Germany, and in a sense it brought Beckett full circle: he collaborated on it with Barney Rosset, who brought tapes to Beckett in Paris for his review.[51]

Beckett scholars often quote Beckett's assessment of *Film* as "an interesting failure" to justify a critique of the work. Yet Beckett revised that statement, which he declared "much too severe": the more he watched *Film*, the more he appreciated its "sheer beauty, power and strangeness of image."[52] Regardless of one's evaluative stance on *Film*, Beckett discovered in the experience of making it how to harness the mechanisms of television to powerful visual effect: in extreme close-ups on specific body parts, quick fade-ins and fade-outs, and intense lighting contrasts, all of which would come to characterize

Figure 7: Screenshot from Samuel Beckett's *Film* (1965)

Figure 8: Screenshot from Samuel Beckett's *Film* (1965)

his televisual works. If *Film* allowed Beckett to carve out a niche for himself, it is noteworthy that his television audience resided exclusively in the anglophone and German-speaking worlds—just one more sign that, vastly unlike the world of cinema, France continued to occupy a peripheral position in the development of avant-garde TV.

Television as Parody: Ionesco's Social Critique

By the end of the 1950s, Ionesco had cemented his reputation as a masterful playwright, whose comical character dialogues satirized the absurdities of bourgeois life, the dangers of political ideologies, and the farce of pseudo-intellectualism. His plays were written for the stage, where they were performed in theaters across Paris and in cities across Europe.[53] Despite some critics' laments that Ionesco had turned away from parody and subversion in his theatrical productions of the 1960s, the screenplay that he wrote for Grove, "*The Hard-Boiled Egg*," suggests instead that he channeled that parodic impulse in innovative ways.[54] The task of writing for television, and particularly for an audience of American viewers, enabled Ionesco to engage with social issues that he had yet to confront in his theatrical writings and that he saw as necessitated by new media forms.

Ionesco's interest in alternative modalities likely stemmed, in part, from his previous, brief foray in radio, as well as from the recent adaptations of his theatrical productions to new media. In wartime France, as Julia Elsky has shown, Ionesco was intimately involved in writing and producing radio plays as part of his employment for the Romanian delegation to Vichy. These productions, problematic as they were from a propagandistic point of view, dramatized questions of national identity and language that would become formative in his theatrical writing.[55] Years later, Ionesco would again encounter his theater on the radio. One of the first performances of *Rhinocéros*, even before its 1960 opening at Paris's Odéon-Théâtre de France, appeared in a 1959 English translation for the BBC radio, and *Les chaises* (*The Chairs*) aired in 1961 as a live-performed television production. Ionesco was not personally involved with either staging, but he became intrigued by the idea of adaptation, for aesthetic and conceptual reasons, and probably for financial ones too. At his request, *Variety magazine* published an advertisement in their January 2, 1963, issue stating that "MR. EUGENE IONESCO"—his name bolded in large capital letters—personally "requests alll [sic] agencies, theater directors and producers in the realms of theater, motion picture, radio, recording companies, etc." to send proposals to him through his publishers in the United States or France.⁵⁶ The advertisement, which Ionesco had drafted in French in a December 1962 letter to Rosset, reflected his eagerness to support new versions of his work across languages and genres.⁵⁷

In contemplating screenplay ideas for Rosset's Evergreen project, Ionesco came up with two possible options. The first, "Last Saturday in Hammambad" ("Samedi dernier au hammam-bad"), was a not-so-subtle sendup of Robbe-Grillet and Resnais's recently released *Last Year in Marienbad* (1961). In Ionesco's version, the setting would shift from a countryside estate to the Marais district of Paris, where a man would be searching for a young blond woman whom he had seen before. She would appear in the most improbable of places—traversing deserted streets, exiting a urinal, buying meat at a Kosher butcher—and only at the end of the film, when the blond woman is replaced by a black woman, will the man declare "c'est bien elle" ("that is her").⁵⁸ His second project proposal was for "L'oeuf dur" ("The Hard-Boiled Egg"), in which Ionesco imagined two parallel storylines that ostensibly converged around the dual meanings of "*hard-boiled*": "un film de faux suspens" ("a fake suspense film"), in the style of an American western, and a cooking demonstration for preparing a hard-boiled egg.⁵⁹ An undated telegram in Ionesco's personal papers from Richard Seaver declares the press's decision:

CONTRAT FILM PREPARE PAR SALISBURY A ETE SIGNE PAR BARNEY AUJOURDHUI STOP NOUS PREFERONS FINALEMENT OEUF DUR COMME SCENARIO AMITIES DICK

FILM CONTRACT PREPARED BY SALISBURY WAS SIGNED TODAY BY BARNEY STOP WE ULTIMATELY PREFER THE HARD-BOILED EGG SCRIPT REGARDS DICK⁶⁰

Regardless of Grove's selection, Ionesco made clear in both project ideas his explicit interest in exploring the possibilities of parody. Such was not a new mode for Ionesco, given the political and ideological critiques embedded in his previous plays like *La Cantatrice chauve* (*The Bald Soprano*) (1950) and *Rhinocéros* (1960). Ionesco was drawn to theater's capacity to center the "extreme exaggeration of feeling, an exaggeration that shatters mundane reality" ("exagération extrême des sentiments, exagération qui disloque la plate réalité quotidienne").[61] In turning from theater to film, Ionesco seemed particularly keen to experiment with how this idea—of exaggerating or adding shock value to the quotidian—might translate to other media, particularly visual ones. As a *Herald Tribune* article aptly put it after an interview in 1962 related to *La colère*, "Mr. Ionesco says he has tried to translate his subject matter into pictorial terms, that is, into a series of images each growing out of its predecessor 'organically,' through a chain of inevitable circumstances."[62]

A closer look at the short film *La colère* provides important context for situating "The Hard-Boiled Egg" as a work satirizing the medium of television. The sketch was part of *Les sept péchés capitaux* (*The Seven Deadly Sins*, 1962), a compilation of short films by seven authors and filmmakers—including Claude Chabrol, Jean-Luc Godard, Claude Mauriac, and Roger Vadim—each of whom tackled a different deadly sin; Ionesco was charged with anger. *La colère* depicts a traditional Sunday afternoon—families leaving church, lunch gatherings in outdoor cafés and apartments—that devolves into a series of monumental catastrophes, including the threat of nuclear war. The short film bears all the traces of Ionesco's irony, in which appearances belie the tragedy of existence. As one woman in the film brags to another, her husband is "very happy, you know; he has adjusted quite well to paralysis" ("très heureux, vous savez, il s'est très bien habitué à sa paralysie").[63]

The film takes the viewer through a series of domestic scenes in which seemingly blissful couples about to enjoy a Sunday lunch suddenly discover a fly lurking in their soup, prompting total chaos. The film flashes from one household dining room to the next, in which men of various ages, accents, and professions exclaim to their wives that, for the last twenty-five years, they have consistently found "a fly in my soup!" ("une mouche dans ma soupe!"). No longer able to take it, couples throw dishes at each other and spout verbal insults. Their anger spills from the home into the street—literalized by flooding water that seeps under doorframes and by fires that erupt from unattended stovetop burners—and culminates in widespread rioting on streets around the world, including actual news footage of antiwar protests and atomic bomb explosions. The film foreshadows this turn from the local to the global. "How about we listen to the news?" ("Si on écoutait les nouvelles?"), asks the husband in the film's first home scene, to which his wife replies by turning on the television in their dining room. It is by way of the television set that viewers are narratively transported from one home to the next, widening their gaze from the TV frame to its placement in each domestic space. In a half dozen dining rooms, the television is given pride of place, transmitting news headlines from the same female newscaster as an audiovisual backdrop to the film's staging of the couples' marital bliss.

It is noteworthy that Ionesco, in 1961, would center the television set as a common fixture of domestic living space. His representation of television indexes the recent transformation in France that had expanded the network grid across the nation, while it also played into tropes, circulating widely in 1950s America, that television held the promise of domestic harmony and could be functionally integrated into central eating and living spaces.[64] Whether Ionesco witnessed that for himself in his recent visits to the United States—he had, for instance, traveled to New York in 1961 for the opening of *Rhinocéros*—we cannot be certain. But we can be sure that television was at the forefront of his mind. On the cover page of a screenplay draft of *La colère* that includes a few scribbled, handwritten notes, Ionesco circles the word "télévision" and ends with the parenthetical note "et peut-être plusieurs télés—" ("and maybe a few TVs—").[65]

During film production, Ionesco expressed his dissatisfaction with the producer's lack of attention to the placement of the television sets:

> In the part of the film where we see happy homes, the TV announcer and the television set itself must play a big role: yet that cannot happen because the television is invisible, relegated to the background.
>
> Dans la partie du film où l'on voit les intérieurs heureux, la speakerine de la télévision et la télévision elle-même doivent jouer un grand rôle: or, cela ne peut se faire car la télévision est invisible, reléguée qu'elle est au second plan.[66]

Ionesco sought to represent the ways in which the advent of television into the home could disrupt the boundaries between public and private. In the narrative universe of *La colère*, the television operates as a tool of trickery and a threat to domestic life. The newscaster's repeated claims of good news from around the world ("Les nouvelles sont bonnes!" Figure 9), set against the ensuing scenes of global havoc, enact the film's dramatic irony. Flies may very well have been present in Sunday soup bowls for twenty-five years, but it is the arrival of television technology—the tool that brings that outside world in—that breaks family harmony. Ionesco's take on anger, in all its exaggerated forms, narrativizes anxieties about television as a threat to domestic life.

At the same time, the TV set functioned strategically for Ionesco as a narrative tool for swift visual storytelling. The rapid succession of images on an identical and identifiable visual object, from one home to the next, usefully communicated the ubiquity of collective anger. In that sense, the move from theatrical to cinematic modes of storytelling allowed Ionesco to extend his satirical gaze more quickly from the specific to the general. What seems to have intrigued Ionesco about the prospect of writing for the screen was the translation process by which words could transform into a series of images; in agreeing to Rosset's proposal, he described an idea for "a culinary recipe to put into images" ("une recette culinaire à mettre en images").[67] This intersemiotic process of translation is one that Ionesco would continue to sharpen by reflecting concretely in his American screenplay on the nature of images circulated on television.

Figure 9: Screenshot from Eugène Ionesco's *La colère* (1962)

"THE HARD-BOILED EGG" IN THE AGE OF HOMEMAKING SHOWS

Given Ionesco's recent interest in representing television, it seems fitting that he would have been asked to produce a work directly for TV. The original French script of "L'oeuf dur," early drafts of which can be found among Ionesco's papers at the *Bibliothèque nationale de France,* begins with three "gangsters" who open fire with machine guns on an old French farm. One comically instructs all the farmworkers to put their hands up, while the other two sneak into the henhouse. Scared by the commotion, the hens start laying eggs at an alarming rate; the thieves gather up the eggs and stash them in their bags. Moments later, a driver arrives in a getaway van to rescue the gangsters from the scene, and "on the van is written, in big letters, 'radio television'" ("[s]ur le camion, en grosses lettres, est écrit: radio télévision").[68] Ionesco's villain is clear—in France, the two media were closely aligned in the 1960s under the umbrella title Radio-Télévision Française (RTF)—but the egg thieves do not get far: they are eventually defeated in a shootout with the police, and the eggs and weapons are left on the side of the road.

These opening pages of the screenplay do not make it into the English translation. Instead of an alternating narrative sequence, the English translation maintains only the cooking demonstration, thus making the script easier to follow, less visually complex, and less expensive to produce. Moreover, Ionesco's knock on RTF would have been more legible for French audiences than for Americans.[69] Yet the idea that television was complicit in a crime seems to have permeated his thinking at the time of writing the screenplay, and he found other ways of making that satire manifest for American viewers—in particular, through a wider critique of the ways that gender and race are distorted by commercialized culture.

The storyline of "The Hard-Boiled Egg" is carefully attuned to the role of television in the 1960s home. The English script begins with a "shot of a modern kitchen," in which a woman wearing an apron holds an egg in her hand. The directions for the earliest shots in the film insist on its pedagogical mode: a blackboard displays chalk-drawn images of an egg's formation and dimensions, while the woman narrates instructions for cooking the egg, both on-screen and in voice-over:

> "To prepare a hard-boiled egg, first go to your local dairy. . . . To make sure the egg is fresh ask your dairyman to candle it. . . . It's preferable to cook the

hard-boiled egg on a stove. Don't put the egg directly on the stove.... You must put water into the saucepan, a sufficient amount so as to cover the egg."⁷⁰

Yet despite any appearance of conformity to the genre of the cooking show, the script quickly makes clear that something is awry. The camera is instructed to pan slowly over standard kitchen objects and materials (e.g., refrigerator, sink, faucet, Formica table) until

> [w]e see a drawer open slowly by itself. Inside, we can catch a glimpse of neat rows of knives, forks and spoons. Another drawer opens, and inside we can see some cups and saucers. Then the camera shows a white cupboard, inside which we can see three onions, a tomato, a dry loaf of bread and a surprised white mouse, which turns away.⁷¹

This ironic subversion of cooking show conventions proceeds throughout the woman's lesson, in which visual images projected for the audience complicate the apparent simplicity of the cooking task. Alongside her banal instructions for proper saucepan diameter and optimal water quantity for the egg's preparation, we are presented with outdoor street scenes: houses in a small village, snowflakes falling, a dog jumping away from a car's headlights. The images become increasingly catastrophic: as the woman prepares to light the stove, we see a

> very enlarged close-up of the pipes, the burner openings, the little flames, which grow even larger. A forest fire, incandescent polycanders in the sky above the forest. A woman catches on fire. Fish on fire. A house on fire, etc.⁷²

As people, animals, and cities erupt in flames, the camera returns to the woman, whose face is locked in a "gracious, serene smile."⁷³ The world burns, but the cooking demonstration continues.

The parodic script makes clear Ionesco's familiarity with the televised cooking show. In the United States, so fundamental were cooking shows to the emergence of postwar television that by 1952 two thirds of all local television stations included a kitchen set.⁷⁴ Cooking shows in France were similarly adopted early in RTF's history because they could enact all three of the network's broadcasting goals of educating, informing, and entertaining. Raymond Oliver's *Art et magie de la cuisine*, for one, had been a successful weekly program since 1954, in which Oliver—the owner of Paris's three-star Michelin restaurant Le Grand Véfour—instructs his assistant, Catherine Langeais, on proper cooking methods, and she, cast as a devoted and somewhat naïve protégé, happily echoes back his instructions. In one episode aired in September 1962, Oliver teaches Langeais how to cook an omelette: the opening credits, in which eggs dance their way into a saucepan without any human intervention, would have amused and inspired any viewer with Surrealist or absurdist narrative inclinations (Figure 10).⁷⁵

Eggs featured frequently in Oliver's cooking demonstrations, as they also did on the other side of the Atlantic, catalyzing Julia Child's television career.⁷⁶ Child's very first appearance on TV was in 1962, following the publication of *Mastering the Art of French Cooking* (1961), when she and her co-writer Simone Beck were invited to the *Today Show* to cook an omelette live on air. The cooking experiment was a near failure—the hotplate on set did not work as planned—but it taught Child, according to Dana Polan, "to train oneself to shrug off the accidents and contingencies that inevitably would still creep in and needed to be turned into lessons that one could learn from."⁷⁷

Such would become the aesthetic of Child's shows—a blend of techni-

Figure 10: Screenshot from the opening credits of *Art et magie de la cuisine* (1962)

cal instruction and whimsy—and after this first televised performance, she pitched her own show to WGBH TV in April 1962. The three pilot episodes of what would become *The French Chef* aired in July 1962 and showcased cooking demonstrations of the French omelette, the soufflé, and coq au vin.[78] The pilot episodes have been lost from WGBH's archive, but an episode from the first season, "The French Omelette," broadcast on February 23, 1963, gives us a clue as to what the pilot episode on eggs looked like: Child goes on a long riff about the diameters of pans and the proper cooking time for eggs. Where she talks at length about how using two or three eggs will vary the cooking time, Ionesco's chef in "The Hard-Boiled Egg" says, "If you want to have two or three egg [sic] . . . you quite naturally double or triple the amount. . . . The number of eggs does not affect the cooking time. This characteristic is no discredit to the eggs. If, despite all precautions, the egg is rotten . . . don't eat it."[79]

There is no saying with certainty that Ionesco watched these exact episodes of *Art et magie de la cuisine* or *The French Chef*, although the timing of his script, written shortly after Oliver's and Child's egg episodes aired in 1962, make it plausible. There can be no doubt, though, of the parodic intent of "The Hard-Boiled Egg." The success of the script's parody hinges on the audience's familiarity with the conventions of the cooking show—in everything from the kitchen set, to the exacting cooking details, to the host's calm affect in the face of potential disaster. Ionesco knew enough about television to expect his American viewers to recognize the conceptual frame of the cooking show. In turning to parody, he did what any avant-garde artist does best: he tapped into the zeitgeist of an era and issued a social commentary on the mechanisms that undergirded the very medium he was deploying. "The Hard-Boiled Egg" keenly registered television's representation and manipulation of women and cultural minorities. Early TV's homemaking shows actively targeted women as viewers—housewives in particular—and they sought, as Marsha Cassidy has shown, to foster a sense of intimacy and connection through kitchen sets that looked like they could belong in anyone's home. Shows like Oliver's and Child's conveyed the idea that *haute cuisine* could be accessible even for the untrained home cook, and their wild success in the 1950s and 60s, alongside that of other homemaking shows, testified to the role of women as influential media consumers.[80] In the narrative logic of *Art et magie*, Langeais—the unpracticed, smiling apprentice—could be any woman watching from home, ready to learn and eager to please her male counterpart.

REPRESENTING RACE AND GENDER ON TV

If in *La colère* Ionesco presents images of devoted housewives who watch TV and turn angry when their husbands cast aspersions on their cooking, "The Hard-Boiled Egg" goes a step further by insisting on TV's manipulation of female bodies and the gaze. The script enumerates in detail how the woman's body should be filmed:

> The camera parades slowly along her bare arm, reveals the suggestion of a breast, the neck, the back of the neck, then the woman's face, starting with her chin then ascending to her lips, her nose, her eyes, her ears. Then we see a close-up of large eyes, blinking, then the woman's whole face.[81]

The camera directions adhere to film's conventional sexualized gaze, what Laura Mulvey (and other feminist film scholars since) identify as "the indispensable element of spectacle in normal narrative film" whereby a woman's "visual presence tends to . . . freeze the flow of action in a moment of erotic contemplation."[82] Ionesco's directives apprehend those visual dynamics, scanning the woman's body in a manner akin to the egg, both objects to be consumed.

As it unfolds, the script clarifies the young woman's role as a "housewife"—"la ménagère," in the French text—and in glimpses between her exaggerated, overperformed smiles, we see signs of her agitation: "Shot of the face and bust of the young woman who, as she says the next sentence"—which will be another bland commentary on cutting an egg—"looks almost furious and speaks aggressively. She reverts to her smiling attitude."[83] The housewife's body betrays her efforts to maintain a veneer of happiness: as she hiccups uncontrollably, while trying to insist on the nutritional value of eggs, "[w]e clearly see that it is she speaking, but she speaks with the deep voice of a man."[84] In this act of defiance, Ionesco desacralizes the woman's body as a sexualized object, while rendering visible and audible her physical rejection of conventional ideals of fertility and motherhood. By defamiliarizing the woman's speech through a male-ventriloquized voice-over, Ionesco centers attention squarely on fixed ideas of gender that condition our gaze. Like the egg in the woman's hand that will transform into something inedible and rotten, this moment of re-gendering allows her to break out of the role, both in society and for the camera, that had attempted to contain her.

In a gesture that seems noteworthy for its time, "The Hard-Boiled Egg" extends its critical observation of visual culture from gender to race. Ionesco's theatrical productions had denounced racist discourses before: his satirical play *L'avenir est dans les oeufs* (*The Future Is in Eggs*, 1951) had even done so through the figure of eggs, offering a blistering critique of fascist anxieties of reproduction in hen-like women whose eggs guarantee the survival of "la race blanche" ("the white race").[85] Already attuned to racist ideologies, Ionesco registers in "The Hard-Boiled Egg" an awareness of the problematic representation of black bodies on screen. As the housewife's body is about to undergo its physical transformation, the camera reveals a new image:

> Close-up of a fat Negro woman, and of her hand bearing the egg to her mouth; close-up of the mouth alone, which opens, the teeth, the larynx, the enormous fingers in an exaggerated close-up holding the peeled egg, the teeth biting into the eggs four times and swallowing it, then the lips, the chin and the glottis moving as the egg is being swallowed. The lips close, the remains of the egg can be seen around the lips. As we see these unhurried shots, the young woman is speaking, off. . . . The egg is swallowed. Shot of the lips surrounded by the remains of the egg.[86]

As soon as the black woman consumes her egg, the housewife will eat hers, prompting her relentless hiccups and the change in her voice, signals of her body's physical revolt.

The script doubles down on that revolt through a narrative alignment with the black body, represented here through tropes that recall the infamous mammy figure of early American cinema and television. Images of what Patricia Turner has called "the good-humor, stocky, asexual, dark-skinned black woman" of Aunt Jemima ads, early twentieth-century Hollywood films (e.g., *The Birth of a Nation*, *Gone with the Wind*, *Imitation of Life*), or 1950s TV shows like *Beulah* invariably confined African American women to the kitchen and portrayed them as flat, uncomplicated characters who lacked internal agency.[87] "The Hard-Boiled Egg" seems both to index and chafe against such stereotypes, in ways that echo Lauren Berlant's reading of Delilah in *The*

Imitation of Life: countering dominant readings of the film's racist portrayal, Berlant argues that the "grotesque hyper-embodiment" enabled by the "extreme close-up" of Delilah's face "ironizes the tradition of grotesque African American representation in American consumer culture."[88] Ionesco's script suggests a similar effort by emphasizing these "exaggerated" and "unhurried" close-ups. The text's claim to visual hyperbole—an image of "grotesque hyper-embodiment"—situates the representation within Ionesco's wider absurdist project, which consistently turns on ridicule and embellishment as drivers of parody. In that way, race becomes an element of the parody, folded into the script's broader critique of consumer culture and gender.

Ionesco's contribution to the Evergreen project demonstrates how the task of writing for an audience in translation provided an impetus to address issues of visual representation that had yet to occupy his theatrical work. Through his outsider's gaze, Ionesco could mobilize his propensity toward satire in relation to both new media technologies and the specificities of American cultural dynamics. "The Hard-Boiled Egg" was written at a time, in the early 1960s, when American television began to signal an awareness of problematic racial dynamics in the United States. Had Ionesco's film aired on American TV, it might have been understood in the context of this turn toward what Donald Bogle has called "socially conscious" television that challenged racist stereotypes—albeit in a more experimental guise than typical prime-time drama series.[89]

The manuscripts of "The Hard-Boiled Egg" suggest that Ionesco's decision to address questions of race was both deliberate and belated: on a typed French draft, he handwrites the word "noire" ("black") in the margins to refer to the female character, a change that gets incorporated into the English translation. This addition, alongside the summary he had submitted for *Samedi dernier au hammam-bad*, shows that Ionesco became determined to think through the representation of black characters for his American production. From the vantage point of France, where decolonization and the recent war in Algeria constituted the major political upheavals of the moment, Ionesco's script indexes a burgeoning cultural consciousness about race and representation.[90]

It would be reckless, however, to overstate his race consciousness: in a brief moment in "The Hard-Boiled Egg" script, Ionesco refers to a passing image of "a Negro's hands beating a rhythm with drumsticks. A few notes of jazz,"[91] a resoundingly reductive depiction whose purpose beyond flat stereotype is unclear. But at a time when black characters were virtually absent from the French screen, both large and small, Ionesco's script cracks open a space for discussion and contestation, even if imperfectly.[92] The medium of television enabled Ionesco both to translate a theatrical mode of extreme exaggeration into images and to wrestle with specific representational problems endemic to visual culture and its mass circulation of images. Read in this historical context—even in the absence of a fully produced, televised counterpart—"The Hard-Boiled Egg" should be understood within the broader social fabric of the 1960s: as a work eager to confront the representation and consumption of gender and race on both sides of the Atlantic.

Reading Duras Otherwise

In this final section of the chapter, I want to return to the anecdote that opened this book: how might the archival record of Marguerite Duras's *The Ravishing of Lol Stein*—from my discovery of her screenplay draft in the Grove archives, to the baffling manuscript pages on which she wrote, which are part of the collections at IMEC—reframe our understanding of what has been one of the most critically acclaimed books in twentieth-century French literature?

Most scholarly readings of the novel tend to center on the dynamic between Lol V. Stein's story and the first-person narrator Jacques Hold, who attempts, as would an analyst, to reconstruct the pivotal moment in Lol's youth when her fiancé, Michael Richardson, abandons her at a local ball for his new love interest, Anne-Marie Stretter. The novel's vivid staging of Lol's suffering—her primal scream in the ballroom, her subsequent vacant and inscrutable gaze, her tendency to rehearse a triangular dynamic in future relationships—explains why so many critics have privileged psychoanalytic approaches, reading this and other Duras texts as meditations on "jammed repetition" and "impossible mourning" (Kristeva); highlighting the curative role of hypnosis (St. Amand); characterizing Lol as a figure of blankness in which Duras "mak[es] the lack speak" (Willis); or suggesting the feminist underpinnings of Hold's analytic stance (Suleiman).[93] These and other related readings have defined the critical legacy of *Le Ravissement*, and if we remember and still teach the novel today in advanced undergraduate or graduate seminars, it is most likely to probe the intersection of psychoanalysis, literature, and feminist writing and to reveal the pivotal role the novel played in shaping Duras's literary and cinematic works of the next decade.[94]

As fruitful as this critical lineage has been, it misses a key beat in the Lol story: *Le Ravissement* was first written not as the novel we read today but as a commissioned screenplay for an American television audience. This fact earns a passing mention in the *Pléiade* edition to Duras's works, but since the early screenplay is absent from Duras's papers, apart from a brief synopsis, scholars have not been able to properly account for it either in general literary criticism or fine-grained textual scholarship.[95] The *Ravissement* screenplay was never produced, but it *was* completed, translated into English, and catalogued in the Grove Press archives. This early manuscript enables an alternative reading of a novel that has been crucially embedded in twentieth-century French literary studies, and in what follows, I offer the first comparative analysis of the American screenplay and the French novel.

A transnational, cross-linguistic, and intermedial reading not only clarifies what genetic critics would call the *avant-texte* of *Le Ravissement*; it also illustrates Duras's embrace of—and fraught relationship with—visual culture and new media technologies, in ways that align broadly with the ways that French avant-garde writers engaged with the televisual medium in the postwar decades, as this chapter has shown. My reading of *Le Ravissement* asks that we also critically confront the very idea of archival discovery, to draw on what the philosopher Judith Schlanger has elegantly theorized in *Présence des oeuvres perdues* as the critic's "joy of receiving the old as new" ("joie de recevoir le vieux comme neuf") upon encountering a forgotten, lost, or neglected text.[96] Following Schlanger, what does it mean (as I have been suggesting throughout this chapter, and as I will address in greater detail later) to "find" a text and to integrate it into our scholarly framework—and this especially for a novel that has been haunted by a "script perdu" and that is itself so fraught and complicated on questions of loss?[97]

LOL IN THE ARCHIVES

By the early 1960s, Duras had written nearly a dozen novels and plays and had begun to explore the medium of film. Though she would eventually have a prolific career as both a screenwriter and director, she fell into the film industry by accident in 1958, when Alain Resnais asked her to write the script for

Hiroshima mon amour after other writers had turned him down. Resnais had been drawn to the sound and style of Duras's fiction, and after she nervously agreed to take on the project, he famously advised her to write *Hiroshima* as if she were composing a novel, not a film: "Make literature. Don't worry about me. Forget the camera" ("Faites de la littérature. Ne vous occupez pas de moi. Oubliez la caméra").[98] The film would achieve immense success, earning international accolades including Duras's nomination for an Academy Award for best screenplay. When in 1961 Grove Press launched its Evergreen paperback imprint dedicated to the publication of original screenplays, the editors chose *Hiroshima mon amour* to debut the series.

Duras was, in that sense, a natural choice for Rosset when he solicited screenplays for his Evergreen television project the following year. "I was thrilled to see you in Paris," Rosset wrote Duras on October 17, 1962, "and I'm happy you were interested in letting us try to put together what would be, if we succeed, the most exciting American television program there could be."[99] It seems sensible that the opportunity appealed: in the context of being temporarily barred from television in France for having signed the "Manifesto of the 121," here was a chance for Duras to participate in a rapidly expanding medium through a script of her own design.[100] Duras agreed to the project in late 1962, and on February 28, 1963, signed over the rights for a screenplay to Grove.[101] That screenplay was sent to Grove and translated into English as "An Original Film Script by Marguerite Duras, Working Title: *Lol Blair*," well before the novel's publication in France (1964)—a fact that is crucial for establishing the chronology and genetic history of *Le Ravissement*, and, by extension, for showing how the project's made-for-TV origins should critically inform our reading of the novel.

Duras's extensive archives housed at IMEC offer only a partial account of that history, in fragmentary details that provocatively point to the existence of a text elsewhere. A slim folder titled "Script Grove Press: manuscrit" suggests, for instance, that Duras sent Grove a single typed synopsis, in French, totaling ten pages and describing the planned film. Written entirely in third-person narrative with no attempt yet at dialogue, the synopsis offers a rough description of what would become the novel's main plot contours: Lol is abandoned by Michael Richardson at the ball, with her best friend Tatiana Karl by her side; Lol suffers a mental breakdown (and in this version spends time in an "asile psychiatrique," a narrative detail later removed); she marries Jean Bedford and reunites with Tatiana, whose lover, Jacques Hold, fascinates, and is fascinated by, Lol—thus re-enacting the triangulated love at the core of Lol's experience. At the end of the synopsis, we read that Jacques believes that he alone has cured Lol ("il a guéri Lol de lui-même"), and the film plans to close with Lol gazing upon the hotel window where Jacques will end his relationship with Tatiana once and for all.[102]

One of the problems identified in textual criticism on *Le Ravissement* is the challenge of constructing a proper chronology in Duras's French papers.[103] For one, none of the manuscripts related to *Le Ravissement* are dated. Some sense of a chronological sequence is evident, such as the earliest traces of the novel: in a notebook filled with handwritten, untitled dialogues, Duras writes of Lol and Tatiana, characters ostensibly named for the theater actresses Loley Bellon and Tatiana Moukhine, whom Duras might have seen in 1961 productions in Paris (Bellon had starred in Giraudoux's *Judith* and Moukhine in Genet's *Les Bonnes*). The fragmented dialogues—likely written with the British theater director Peter Brook in mind, since he had commissioned a play from Duras—were never completed and bear little resemblance, apart from the characters' first names, to the completed novel.[104] The other manuscripts in the collection contain clues about a probable order—we learn from them, for example, that the early drafts were titled "L'Homme de Town Beach" or "Lol Blair," long before Duras settled on the name "Lol V. Stein," and that Duras radically changed narrative tactics when she converted the novel from a third-person perspective to Jacques Hold's first-person delayed reveal.[105]

The biographer Jean Vallier has surmised that Duras may have written two film scripts: the first, destined for Grove, left no archival trace at the IMEC apart from the synopsis, while the second was written a couple of years after the Gallimard publication (1964), when the film director Joseph Losey considered turning the novel into a film. Vallier's timeline logically follows the IMEC collection, which includes five folders labeled "Projet de film avec Joseph Losey." Losey did indeed express an interest in transforming the novel into a film, as by that point he had been blacklisted in the U.S. for his communist leanings and was living and working abroad, mainly in England. The idea, however, was abandoned upon Duras' insistence: "I would much prefer that you ask me for an original script, written especially for you," Duras wrote,

"Lol V. Stein has made a huge splash here—you'll forgive me for saying it in those terms, but it's the truth—especially among the most literary readers. And those readers are telling me not to touch it, that a text should be left as a text, and to make a movie elsewhere."[106] What the IMEC folders contain are thus not a Losey screenplay but fragments of the original Grove script—not the complete text, but bits and pieces, scattered and out of order, that correspond quite clearly with the Grove translation. One file includes what would become the final thirty pages of the English script;[107] another is comprised of three incomplete segments that align with portions of the English translation: Lol's visit to Tatiana's house (pp. 42–52 of the Grove translation); the opening scene of the film, which begins with Lol meeting her future husband Jean Bedford on the street (pp. 1–22); and a brief portion of the scene when Jacques, Tatiana, and her husband Peter Beugner convene for dinner at Lol and Jean's house (pp. 58–63).[108]

Cross-referencing Duras's work across transnational archives confirms Lol's screenplay origins; but it also shows, through the textured materiality of the pages themselves, how Duras engaged in a dual process of construction, writing the screenplay and novel in tandem, with sections transplanted, pasted, and modified across versions. The messy French drafts of both the novel and what we can now call the original screenplay, a collage of handwritten notes and glued pieces of typed text interspersed throughout, sometimes include cut-out sections from the other version. The screenplay is composed along two columns of text, the left side narrating the scene, the right side devoted to dialogue. In one such draft, Duras's hand crosses out Jacques Hold's first-person narration and converts the left-hand column narrative into the descriptive third person—an appropriate adaptation from a novel to a screenplay. We see this process flipped as well. The drafts of the novel, collated in separate IMEC files, contain interspersed references to the drafts of the screenplay. "Film opening" ("Début film"), Duras writes in one draft, pointing to the sentence, "Jean Bedfort [sic] was walking down the street" ("Jean Bedfort [sic] marchait sur le trottoir").[109] In another, a "NB" after one sentence from the novel reads, "The whole film will be treated as 'scenes.' Example: They don't go to the ball, they are at the ball. Theatrically" ("Tout le film sera traité en 'scènes.' Exemple: Ils ne vont pas au bal mais ils sont au bal. Théâtralement").[110]

The American film, in other words, was embedded into the very fabric of the novel. In the Introduction to this book, I mentioned the fascinating paper upon which Duras drafted her work, those cardstock binder dividers, stamped along the header with the names of various American publishers. To be clear, Duras could not possibly have written on these page scraps from the United States itself; her first visit to the U.S. did not take place until 1964, after *Le Ravissement* was already on the shelves in French bookstores.[111] The binder pages likely served as organizational dividers that a French publisher would have used to track translation rights deals with American publishers, an activity in which someone like Dionys Mascolo—Duras's ex-husband, close friend, and rights officer at the Librairie Gallimard—was firmly entrenched in the late 1950s and early 60s. The fact that some of the manila pages among Duras's drafts bore the letterhead "Le Gérant: Dionys MASCOLO. Impr. Edit. Polyglottes. 232, rue de Charenton" would further support this theory.[112] Though we may never know with certainty exactly how Duras acquired these pages, they nevertheless index, at least symbolically, the novel's literary history as firmly rooted in the American publishing world: every draft page of *Le Ravissement* marks its ties to American culture.

It's with this in mind that a close reading of the television script offers a chance to reread the novel within the context of its transatlantic passage. For scholars who have understood *Le Ravissement* as anticipatory of Duras's subsequent cinematic productions, this recovered literary history should confirm the novel's origins in visual media.[113] If unproduced films, following Jean-Louis Jeannelle, can indeed generate meaning, what we find in the *Ravissement* script is not just how Duras wrote, quite literally, at the crossroads of visual and textual genres, but how she explicitly engaged the question of gazing—a question fundamental to Lol and to the television culture from which she emerged.

DURAS'S RAVISHING SCREEN

In the opening pages of the novel, long before Jacques Hold has identified himself as the narrator, he describes Lol in terms of her problematic gaze. The scene he depicts is the crucial ball of her past, and as all eyes in the room fixate on Anne-Marie Stretter's "self-assured boldness," Lol gazes on, without exactly seeing:

> Had she [Lol] looked at Michael Richardson as she passed by? Had this non-look of hers swept over him as it took in the ballroom? It was impossible to tell, it is therefore impossible to know when my story of Lol Stein begins: her gaze—from close-up one could see that this defect stemmed from an almost painful discoloration of the pupil—was diffused over the entire surface of her eyes, and was hard to meet.[114]

The first glance at Lol's face, with its emphasis on the visual as metaphor, stages the stakes of the novel. For Jacques Hold, these stakes are of a narrative order: the inability to meet Lol's gaze reflects the challenge of narrating her story from a clear and fixed origin point. This idea will be rehearsed over the entire novel, for try as Jacques Hold and Lol might to recover her past and confront the scene of the trauma, they will never entirely succeed. Yet Hold's visual description of Lol also calls forth another reading: from Lol's position as observer of the scene, and not just from Hold's as narrator, what might be at stake in the act of watching without seeing?

The screenplay affirms just how much this question was core to Duras's Lol project. It is no surprise that Duras was hyper-attuned to the interplay between visual and textual modalities; scholars have suggested terms like "cinémato-graphie" or "entrécriture" to refer to Duras's tendency to blend the visual and literary in unpredictable and often conflicting ways.[115] In the case of the Lol screenplay, we encounter Duras's particular interest in identifying narratively that which escapes the visual frame, what *cannot* ostensibly be seen. In one scene, as Lol stands outdoors in a field of rye, gazing up at the hotel room where Jacques (here, "Jack") and Tatiana conduct their affair, she is blocked from fully seeing them:

> Tatiana Karl, naked, with her black hair let down, in turn crosses the stage of light, slowly. She pauses in the rectangle of Lol's vision, turns toward the back of the room, where the man has disappeared. The window is small, and all Lol can see is the lovers' busts, cut off at the level of the waist. Thus we cannot see the lower part of Tatiana's tresses.[116]

The scene is written for film, with lighting and framing instructions for a production crew embedded into the narrative. The cinematographic feel of the passage makes its way into the published novel:

In turn, Tatiana Karl, naked in her black hair, crosses the stage of light, slowly. It is perhaps in Lol's rectangle of vision that she pauses. She turns back to the room where the man presumably is. The window is small, and no doubt Lol can see only the upper part of the lovers' bodies, from the waist up. Thus it is that she cannot see the full length of Tatiana's tresses.[117]

Rereading *Le Ravissement* comparatively, through the *avant-texte*, elucidates just how clearly the novel emerged from its screenplay origins, written as a series of frames to be captured and filmed. Yet the differences between screenplay and novel are equally revealing: in the former, Duras's slippage of perspective between Lol's vision and ours—"*we* cannot see"—locates the spectator's position alongside Lol's, as outsiders who, together, fail to see beyond the window frame. This position not only aligns our gaze with Lol's, but in so doing also suggests, *contra* Jacques Hold's implied reading of Lol's eyes as meaningfully unique, that her limited sight—gazing without seeing—is symptomatic of a more general condition of spectatorship.

Duras's interest in that which exceeds one's visual frame echoes across the screenplay. We read frequently of what characters fail to see: "Jack, still walking with the same even step, leaves the billiard room when Peter ("Pierre") Beugner isn't looking. Peter doesn't notice that he leaves."[118] In some instances, we see with and alongside Lol. In others, her visual frame is narrower than the imagined viewer's: "All that follows is seen by Jack Hold from behind the bay window. Lol is seated facing the bay window behind which Jack Hold is standing, but she does not see him immediately."[119] This image accords with Duras's "NB" inserted shortly thereafter—"as soon as Jack Hold appears in the film, we'll see the film through his eyes"—and anticipates how his dominant position vis-à-vis the camera will translate into his narrator function: Jacques Hold's perspective will become the one through which we access Lol's story.[120]

At the same time, Duras directs readers of the script not to be too trusting of the narrator/camera:

> A field of rye stirs very softly in the breeze. Afternoon. The weather is lovely. We see the field from above. Nothing, not a wrinkle disturbs its surface. Then suddenly, when the wind has died down, a certain spot in the field stirs. (Some spectators will see it, others will not. There must be some doubt about whether it moved or not.) This is all we shall see of this incident.[121]

Just as Jacques Hold's novelistic rendering of Lol is punctuated by doubt, with its recourse to unanswered rhetorical questions, its sentences that frequently begin with "je crois"—this is what Suleiman identifies as the discursive signs of the novel's "feminine writing"—so too does the camera resist an idea of certainty.[122] Duras's imagined spectators are, in turn, cast collectively as unreliable viewers, reminded to doubt their own visual perception. As spectators, we are, in that sense, very much like Lol herself: even in looking, we cannot be sure of what we have seen.

Duras's subversion of an all-seeing gaze is consistent with works by other writers of her generation loosely affiliated with the New Novel—one can think most obviously of Robbe-Grillet's *Le Voyeur*, or the many characters across Beckett's novels and plays who progressively lose the power of sight. In explicitly challenging the authority of visual perception, Duras neatly conforms to the "denigration of vision" that Martin Jay identifies as widely emblematic of twentieth-century French literature and thought. Duras receives just a passing reference in Jay's *Downcast Eyes* (as one of many post-1968 feminist thinkers who sought to challenge the ocularcentrism pervading patriarchal discourse), but her work broadly supports his central claim that from Surrealism to postmodernism, and through phenomenology, the Situationist movement, and even the *nouveau roman* project, novelists and theorists alike displayed a deep ambivalence about the authority of visual experience.[123] That ambivalence was due in no small part to the expansion of visual technologies in the twentieth century, and it is worth pausing on Jay's observation that "by the 1970s," following the Situationists' radical critique of "the society of the spectacle," "scarcely any discussion in France or elsewhere of the manipulative power of mass culture could resist blaming its spectacular dimension."[124] The Situationists were more concerned in the 1950s and 60s with cinema than with television, Jay reminds us, yet misgivings about the mass consumption of visual media, in France and the U.S., were certainly familiar to Duras in the 60s. While Duras enthusiastically watched television and emblematized in her own practices "TV's power to fascinate and activate viewers," she also, as Anne Brancky attests, used her platform as a journalist, writer, and intellectual "to as[k] that readers be more critical and analytical consumers of the media."[125] Duras would go on to reiterate that message years later, calling upon television consumers to question the falsity and ineptitude of what they saw on TV.[126]

That Duras's television screenplay would overtly question the power of visual experience provides crucial insight into the thinking behind, and the making of, the Lol project. The novel ends with Lol in her standard spot, outside the *Hôtel des Bois* where Tatiana and Jacques rendezvous, except this time, she's asleep: "Night was falling when I reached the Forest Hotel. Lol had arrived there ahead of us. She was asleep in the field of rye, worn out, worn out by our trip."[127] The novel's conclusion marks the physical change that has taken place for Lol—fatigue; her body's shift to a horizontal, prostrate position; her upturned gaze now shuttered, interrupted—while suggesting that little, after the journey she undertook with Jacques to the site of the ball, has functionally changed; she remains, after all, stuck outside, bound to repeat the triangular structure of their dynamic.

The screenplay, meanwhile, had imagined a quite different ending. Not only does Lol's husband make his way to the hotel, presumably to rescue Lol from this quasi-affair, but in the final instant, "We see Lol who wakes up, stretches and plays with the stalks of rye, her eyes riveted on the window of the hotel. THE END."[128] With this closing *mise-en-abyme* image of Lol's riveted gaze fixed ahead on what amounts to a screen, the script gestures at the medium into which it's written. Like a television spectator, Lol stares intently at an object within a frame—a window, a television set—that remains physically out of reach. This view of Lol echoes the first time in the novel when she stands outside the hotel to watch Tatiana and Jacques: "Her eyes riveted on the lighted window, a woman hearkens to the void—feeding upon, devouring this non-existent, invisible spectacle, the light from a room where others are."[129] Lol's gaze, figured as an act of spectacular consumption, is thus not only a sign of psychic trauma, as so many psychoanalytic critics from Lacan onwards have read her; nor is it entirely precise to say, as others have, that such figurations of gazing reflect Duras's general cinematic impulse, a diegetic staging of film spectatorship.[130]

We can also see the traces of the novel's television screenplay origins in the staging of Lol's gaze. Devouring the nonexistent spectacle, Lol performs the role of the television viewer, a parallel that Duras encouraged by aligning our gaze with Lol's across the screenplay text. It is striking that Lol peers repeatedly into a private space—the intimacy of a home, a room, one could imagine our room, even—that epitomizes the domesticity of the television experience.

In that sense, her gaze, like those of other characters imagined by avant-garde writers of the period, reinforces Spigel's point about widespread anxieties about television circulating in the 1950s and 60s that resulted in tropes of windows and "prying eyes": "the new TV eye threatens to turn back on itself, to penetrate the private window and to monitor the eroticized fantasy life of the citizen in his or her home."[131] The novel's rootedness in its television origins encourages us to situate Lol in this context, a framework aimed not to reduce her to a single interpretive reading, but to reveal her in all her extraordinary complexity, as one who emerges out of a specific cultural moment. In that sense, we see how Lol embodies the temptations and anxieties of television culture, the dual fascination with, and stark alienation from, the object of her gaze. This meditation on television's cultural role is thus Duras's rejoinder to Rosset's request: Lol's *ravishment*, entranced as she is by the visual spectacle in the frame, is just as much ours, as it is hers.

Coda: On Lost Texts and Archival Finds

In January 1979, fifteen years after Gallimard published *Le Ravissement*, Duras wrote a short essay titled "Le cinéma de Lol V. Stein" for *Art Press International*. The title of the piece explicitly echoed a passage in the novel that describes Lol's emotional state after being abandoned by Michael Richardson: "the eternity of the ball in the cinema of Lol Stein" ("l'éternité du bal dans le cinéma de Lol V. Stein") registers the psychic manifestation of Lol's trauma, the endless replay of the scene in the days and years after the event.[132] If in the novel cinema functions as a metaphor for Lol's mind, in the essay Duras treats it literally, as a filmic object that never quite existed. "I lost the shot-by-shot breakdown of the ball scene" ("J'ai perdu le découpage du bal"), Duras writes in the essay's opening sentence, recalling a film script she might have made for it, and proceeds to imagine through the conditional past what the film could have looked like: "The weather would have been gray. The first long shot would have been of an aging Lol V. Stein, etc." ("Le jour aurait été gris. Le premier plan très long aurait été celui de Lol V. Stein vieillie, etc.").[133] In Duras's reconstructed memory, a filmed version of the Lol narrative obtains as a kind of elusive phantom text, a hypothetical film that never reached fruition.

It's unclear whether the lost film script Duras had in mind was the same one as the Grove screenplay; one of the early long shots in that version *does* describe the weather as "gray," but there is no mention of an aging Lol V. Stein.[134] When Duras evokes this "lost script" again in her 1987 work *La vie matérielle*, it is even less clear what script she was recalling (". . . this script that I lost. Why did I have the idea for that script? I don't know anymore"; ". . . ce script que j'ai perdu. Pourquoi j'ai eu l'idée de ce script? Je ne sais plus").[135] For Duras, the idea of loss was not just constitutive of the Lol character, but had become entrenched in the retrospective imaginary of the Lol project—a framework that makes the idea of recovery, of filling an absence, of *finding* a lost text, uncomfortably incongruous with *Le Ravissement* as a literary object.

Judith Schlanger's work on the "presence of lost texts" helps to think through this disjunction between the lost and found. Schlanger points up the critic's thrill in discovering presumably vanished texts, the moment when "found texts thrust us into the opposite of the irreversible: no longer absence, destruction, or loss, but rather a supplement of presence . . . the newly recovered arrival gives us the joy of receiving the old as new" ("les oeuvres retrouvées nous plongent dans l'inverse de l'irrémédiable: non plus l'absence, le dommage et le manque, mais au contraire le supplément de présence . . . le nouvel arrivant retrouvé nous donne la joie de recevoir le vieux comme neuf").[136] This abundance of presence appears to cancel out the loss, the "manque," giving the impression, in that joy of discovery, of having filled a void. What we love in anecdotes of discovery, Schlanger suggests, is the reversal itself, the spectacular notion that absence has become presence, that "destruction and loss can change signs and turn into finding and gain" ("le moment spectaculaire où le dommage et le manque peuvent changer de signe et devenir trouvaille et gain").[137]

Schlanger theorizes the experience of archival discovery, the uncanny *frisson* of realizing one has found what has been lost. Yet that joy of reversal—the belief, for the literary critic or historian, that one is making present what has been absent—can also be a trap, one that risks foreclosing an appreciation for the limits of the archive. Loss, Schlanger contends, can never entirely be eradicated, just like archives can never be totally filled, mastered, or even delimited. Try as we might to fill a void, we must also acknowledge the productive potential of seeing loss as "constitutive" and "essential" of textual production and archival discovery ("Not only is a lot missing, but in a way this lack is constitutive, essential" ("Non seulement beaucoup manque, mais d'une certaine façon ce manque est constitutif, essentiel").[138]

This is the ultimate lesson of Duras's Lol project, informed as it is by the recovered "script perdu": to purport to fill in the gaps, to cover a loss with a find, not only runs counter to the Lol figure—herself discursively bound to loss—but reminds us of that which is constitutively and irrevocably missing. Duras defies any critical tendency towards a conclusive read that would privilege meaning at the expense of meaningful absences.

We can extend this lesson, too, to all of the lost screenplays I have "recovered" and discussed in this chapter—screenplays that were always "there," but had just not yet been placed into conversation with other documents and materials located elsewhere. This chapter speaks to the generative potential of transnational archival research, while it should also remind us that discoveries are always partial and mediated. Even with their discovery, the Evergreen screenplays exist only in their textual form (with the sole exception of Beckett's), and in that sense remain lost to us still, phantom films that we can conjure through reading but not seeing. I have argued throughout this chapter for integrating these TV scripts into our understanding of French literary history, whether that was through a subsequent creative turn towards experimental visual media (Beckett especially), a willingness to explore questions about race and gender that was unusual in early 1960s France (Ionesco), or a self-reflexive meditation on the risks of television intruding into the private sphere, as we saw in every case. The screenplays remind us just how much literary history can often be informed by incomplete, absent, or lost materials. I offer up this set of readings as anything but definitive, and with the hope that other lost texts might one day surface and complicate all that I have suggested here.

When France's New Novel Met the American Textbook
French and the College Classroom

> A novel which is no more than the grammatical example illustrating a rule—even accompanied by its exception—would naturally be useless: the statement of the rule would suffice.
> —ALAIN ROBBE-GRILLET, *For a New Novel*[1]

OVER THE COURSE of the 1960s and 1970s, many of France's experimental writers had become known quantities in the United States. The American university system helped enormously to catapult them onto the literary stage: it was thanks to a "rapidly expanding university population for knowledge of the world," as Loren Glass argues, that "modernist masters" like Beckett, Robbe-Grillet, and Genet could gain such traction among readers.[2] François Cusset similarly identifies the 1970s as a critical time of "direct encounters between French authors and their American readers" because of American higher education; by 1980, French writers—and for Cusset, this means Derrida, Foucault, Deleuze, Lyotard, and other French philosophers eventually called "theorists" in the U.S. context—were "translated, commented upon, and placed on the reading lists of literature courses" in an effort by literature departments to legitimate their existence and galvanize energy for the humanities.[3] The American university had, in these respects, a critical effect on how, and whether, French writers and philosophers were read beyond national borders. American universities played an instrumental role not just in disseminating French literary and philosophical works; they also, as this chapter suggests, led to the production of new works, originated on college campuses, that in turn shaped the course of French literary history.

In 1981, Alain Robbe-Grillet published an exceptionally idiosyncratic book, even for an author whose work had already come to be known as unusual. *Le rendez-vous* (*The Meeting*), as it was called, billed itself as a grammar manual designed to teach intermediate French to American college students. Published with one of the leading American textbook publishers at the time—Holt, Rinehart and Winston—*Le rendez-vous* comprises two discrete but integrated parts: an original novel penned by Robbe-Grillet and a series of grammar exercises that Yvone Lenard, a successful textbook author and professor at California State University, Dominguez Hills (CSUDH), devised in close collaboration with Robbe-Grillet. As a language-learning tool, *Le rendez-vous* advanced a systematic approach that introduced students to increasingly complex verb tenses and grammatical constructions. Robbe-Grillet's first chapter, for instance, was written entirely in the present tense, while each of the subsequent seven chapters integrated, one by one, more advanced tenses like the imperfect, conditional, and historical past. Lenard's accompanying grammar exercises, interspersed throughout, reinforced each new tense or expression through oral and written activities. By the end of the manual, American students were expected not only to have gained a nuanced understanding of the French language, but, as a final exercise, to formulate a coherent description of the *nouveau roman*—or New Novel as it came to be known in the U.S.—both as a genre and as a radical departure from "le roman classique" ("the classic novel").[4]

The publication of a grammar manual by a highly regarded French author is striking on a number of levels. Few genres seem as spectacularly dissimilar as a language-learning manual—whose success in the classroom hinges on its clarity, ability to teach, and legibility—and an experimental novel, especially the kind of novels Robbe-Grillet usually wrote, which even his staunchest defenders acknowledged were often opaque, hermetic, and illegible.[5] Until *Le rendez-vous*, Robbe-Grillet had published exclusively with France's elite avant-garde press, Les Éditions de Minuit. His early novels—*Les gommes* (*The Erasers*, 1953), *Le voyeur* (*The Voyeur*, 1955), and *La jalousie* (*Jealousy*, 1957)—had quickly catapulted him onto the French literary scene and earned him a reputation as a controversial experimentalist, while his influence at Minuit as a trusted manuscript reader and advisor to the editor-in-chief Jérôme Lindon further helped reshape the field of mid-century French literature.

Robbe-Grillet rallied writers like Claude Simon, Marguerite Duras, Nathalie Sarraute, and Robert Pinget to the Minuit imprint—writers who had already published at prestigious presses like Gallimard—and proclaimed their collective mission as New Novelists, appointing himself leader of the movement.[6] In his foundational formulation published in the collection of essays *Pour un nouveau roman* (*For a New Novel*), Robbe-Grillet defined the *nouveau roman* as a reflection of the increasing instability of the modern world, antithetical to the "image of a stable, coherent, continuous, unequivocal, entirely decipherable universe" that characterized much of nineteenth-century literature.[7] The project of the *nouveau roman* was not to render this world decipherable, as Honoré de Balzac's realist novels had, or to confront contemporary injustices explicitly, as Jean-Paul Sartre had advocated a decade earlier in his call for committed literature, but to map the "difficulty [of] getting [one's] bearings" onto the form of the modern novel, through rhetorical and structural techniques that refused the reader easy access.[8] The constraints imposed by the genre of the grammar manual would seem very much at odds with a literary project that mobilized language and form to contest the transparency of meaning.

That Robbe-Grillet would undertake the grammar manual project suggests, in part, the extent to which teaching and publishing in the United States could condition the production of literature, even in French. Mark McGurl's landmark study *The Program Era* has shown just how influential American universities and pedagogical instruction have been in shaping postwar American literature. The emergence of creative writing programs in the postwar period—what McGurl calls "the most important event in postwar American literary history"—"transformed the conditions under which American literature is produced" and "fashioned a world where artists are systematically installed in the university as teachers."[9] Robbe-Grillet's example at once illustrates this point—*Le rendez-vous* is unquestionably an outgrowth of his position at New York University (NYU), where he regularly served as a visiting professor of French beginning in the early 1970s—and suggests the need to widen McGurl's frame beyond the English department as an exclusive site for fashioning literary forms. Robbe-Grillet's project literalizes the idea, disciplined specifically in the structure of foreign language programs, that the process of achieving grammatical fluency culminates ideally in literary analysis and production. *Le rendez-vous* strikingly attests to the structure of French departments at American universities, where language pedagogy and literature teaching coexist, though often as separate and unequal entities. Up-ending conventional hierarchies, *Le rendez-vous* presents a case in which literary production depended on the expertise and cultural capital of a language pedagogue. A bestselling author of over a dozen published French-language manuals, Lenard exposed Robbe-Grillet to the lucrative textbook industry and helped him produce his greatest commercial success.

A text that began as a grammar manual for American students was repackaged and repurposed for readers back home in France under the title *Djinn: Un trou rouge entre les pavés disjoints* (*Djinn: A Red Gap in the Broken Cobblestones*), published by Minuit, and it would become the bestselling novel Robbe-Grillet ever wrote. The previously unexamined archives of this publication reveal an unknown literary history of transnational collaboration and exchange, one that places new emphasis on Robbe-Grillet's formative involvement with American higher education during his literary career, and on the unrecognized contributions of a woman whose academic and publishing expertise helped to foster his success. Attending to the ways in which this transatlantic literary history encompasses the educational publishing industry, the growth of opportunities for teaching in the United States, and Robbe-Grillet's own increasing fascination with pedagogy helps refine our understanding of his literary legacy.

Teaching French in the Era of the Textbook Boom

Two concurrent developments in the postwar American publishing industry and academy aligned to make a book like *Le rendez-vous* possible: the expansion of the textbook market in the U.S. and the evolution of foreign language pedagogies in the classroom. The demand for college textbooks soared in the wake of the GI Bill and subsequent baby boom. By 1958, the textbook industry had doubled from its prewar size, and it accelerated at such speed that textbook sales nationwide had quadrupled by 1967.[10] The expansion of college divisions in large publishing firms coincided with college population growth, and writers of college-level textbooks earned substantially higher royalties than their counterparts creating books for the K–12 market.[11] When a *Fortune* magazine article in 1959 declared textbook publishing "the fastest-growing, most remunerative, and most freely competitive branch of book publishing," college textbooks grossed $84 million yearly; by 1990, that figure had grown to $2 billion.[12]

Lenard's career coincided precisely with this textbook boom. Lenard had left her native France in the late 1940s and received a BA and MA in French and classics at the University of California, Los Angeles (UCLA), in 1955. Charged with directing the university's French-language program, Lenard remained on the faculty at UCLA until 1968 and devised there a pedagogical technique that, systematizing aspects of the direct method, highlighted verb usage and employed a question-answer format of instruction. What Lenard dubbed in the early 1960s the "verbal-active method" earned her attention as an innovative pedagogue; one former UCLA student, writing in the *Los Angeles Times*, called Lenard "the kind of teacher a student remembers all his life."[13] Learning of her technique, Charles Woodford, an acquisitions editor at Harper and Row, commissioned Lenard to formalize her approach in what would become her first textbook, *Parole et pensée* (*Word and Thought*), published in 1965. An elementary language textbook designed for first-year college French, *Parole et pensée* would go on to have an extensive career. Five new editions were published over the next twenty years, and it became, as one reviewer called it, "something of a classic."[14] By its second edition, the textbook had been adopted in over 400 colleges and universities across the country, spanning community colleges, public universities, and Ivy League institutions (Figure 11). When a history of Harper and Row was published in 1967, *Parole et pensée* was listed as one of the press's nine bestsellers of that year.[15]

Lenard's early commercial success turned her into a regular textbook author for Harper. At Woodford's request, she published nearly a dozen language textbooks, ranging from elementary to advanced, and targeted separately for universities and secondary schools. Throughout the 1970s, Lenard toured the country as a pedagogy expert. She spoke before the board of education in New York City in 1971 to voice support for foreign language instruction and gave workshops for high school and college teachers, earning praise such as the following from the chair of romance languages at the University of North Carolina, Greensboro: "Before we invited you to come, we were convinced of the excellence of your books. Now that we have seen them come alive through you in person we are thrilled with the possibilities of a renaissance in language teaching through your methods."[16] Recognizing her achievements, and making explicit reference to her textbook successes, the French government awarded Lenard the rank of chevalier in the Ordre des

Figure 11: Promotional flyer for Yvone Lenard's *Parole et pensée*

Palmes académiques in 1970.[17] Notwithstanding all these successes, Lenard has been entirely forgotten by literary history.

As the field of educational publishing in the United States expanded to serve a growing academic market, it naturally published not only language textbooks such as Lenard's, but also literary readers and anthologies aimed at the sizable population of students studying literature in English and in other languages. The most well-known example, *The Norton Anthology of English Literature*, remained from its first edition in 1962, "the primary source of Norton's growth throughout the 1970s and 1980s."[18]

To support French departments at universities in the United States, American trade publishers such as Appleton-Century-Crofts, Dell, and Macmillan bought the rights to republish French novels and plays, in French, and packaged them in fully annotated editions. These teaching editions enabled contemporary French texts like Samuel Beckett's *En attendant Godot* (*Waiting for Godot*), Albert Camus's *Le malentendu* (*The Misunderstanding*), Marguerite Duras's *Le square* (*The Square*), and François Mauriac's *Thérèse Desqueyroux* to circulate in the U.S. at less than two dollars each, allowing publishers to avoid the high cost of importing texts from France.[19] Books in Dell's series, such as Molière's *Tartuffe* (*The Imposter*), Balzac's *Peau de chagrin* (*The Magic Skin*), and Jean Giraudoux's *La folle de Chaillot* (*The Madwoman of Chaillot*), sold to American students of French for only fifty cents.[20] Germaine Brée, a professor of French at NYU and the University of Wisconsin, Madison, bridged the gap between academia and trade publishing, serving as the general editor for both Dell's Laurel French Series Language Library and Macmillan's Modern French Language Series, each of which published dozens of teaching editions of French novels in the 1960s. These editions targeted the college classroom: they provided instructional support for professors and often added reading comprehension exercises and vocabulary appendices for students. While the original Gallimard or Minuit editions of French novels did, of course, also circulate in the United States, the investment by American publishers in teaching editions reflected their desire to tap the niche market that was the French literature classroom in America. Brée and Carlos Lynes Jr. summed up this goal in their introduction to Marcel Proust's *Combray*, the first part of *A la recherche du temps perdu* (*In Search of Lost Time*):

> Our experience in presenting Proust to undergraduates in a liberal arts college and in a large university confirms our belief that *Combray* is an ideal choice for this purpose. . . . We have felt that our task—and the task of our colleagues in other institutions—would be greatly facilitated if a separate edition of this part of Proust's novel could be made available to students and teachers.[21]

That French literary texts were explicitly mobilized and marketed for their use in American colleges and universities illuminates the publishing context that would support a blended literary and pedagogical project like *Le rendez-vous*.

More than any other precedent for *Le rendez-vous*, it was Michel Benamou's 1969 elementary French-language textbook, *Mise en train: Première année de français* (*Warm Up: First-Year French*), co-authored with Eugène Ionesco, that set the stage for Robbe-Grillet and Lenard's project. In fact, the earliest review of *Mise en train* traced the book's direct lineage to "Lenard's method."[22]

As language-learning pedagogies in the 1960s began to evolve from the prevalent audio-lingual method that had deemphasized literature in the classroom, Benamou sought to infuse the language classroom with literary models, as Lenard too had done by integrating poetry and prose excerpts in *Parole et pensée*.[23] A linguist and professor at the University of Michigan, Ann Arbor, Benamou served as the managing editor for the journal *Teaching Language Through Literature*, a publication of the Modern Language Association Conference that commenced in 1961 and that concretized the position of many college professors seeking a better way to connect linguistic and literary pedagogies. Benamou articulated a systematic pedagogical approach to combining language and literature instruction in his monograph *Pour une nouvelle pédagogie du texte littéraire* (*For a New Pedagogy of the Literary Text*), arguing that a student's ability to differentiate between "discours normal" ("normal discourse") and "discours littéraire" ("literary discourse") was a crucial phase of foreign language learning.[24] Benamou explains, "Tout ce que nous voulons, c'est une *pédagogie de la découverte, du choc, de la surprise*" ("What we want, is a *pedagogy of discovery, of shock, of surprise*"), achieved by exaggerating the difference between discourses so as to render students acutely aware of various linguistic registers and styles.[25]

As an illustration of Benamou's approach, *Mise en train* centers on twenty dialogues, all originally penned by Ionesco for the textbook, that self-reflexively parody the experience of language learning and, in recognizable Ionescoian fashion, foster an acute appreciation for the absurd. Within the diegetic frame, students speak in a syntactically flawless but semantically outrageous French. In one dialogue, after their professor commands them to formulate sentences based on recent vocabulary—or else risk a bad grade—one student, Jean-Marie, rattles off a dozen sentences like the following:

> La table est dans le cahier. Le professeur est dans la poche du gilet de la montre. Le tableau noir écrit sur la craie blanche et la craie efface l'éponge
>
> The table is in the notebook. The professor is in the pocket of the watch's vest. The blackboard writes on the white chalk and the chalk erases the sponge.[26]

Even first-year students of French can grasp the humor of Jean-Marie's phrases, seeing in him a textual echo of themselves as imperfect language learners. In fact, the logic of *Mise en train* rests entirely on this spirit of playful identification and self-conscious performativity. "The best way to overcome the artificiality of teaching French outside France is not to ignore this artificiality," Benamou writes in his introduction, but

> to make the most of the artificiality by exaggerating it, somewhat like the avant-garde dramatists underscoring stage conventions in order to free themselves from stage conventions. In other words, the teacher must recognize that an American student learning to speak French is actually playing a role.[27]

The principles of avant-garde drama, for Benamou, naturally aligned with his pedagogical approach of exaggerating discourses and registers. In asking Ionesco to write dialogues for the express purpose of teaching grammar, he aimed to bring a writer's aesthetic project to bear on the particular demands of the American foreign language classroom.[28]

Mise en train provides an instructive backdrop for *Le rendez-vous*, since in many ways Ionesco was a far more natural literary contributor for a grammar textbook. Unlike Robbe-Grillet's early works, Ionesco's plays explicitly dramatized pedagogical scenarios, as in the parodic representation of a professor's tutoring sessions in *La leçon* (*The Lesson*, 1951). In fact, as Ionesco sometimes explained, his entire project owed to a language textbook he had consulted to learn English, *L'anglais sans peine* (*English Without Toil*). In writing his first play, *La cantatrice chauve* (*The Bald Soprano*), he borrowed many lines of dialogue from the textbook, hoping "to communicate to my contemporaries the essential truths of which the manual of English-French conversation had made me aware."[29] Recent scholarship has nuanced Ionesco's proclaimed literary origin story, showing a wider array of language manuals and experiences that influenced his writing.[30] His attunement to the process of language learning made Ionesco singularly well-positioned to write a grammar manual—a fact that Benamou highlighted, somewhat hyperbolically, in his first letter to Ionesco: "J'obtiendrai votre aide, sinon je n'écrirai pas de manuel" ("Either you'll help me write it, or I won't write a grammar manual at all").[31]

News of *Mise en train* circulated to university professors as early as 1965, well before the book was in press. The 1965 Modern Language Association convention in Chicago was abuzz with anticipation for its publication, which would not happen for another four years.[32] Though precise records of *Mise en train*'s distribution do not seem to be available, there is evidence that it was taught throughout the 1970s and 1980s at many North American universities and secondary schools, including Columbia University, where one former undergraduate recalled, in a letter to the editor of the *New York Times* after Ionesco's death, his fond memories of studying the "uproarious" dialogues in his first-year French class.[33] The potential market for Ionesco's textbook is nonetheless clear, emerging as it did at the pinnacle of French-language study in America. In the late 1960s, each fall semester the enrollment in French courses nationwide was between 350,000 and 400,000 students, and even when this number dropped in the mid-1970s, there were still on average 250,000 student enrollments in French undergraduate and graduate courses in a given semester.[34] By the time that Robbe-Grillet and Lenard embarked on *Le rendez-vous* in 1979, not only were there strong precedents for integrating literature into the American foreign language classroom, but the financial power of the textbook industry, and Lenard's success in it, suggested the potential to reach an audience of hundreds of thousands of American students learning French.

Robbe-Grillet and the United States

In his preface to Bruce Morrissette's *Les romans de Robbe-Grillet* (*The Novels of Robbe-Grillet*), the first published monograph devoted to the author's work, Roland Barthes identifies two contesting critical approaches to reading Robbe-Grillet. The first, what he calls "chosiste," reads Robbe-Grillet as a "destructeur de sens" ("destroyer of meaning"), a writer whose obsessive descriptions remain on the surface of things, blocking any attempt to locate a deeper narrative order.[35] The second, a humanistic approach that, Barthes says, Morrissette will go on to model in his study, performs the hermeneutic gesture of interpretation, deciphering the sense and symbols embedded in Robbe-Grillet's narratives. Whereas the first favors a vision of Robbe-Grillet as revolutionary, the second, in its recourse to traditional interpretive modes, demystifies Robbe-Grillet's work and situates him in a classical lineage. It is the tension between these two modes that Barthes highlights in his preface: between, implicitly, the earliest French criticism, notably by Barthes himself ("Littérature littérale" and "Littérature objective") and Maurice Blanchot, that positioned Robbe-Grillet's work as radical because of its resistance to interpretation, and the humanistic readings offered by Morrissette, the first American scholar to "discover" Robbe-Grillet and to help bring his novels to the attention of American readers.[36]

Without overstating a distinction between French and American approaches to Robbe-Grillet's work, his preface anticipates the transformations that Robbe-Grillet scholarship would undergo as a result of transatlantic encounters. In his 1984 semiautobiographical text *Le miroir qui revient* (*Ghosts in the Mirror*), Robbe-Grillet depicts his first meeting with Morrissette in the form of a literary legend. While on a research trip in France, Morrissette, then a professor of French at Washington University in St. Louis, first heard of Robbe-Grillet, who was promoting his recently released novel *Le voyeur* on the radio, and he set out to meet the author at his family home in Brest. After a couple of days with Robbe-Grillet and his family, he claimed to have "found what he was looking for" and was determined to "devote" himself to the study of Robbe-Grillet's writings. Morrissette "wanted to be sure that I was a genuinely great writer; now, geniuses necessarily have exceptional mothers; and now he knew that mine was!"[37]

The encounter with Morrissette also proved crucial for convincing an American press to publish Robbe-Grillet's novels in English. Barney Rosset at Grove had already turned down a literary agent's offer to translate Robbe-Grillet's novels into English—citing the unlikelihood "that these books would prove to be a great commercial success in this country"[38]—when Morrissette contacted Rosset for the first time, in March 1957, and mentioned his critical study of Robbe-Grillet, then in progress. Within two months, Grove, already the exclusive American publisher for Beckett and Jean Genet, reversed course and signed a contract with Minuit to translate one of Robbe-Grillet's novels, although it had yet to determine which one. In his offer letter to Rosset, Robbe-Grillet's agent Georges Borchardt included a sample translation of *Les gommes*, prepared by Morrissette, "who is, as you know, working on a full-length study of Robbe-Grillet's novels."[39]

Morrissette became the trusted advisor to Rosset on all matters related to Robbe-Grillet. He reviewed various English samples of *Le voyeur* and *La jalousie* to select the best translator; he provided detailed notes and corrections on drafts of the English manuscripts; he weighed in on cover design and layout; and his scholarship oriented Grove's framing and marketing of Robbe-Grillet's works. Robbe-Grillet's presence on the American literary scene owed to this collaboration between a literary scholar and a trade publisher. Rosset recommended Morrissette for a Guggenheim Fellowship in 1958, which he was subsequently awarded, an indication of how the triad of Robbe-Grillet, Grove, and Morrissette positioned all three for literary success in America. As Rosset explained in his letter of recommendation:

> We feel that Alain Robbe-Grillet is one of the most important of living French writers, whose work has not as yet been published in this country. . . . We will be the American publishers of Robbe-Grillet's works, and we will bring out one of the novels as soon as we have a good translation completed. We have been working very closely with Professor Morrissette in our plans to publish Robbe-Grillet's work. . . . We are amazed at the ability and insight of Professor Morrissette and we have found his work on Robbe-Grillet extremely valuable to us.[40]

Robbe-Grillet's initial entrance into the U.S., then, happened by way of this collaborative synchronicity between academic and trade fields, in a joint effort to render his literary work meaningful and accessible to American readers.

The circulation and translation of his works in the United States had the immediate effect of bringing Robbe-Grillet into close contact, both geographically and intellectually, with the American university. Robbe-Grillet recognized as much: "It was only in the 60s—and no doubt in part thanks to [Morrissette]—that I became a star in North American universities."[41] Grove sponsored Robbe-Grillet's whirlwind author tours to colleges across the United States, beginning in 1963 to promote the film *Last Year at Marienbad*, for which he wrote the screenplay, and repeated the next year following the release of *Les gommes*.[42]

Robbe-Grillet immediately seized on the importance of a classroom audience for his books. In a letter to Rosset regarding the pending English translation of *Le voyeur*, he appealed to the publisher's sensibilities regarding market and readership:

> Avez-vous déjà choisi le titre anglais du livre? Quand celui-ci doit-il paraître? Beaucoup d'américains me l'ont demandé: surtout des professeurs d'universités qui ont fait (ou qui vont faire) des cours sur cet ouvrage dans leurs classes de littérature française.

Have you already chosen an English title for the book? When will it be published? Many Americans have asked me this, especially university professors who have offered (or who are going to offer) classes on this book in their French literature courses.[43]

A French-language American teaching edition of *La jalousie* was published in 1963, only a few years after the release of Grove's English translation, followed in 1970 by a teaching edition of *Le voyeur*. From his post a decade later as a visiting professor at UCLA, Robbe-Grillet congratulated Grove on their widespread distribution of his novels while he taught them to American students:

> Je tiens à dire comme je suis satisfait des services de Grove Press! Au cours du trimestre que je viens de passer à UCLA (où j'ai enseigné le Robbegrillet, comme d'habitude!), je suis entré dans de nombreuses librairies, et j'y ai trouvé partout mes livres, en plus ou moins grande quantité.

> I must tell you how satisfied I am with Grove Press's service! At the beginning of the trimester that I just finished at UCLA (where I taught Robbe-Grillet, like always!) I went into numerous bookstores and I found my books in every store, in more or less large quantities.[44]

Robbe-Grillet benefited from what Loren Glass has described as Grove's main publishing innovations: "democratizing the avant-garde" by producing widely available and affordable paperbacks by modernist writers, and marketing actively to college campuses.[45] Attentive to the use of his novels in American classrooms, and aided by Grove's distribution networks, Robbe-Grillet discovered a market for his novels both in and around the university.

This appreciation for classroom audiences intensified in the 1970s when Robbe-Grillet was hired to teach in American universities. After a 1971 conference in Cerisy dedicated to Robbe-Grillet's work, Tom Bishop, professor and chair of NYU's French Department, extended an invitation to Robbe-Grillet to teach for one semester the next year. Robbe-Grillet's visiting position lasted two decades. From 1972 to 1991, Robbe-Grillet taught on a nearly annual basis two courses—Le Nouveau Nouveau Roman (The New New Novel) and Cinéma et Littérature (Cinema and Literature)—to packed crowds of undergraduate and graduate students in French and comparative literature. His syllabi suggest that he was keenly attuned to the possibilities afforded by anchoring his courses in a theorization of his own role as pedagogue. The course description of Le Nouveau Nouveau Roman begins self-reflexively:

> Je ne suis pas professeur de littérature, mais romancier: tentative de définition de ce que peut être l'enseignement littéraire d'un écrivain. Théorie et pratique du roman. Critique des formes périmées. Fonction auto-critique de l'écriture moderne.
>
> I am not a literature professor, but a novelist: attempt to define what a literary teaching of a writer might entail. Theory and practice of the novel. Critique of outdated forms. The self-critical function of modern writing.[46]

In this brief theoretical sketch, Robbe-Grillet offers a rationale for his pedagogical position as organically linked to the function of the modern novel. The self-criticism inherent in the *nouveau roman*'s form would be extended into a teaching method, especially insomuch as the main subjects of Robbe-Grillet's courses were his own novels and their evolution in relation to other writers of his generation, like Robert Pinget and Claude Simon. "Not a literature professor," but compelled to think like one, Robbe-Grillet packaged the *nouveau roman* into a pedagogical form. Jérôme Lindon, Robbe-Grillet's longtime editor at Minuit, implicitly endorsed the potentially fruitful interactions between pedagogy and literature, noting in one letter,

> Je pense de plus en plus qu'un ouvrage où, à partir de tes cours, tu ferais un peu le point serait le bienvenu. As-tu pu avancer ce projet et nous rapporteras-tu des États-Unis un beau manuscrit?
>
> I've been thinking more and more that a work in which you take stock of your courses would be most welcome. Have you made any progress on that project and will you bring us back a fine manuscript from the United States?[47]

Though Robbe-Grillet never followed through with that specific project, his experience in the academy in the United States eventually cultivated a pedagogical impulse in his writing. "When I write," he declared in a 1976 lecture delivered at the University of Chicago, "I write with great care, organizing structures that seem to me beautiful, demonstrably provable, even almost pedagogic."[48] He likened his writings to what a schoolchild might write before academic settings imposed conventional narrative rules, implicitly advocating a return to "naturalness" over tradition as an alternative instructional method.[49] Always eager to self-theorize, Robbe-Grillet had reimagined his literary project in explicitly pedagogical terms. At the same time, he benefited from his institutional position as a university lecturer to reproach schools, universities, and literary prize committees for reinforcing the established order and failing to promote aesthetic innovation. Such an approach was consonant both with Robbe-Grillet's general ambivalence toward institutions—this was the writer who would later forgo a seat in the Académie française by refusing to follow the simple protocol of submitting an advance copy of his acceptance speech—and with his self-promotional style. Teaching the *nouveau roman*, in his estimation, could counteract outdated pedagogical models and bring acclaim to himself and other writers loosely collected under the same label. As his invitations to speak and lecture in American universities proliferated, Robbe-Grillet began to see himself as a "voyageur de commerce du Nouveau Roman" ("business traveler for the *nouveau roman* movement"), who would "pas perdre une occasion de parler du Nouveau Roman" ("not miss an occasion to speak about the New Novel").[50]

It was in this context that, two years later, *Le rendez-vous* was conceived. Not only did the textbook emerge from Robbe-Grillet's institutional presence in the university—a presence that naturally increased his network of academic contacts—but it provided a formal outlet for channeling his thinking on the intersections between pedagogy and literature that teaching in a university had activated.

Rendezvousing Across the Atlantic

When she met Robbe-Grillet in 1978, Lenard had moved from UCLA to CSUDH, where she received tenure and chaired the Foreign Languages Department. She remained in close contact with her former colleagues, and at a dinner she hosted for them on June 4, 1978, was introduced to Robbe-Grillet, then a visiting professor at UCLA. As Robbe-Grillet wrote to his wife, Catherine,

> Le soir dîner chez une dame Lenard, qui récolte 150 000 $ par an sur des livres scolaires et habite une maison en conséquence, elle voudrait que je fasse un texte didactique pour apprendre le français aux élèves de 1ère année d'univer-

sité. . . . [E]n principe ça m'intéresse et j'ai accepté de réfléchir à la question. On doit se revoir en Provence, cet été, où elle a une maison de riche (reproduite dans *Plaisir de France*!).

Dinner at the house of a woman named Lenard, who earns $150,000 a year writing textbooks and lives in a sizable home. She would like me to write a didactic text to teach French to first-year university students. . . . [I]n theory that interests me, and I told her I'd think about it. We will see each other in Provence this summer, where she has a rich person's home (featured in *Plaisir de France*!).[51]

Unabashedly impressed by Lenard's wealth, Robbe-Grillet agreed to embark on a collaborative project with her by summer's end.

"*Le rendez-vous* is proposed as an answer to a definite need," begins Lenard in her introduction to the textbook, a need that seems to operate in two directions.[52] On the one hand, the textbook proposed to fill a void for American teachers and students of intermediate French, a course level for which it is notoriously difficult to find accessible supplementary literary texts. On the other hand, the textbook enabled Robbe-Grillet to tackle a particular aesthetic problem: could he write a compelling text under grammatical and lexical constraints? The introduction boldly advertised the literary stakes of this experiment: "Would these restrictions impair the writer's expression to the point where his identity would be lost? Is it inherent in the text, written with a didactic intention, to be flatly expository, devoid of dynamic tension and mystery?"[53] The challenge was a familiarly Oulipian one, as the next chapter will develop in more detail—and certainly novels like Georges Perec's lipogrammatic *La disparition* (*A Void*) had already demonstrated that, quite to the contrary, formal constraints could elevate dynamic tension and mystery.[54] In Robbe-Grillet's case, however, these constraints were distinctly transnational in nature. His task was both to adhere closely to the grammatical progression of French-language acquisition prescribed by an American university professor and to write with a readership of non-native speakers in mind. Such a project, the introduction maintained, would paradoxically position *Le rendez-vous* as exemplary rather than peripheral in Robbe-Grillet's corpus: "Alain Robbe-Grillet feels that *Le rendez-vous* is an integral part of his *oeuvre*" and "he sees it as an ideal introduction to the study of his other works."[55]

Unsure how to categorize *Le rendez-vous* in Robbe-Grillet's literary corpus, one critic has suggested "casting it aside" ("le laisser de côté") as a "bastard text" ("petit bâtard").[56] Yet despite the unusual circumstances of its production, *Le rendez-vous* retains familiar plot elements and a narrative structure consistent with his previous novels. A first-person narrator named Boris, responding to an advertisement in the newspaper, meets an American named Jean—spelled "Djinn" in the text and pronounced "Gene" as it is in American English—who offers him employment. Captivated by Djinn's musical voice, androgynous appearance, waxlike features, and generally mysterious air, Boris is led on a series of strange encounters.

Part police thriller and part dream fantasy, the novel follows Boris's adventures through the city of Paris on foot and in taxis, from the rue Vercingétorix near Montparnasse up to the Gare du Nord. He meets two ageless children, Marie and Jean, who rename him Simon Lecoeur and guide him, blindfolded, to a room where a recording of Djinn's voice laments capitalism, technology, and man's alienation to a group of similarly blindfolded men, calling on all of them to resist the "machine" of society.[57] After a shift in narration in later chapters, in which a now female narrator describes meeting Simon, also known as Boris, who appears and disappears mysteriously from her life, the novel produces a series of *mises en abyme* and rehearses many of Robbe-Grillet's standard aesthetic tricks: metamorphoses of identities, names, and settings; repetition as a means of advancing, contradicting, and subverting plot; and playing with visual acuity and blindness to undermine perspective. The novel is also uncharacteristically funny. "Et ne dis pas O.K., c'est très vulgaire, surtout en français" ("Don't say O.K., it's a very vulgar word, especially in French"), Djinn instructs Boris, in one example of the novel's light, parodic tone.[58] While the complexity of plot, lexicon, and grammar increases with each chapter, the novel remains insistently readable. Vocabulary is translated in footnotes throughout, and Lenard's exercises break up chapters after every few pages of narrative, careful to practice recently introduced grammatical content, to probe students' reading comprehension, and to develop their skills in literary analysis.

The publishing archive suggests that Robbe-Grillet was intently concerned with the legibility of his text. In one early, handwritten draft of the manuscript, which he would later send to Lenard, Robbe-Grillet inserted a note at the end of chapter 1: "Lettre à Mme Lenard: corrections: souligner les mots ou tournures trop difficiles; proposer éventuellement les mots anglais étant comme en français; les formes manquantes pour le chap. 2" ("Letter to Madame Lenard: corrections: underline the words or phrases that are too difficult; perhaps suggest English words that resemble French ones and missing grammatical forms for chap. 2").[59]

Lenard responded accordingly, noting places where Robbe-Grillet might simplify his language to accommodate American students. In early drafts, she simply underlined what she perceived as phrases with problematic word choice, such as "les mains <u>fourrées</u> dans les poches de son imperméable" ("his hands <u>stuffed</u> in the pocket of his raincoat"), prompting Robbe-Grillet to change "fourrées" to "enfoncées" ("sunk").[60] As they advanced in the writing process, she took greater liberties in suggesting alternative expressions or turns of phrase. In a penultimate galley version, for instance, she proposed that Robbe-Grillet change both adjectives in the sentence "Tout le charme de cette voix fraîche et fruitée a disparu d'un seul coup" ("All the charm from that fresh and fruity voice quickly vanished"), striking out both "fraîche" and "fruitée" in red and writing in "douce" ("sweet") and "sensuelle" ("sensual").[61] Robbe-Grillet opted for a middle ground, and "cette voix fraîche et sensuelle" made it into the final, published version.[62]

The manuscript drafts abound with such examples, in which not only Lenard offers corrections to Robbe-Grillet's prose but Robbe-Grillet edits her grammatical exercises. Robbe-Grillet brought to the project his well-honed editorial gaze—developed over many years in his role as manuscript reviewer and proofreader for Minuit—to locate spelling mistakes, infelicities of language, and grammatical errors.[63] The production of *Le rendez-vous* reveals, in that sense, not two discretely produced parts of a work but an intimately dialogic process of construction, a transatlantic conversation that took place in cross outs, red markups, and marginal notes.

Before Robbe-Grillet began the process of writing *Le rendez-vous*, Lenard had supplied him with a detailed plan. The chapters were to introduce, in order, the present tense, "er" verbs, and idiomatic expressions using verbs like *être*, *aller*, and *faire* (chapter 1); adjectives, adverbs, and variations on verbs like *porter* and *mener* (chapter 2); "ir" and "re" verbs, color verbs (*blanchir*, *noircir*, etc.), and irregular "ir" verbs like *dormir*, *partir*, and *sortir* (chapter

3); the perfect, imperfect, and historical past (chapter 4); direct and indirect objects, used in affirmative, negative, and imperative sentences (chapter 5); the subjunctive mood and its irregular forms, which Lenard lists (chapter 6); simple and complex relative pronouns (*qui, que, lequel, dont, ce dont*, etc.), as well as the future and conditional tenses (chapter 7); and reflexive verbs, including passive expressions like *ça se dit* and *ça se fait* (chapter 8). "On peut tout employer à partir de ce point" ("You can use everything as of this point"), Lenard writes in her guidelines for chapter 9. Of the tenth and final chapter she writes simply "Liberté totale . . ." ("total freedom").[64] Robbe-Grillet adhered religiously to these guidelines, so much so that the absence of any ninth or tenth chapter in the published version suggests that the "total freedom" on offer may have ultimately been an impediment to writing.

One can picture Robbe-Grillet sitting down to write the novel with Lenard's guidelines at his side. He drafted everything by hand, and his manuscripts are lined with boxed-off sections in the margins that were integrated into subsequent versions. Draft after draft, Robbe-Grillet modified his novel to ensure greater conformity with the instructions. The third draft of chapter 5, for example—in which Robbe-Grillet was to introduce direct and indirect objects in imperative and negative sentences—includes additions to the first paragraph:

> This stubbornness surprised even me. I reproached myself for it, while also taking pleasure in it.
>
> Cette obstination **me** surprenait moi-même. Je **me la** reprochais, tout en **m'y** complaisant.

as well as additions of entire paragraphs that contain such constructions while also modifying the plot:

> The machine is watching you; fear it no longer! The machine gives you orders: obey it no longer! The machine demands all your time: surrender it no longer! The machine thinks itself superior to men: prefer it over them no longer!
>
> La machine **vous** surveille; ne **la** craignez plus! La machine **vous** donne des ordres; ne **lui** obéissez plus! La machine réclame tout votre temps; ne **la lui** donnez plus! La machine se croit supérieure aux hommes; ne **la leur** préférez plus![65]

Grammar, somewhat like this capitalist machine, functions as constraint, ordering the text and the reader. The excessiveness of Robbe-Grillet's repetition of object pronouns seems to nod playfully to the idea of grammatical constraints and especially to the desire to break them. Can a writer both maintain and transcend imposed order? This anxiety, at the heart of Robbe-Grillet's project, seeps from the manuscript's margins into the prose.

The transnational conversation taking place behind the scenes, in letters and manuscript drafts sent across the Atlantic, became the stuff of the novel. We could call the textbook project a performance of a transnational rendezvous, a literary collaboration between a French novelist and a French-language pedagogue in America that becomes inscribed in the fiction itself. Lenard recalls how Robbe-Grillet insisted on the title *Le rendez-vous*, despite the similarity with the title of his earlier novel *La maison de rendez-vous* (*The Meeting House*), and even knowing that he would publish the text under a different title, *Djinn*, in France.[66]

The title signaled the book's status as a transatlantic object, a product of Robbe-Grillet and Lenard's collaborative effort. In the prose, *Le rendez-vous* even recycles the material of transatlantic correspondence. Lenard suggested in one letter to Robbe-Grillet and to possible editors that they might produce "bandes magnétiques" ("magnetic tape recordings") as supplementary pedagogical tools for the classroom;[67] they never did, but instead the "bandes magnétiques" make their way into the novel, part of the machine that projects Djinn's voice for Simon Lecoeur and similar dutiful followers.[68] In the French edition of *Djinn*, Robbe-Grillet added a prologue that frames *Le rendez-vous* as a mysterious manuscript discovered by chance and written by a certain Boris, alias Simon Lecoeur, a professor teaching at an American school in Paris. To insist on the veracity of this narrative frame, the text footnotes Lecoeur's campus address, "56 rue de Passy, 75016 Paris"—the address of what was then NYU's Paris site, emblazoned on the frequent letters Robbe-Grillet received from Tom Bishop.[69] *Le rendez-vous* obsessively reinscribes elements from Robbe-Grillet's American experience, producing a series of textual refractions that jump between life and the page.

The novel itself abounds with rendezvous: appointments whose locations are forgotten; meetings that, trapped between past and future, cannot be clearly located in time; the initial rendezvous between (the American) Djinn and (the French) Simon Lecoeur that becomes a pivotal encounter re-narrated later in the novel.[70] The rendezvous is often a source of anxiety, much like in a dream, evoking fears that the meeting will not take place, or may have already taken place, or is somehow inaccessible. Djinn recalls her first meeting with Simon, when both replied to a newspaper ad for work:

> Toujours est-il que, nous trouvant, Simon et moi, l'un en face de l'autre, chacun de nous a d'abord cru que l'autre était son éventuel employeur.[71]

> The fact is that, Simon and I, finding ourselves face to face, each of us believed, at first, that the other was [their] eventual employer.[72]

No one else shows up to the meeting, and Djinn and Simon, side by side, accompany each other through the streets of Paris:

> Nous nous sommes mis en marche, joyeusement. Simon s'ingéniait à inventer toutes sortes d'histoires, plus ou moins fantastiques, concernant les lieux que nous traversions et les gens qui nous croisaient. Mais il nous a fait prendre un chemin bizarre, compliqué, dont il n'était pas assez sûr. . . . Nous avons fini par nous perdre tout à fait.[73]

> So we set out, happily. Simon did his best to invent all kinds of stories, more or less fantastic, concerning the places we were walking through and the people we came across. But he made us take a strange, complicated path, of which he wasn't sure enough. . . . We ended up completely lost eventually.[74]

With a playful nod to Walter Benjamin, Robbe-Grillet charts the novel's construction: Simon and Djinn, thinly veiled doubles for Robbe-Grillet and Lenard, embark on an uncertain co-authorship, a process of literary flânerie where the writer is an unreliable guide through the city-text.

Given the anxieties of co-authorship palpable in the novel's pages, it may not be surprising that the titular shift from *Le rendez-vous* to *Djinn* formally erases the allusion to a transatlantic collaboration. The title change permitted Robbe-Grillet to assume full ownership of the copyright to the novel, and indeed Lenard's name figures nowhere in *Djinn*'s paratexts. Robbe-Grillet doubled down on that erasure in the prologue he added in *Djinn*, in which police discover a manuscript titled *Le rendez-vous*, penned by Simon Lecoeur, that includes its bibliographic reference, "*Holt, Rinehart and Winston*, CBS

Inc., 383 Madison Ave, New York N.Y. 10017."⁷⁵ Robbe-Grillet displaces authorship fully onto Simon, turning his American publication into a fictional construct that removes Lenard even from citation. We learn in the epilogue, also added for *Djinn*, that the police are drawn to Simon's manuscript because it recounts a crime that would indeed occur—the death of a young woman with a strong resemblance to Djinn, as narrated in chapter 6—leading the police to assume Simon's guilty hand in the murder. It is hard not to read in this plot twist a figural *mise à mort* of the co-author.

Lenard's foundational role in producing *Le rendez-vous* does not, however, escape notice in the letters and drafts that form their literary archive. The manuscripts attest to the ways in which Lenard fueled Robbe-Grillet's creative process, providing him with the constraints and instructions that helped make the novel a success, and her prestige in the field of textbook publishing had unquestionably made *Le rendez-vous* possible and given Robbe-Grillet access to a far more profitable side of publishing than he had previously encountered. His half of the advance for *Le rendez-vous*, $2,250, represented a substantially higher sum than the $400 he had received from Grove for *La jalousie*.⁷⁶ In *Djinn*, the traces of Lenard's role remain visible only in the literary transcription of their co-authorship embedded in the novel's plot and made manifest through the unpublished documents of their archive, which have thus far not figured in the scholarly record.⁷⁷

Djinn, Back in France

The commercial and aesthetic effects of Lenard and Robbe-Grillet's collaboration were nonetheless felt almost immediately in France. On March 3, 1981, *Djinn* came out in Paris, just a month after *Le rendez-vous* was released in the United States. As would be expected, *Djinn* did not include interspersed grammar exercises, but otherwise, besides the added prologue and epilogue, its text was identical to that of *Le rendez-vous*. We know that Robbe-Grillet conceived of *Djinn* as a separate publication from the beginning. In a scribbled note to himself accompanying his initial outlines, he wrote, "S. L. se serait servi de l'alibi du livre scolaire pour rédiger un document, pour lui de la plus haute importance—sur quoi? Espionnage?" ("S. L. perhaps used the scholarly manual as an alibi for writing a document that was for him of the utmost importance—about what? Spying?").⁷⁸ In the first draft—the one that included handwritten notes to Lenard—he already had the foundations of his prologue, in pages that would not be shipped across the Atlantic. While writing a text for American students, Robbe-Grillet was also thinking about how to make it work in France. And work it did.

The novel sold over 20,000 copies in its first three weeks—compared with Robbe-Grillet's previously bestselling novel, *La jalousie*, which sold 150,000 over the course of twenty years—and in interviews Robbe-Grillet vaunted the American origins of the project.[79] The French press widely reviewed *Djinn* as a literary success story. After decades of producing ponderous, overwritten, and inaccessible prose, Robbe-Grillet had finally written a great novel. "Qui eût cru qu'une œuvre de commande révélerait en Robbe-Grillet un maître du roman fantastique?" ("Who would have thought that a commissioned work would show Robbe-Grillet to be a master of fantasy fiction?"), asked Jeanyves Guérin in *L'esprit*.[80] Reviews in *Le monde des livres*, *Le nouvel observateur*, and *Le magazine littéraire* similarly celebrated the novel as the work of Robbe-Grillet at his best, rather than of the author who strayed into more esoteric territory in the 1970s with novels like *Topologie d'une cité fantôme* (*Topology of a Phantom City*) and *Souvenirs du triangle d'or* (*Recollections of the Golden Triangle*).[81]

French critics praised *Djinn* primarily on two scores: for its exemplarity and its legibility. *Djinn* rehearsed tropes familiar from Robbe-Grillet's literary universe: "tout y est" ("everything is there"), wrote Jacqueline Piatier in *Le Monde*, referring as much to Robbe-Grillet's cult objects, settings, and plots as to his maniacal sense of detail. Exemplary of Robbe-Grillet's fictional universe, even to the point of self-parody, the novel was billed by some as an ideal introduction to his work—"la meilleure introduction qui soit" ("the best introduction there could be")[82]—so much so that even lukewarm reviews recognized in *Djinn* a useful point of departure for readers eager to familiarize themselves with Robbe-Grillet's oeuvre.[83] Ironically, then, what made *Djinn* particularly exemplary was its accessibility, a trait previously incongruous with Robbe-Grillet's work. French critics continually reiterated this idea of legibility, describing *Djinn* as an antidote to "illisibilité" ("illegibility"), as a text "fait pour être lu" ("made to be read"), and as a reason to read an author who, though "célèbre" ("famous") was "pas assez lu" ("not read enough").[84] The novel, in other words, was understood to recuperate Robbe-Grillet from decades of unreadable prose and to offer readers unfamiliar with his work the chance to discover him.

In interviews, Robbe-Grillet too attributed *Djinn*'s success to its readability—"il se lit plus facilement que les autres" ("it reads more easily than the others")[85]—and expressed satisfaction that his novels were finally receiving the readership they deserved.[86] Yet what exactly did readability mean with respect to Robbe-Grillet's works? Susan Rubin Suleiman has argued that Robbe-Grillet's novels lose their transgressive edge and become conventionally readable by force of repetition. "The paradox," Suleiman concludes in her analysis of his standard technique of *glissements*, or sliding between voices, "is that after reading a number of Robbe-Grillet's novels, a reader comes to *expect* the *glissements* as part of the code regulating them."[87] Readability—here analogous to breaking the code—inheres in the writer's oeuvre as a whole, attainable only for the experienced, knowledgeable reader of Robbe-Grillet.

This fundamental systematicity of Robbe-Grillet's novels aligned them, for Suleiman, with Barthes's notion of *le lisible* (the readable, pleasurable text) as distinct from *le scriptible* (the writeable text of Barthesian *jouissance*). It was nonetheless this latter category of the *scriptible* to which Barthes seemed to assign Robbe-Grillet, somewhat ambivalently, positioning him in *Le plaisir du texte* against Gustave Flaubert and other writers of pleasurable texts—only later to declare what literary traits they shared.[88] The ambiguity of critical stances vis-à-vis the readability of Robbe-Grillet's work—in Barthes's distinction between readable–pleasurable and writeable–blissful texts, we hear echoes of his distinction between "humaniste" and "chosiste" readings—helps contextualize why a novel like *Djinn* might suggest a vision of legibility different from the one Suleiman describes.

Readers of *Djinn*, as Robbe-Grillet and French critics agreed, did not need to bring to bear a well-honed familiarity with his literary devices. It was the inexperienced, amateur reader, the one with something to learn, that Robbe-Grillet wanted most to reach. Robbe-Grillet's heightened attunement to the instructional value of a text was the legacy of his experiences of publishing *Le rendez-vous* and teaching in the United States. For a text to be *lisible*, for the Robbe-Grillet of the 1980s, did not mean that it occupied a functionally passive position, as Barthes would have it;[89] rather, it meant that the text was *teachable*, a text that a priori imagines its place in the classroom. Robbe-

Grillet vaunted *Djinn*'s pedagogical success to Rosset, who quoted him in a letter to Lenard that the novel "was being used in France to teach French to the French themselves."[90] Inspired by Robbe-Grillet's idea, Rosset hoped that perhaps Grove's English translation of *Djinn*, which he asked Lenard to tackle, might also include English grammar exercises to "teach" English to Americans by helping them focus on written expression.[91] The grammar instruction component was ultimately abandoned, but when the Grove edition appeared in 1982, Lenard's name returned to the cover, reflecting her latest contribution as a French-to-English translator of *Djinn*. Her paratextual reappearance was a kind of poetic return that reinscribed her into the project, though in a way that, ultimately, obscured more than it revealed about her role in it.

Several years after it was published, *Djinn* retained its status as a literary triumph. *Le monde des livres* named it in 1986 as one of the ten best books of the decade from 1975 to 1985, alongside such novels as Annie Ernaux's *La place* (*A Man's Place*), J. M. G. Le Clézio's *Désert* (*Desert*), and Perec's *La vie mode d'emploi* (*Life: A User's Manual*).[92] By that point, though, Robbe-Grillet had turned his attention elsewhere, abandoning fiction writing altogether to dedicate himself to his autobiographical series *Romanesques*. He would write one more novel decades later—titled *La reprise* (*The Resumption*, 2001), a return to the fictional genre, as well as to old plot lines—but by the early 1980s, Robbe-Grillet's practice of the *nouveau roman* had reached a certain end point.[93] The young Robbe-Grillet might never have predicted back in 1955 when he was writing a theory of the New Novel just how vigorously he would go on to undermine his claim, quoted in this chapter's epigraph, that "a novel which is no more than the grammatical example illustrating a rule—even accompanied by its exception—would naturally be useless."[94] What he could not know, at that time, was how an encounter with the American university would transform the conditions under which he could produce a novel, turning attention to grammar into the impetus for literary creation.

That *Le rendez-vous* would be the last textbook of its kind, at least to date, speaks to shifts in foreign language instruction, in both the turn toward multimedia approaches since the mid-1980s and the waning belief that literature can be called on to teach basic language skills. One would be hard-pressed to imagine, now, teachers of intermediate French adopting *Le rendez-vous* in their college courses. The belief that complicated literary texts provided an ideal mode of access to basic French-language skills remains a relic of the past, supplanted by enthusiasm for interactive and visually arresting videos or online materials. I will take up this question in greater detail in the Conclusion, but it is important to emphasize how much *Le rendez-vous,* situated in its place in time, should remind us to give American students their rightful due in the literary history of the French New Novel, providing, as they did, the incentive and motivation (as well as the linguistic limitations) for Robbe-Grillet to write a commercial bestseller. In that sense, this story affirms Rachel Sagner Buurma and Laura Heffernan's call to place "teaching at the center of literary history" and to understand U.S. college classrooms as critical sites of literary and scholarly production where students play an integral role.[95]

Indeed, this literary history that I have been tracing about Robbe-Grillet's textbook-turned-novel participates in a larger narrative about the role of American institutional forces in promoting French literary production. It illustrates, in part, the ways that francophone novelists found, and continue to find, institutional support in departments of French and Francophone Studies in the U.S., both on a visiting basis and in long-term positions like the one Robbe-Grillet held, to teach literature and craft—an investment in creative writing at the college level, as McGurl has shown, that we can trace even beyond the English department.[96] This institutional positioning of francophone novelists explains the proliferation of French-language novels produced in, around, and about American college campuses—a topic I will also return to in the Conclusion as well—and that includes such examples as Michel Butor's novel *Mobile* (1962) inspired by his visiting positions at Bryn Mawr and Middlebury Colleges; Louis-Philippe Dalembert's *Milwaukee Blues* (2021), a novel that in part emerged from Dalembert's observations about campus life and race relations while a visiting professor at the University of Wisconsin, Milwaukee; Maylis de Kerangal's short story collection *Canoës* (*Canoes*, 2023), which evokes the author's time living on a Colorado campus in 1999, where she wrote her first novel, *Je marche sous un ciel de traîne* (*I Walk Under a Stormy Sky,* 2000); and Abdourahman A. Waberi's *Dis-moi pour qui j'existe?* (*Tell Me for Whom I Live?,* 2022), an epistolary novel with repeated references to teaching at George Washington University.[97] Robbe-Grillet's example illuminates one strand in a broader story about how pedagogy and institutional affiliations with American college campuses fuel French literary productions, past and present.

As a case study, *Le rendez-vous* suggests both continuities and shifts that were taking place in the ways that the American market catalyzed French literary works in the second half of the twentieth century. Literary projects like those studied in Chapters 1 and 2, as we have seen, had their own complex transnational histories and outcomes, but they broadly showed the ways that American publishers took risks by investing in works that would have been unconventional or aesthetically inaccessible to readers and viewers. With *Le rendez-vous*, we are confronted with a work that sought to make the experimental commonplace and easily accessible for a U.S. market. To gain firm footing in the college textbook industry, the New Novel needed to lose its avant-garde edge and present itself as readily marketable—a shift that, while for some may have signaled the downfall of an experimental movement, for others would indicate its extraordinary staying power as a cultural force.[98]

In either case, such a shift relied crucially on an insider who knew the mechanisms of college publishing. Like the dozens of novels by women published in French in wartime New York, Yvone Lenard's invisibility from a project in which she commanded a sizable role reveals another way in which literary histories have obscured the participation of women in francophone literary productions. Her odd place in the translation history of the book serves as a reminder of the complicated dynamics at play between translation and authorship—a topic that I turn to in the next chapter.

 # Oulipian New York
On Transatlantic Translators and Intimate Potentialities

> "And you think you would have been better off in America—in New York City—than in Romania or France?"
> —GEORGES PEREC, *Ellis Island*[1]

> Without a plane how can you travel from NY to France on Friday and return on the same Friday?
> —GEORGES PEREC, Handwritten note on a draft of *53 Days*[2]

False Starts

It was April 1980, and my father, a recent PhD in French intellectual history who had just started a career in book publishing, eagerly grasped my hand as he described the lecture we would be attending as the most exciting literary event of his life: Georges Perec, one of his literary heroes, had finally "made it" in the anglophone publishing world after rave reviews of the English translation of his 1978 novel *Life: A User's Manual* in the *New York Times, Time magazine,* and other mainstream venues, and he would be delivering a talk to a packed crowd at Columbia University's *Maison française*. I was too young to understand most of the talk, but I recall glancing around at the audience and being surprised by how intently everyone was looking at Perec and the bursts of laughter and applause that would suddenly erupt as Perec read excerpts from his novel and described the intricate chessboard-like organization that he had used to structure his chapters. Perec was particularly thrilled that New York had finally embraced him as a writer, he said, because the idea for *Life: A User's Manual* had all, in a sense, started there, after he had seen a 1949 drawing by Saul Steinberg that depicted the busy and crowded interior apartments of a New York lodging house.[3] Perec described his thrill at the thought that some of those same New York residents drawn by Steinberg, though considerably older now, might be in the audience that day, which led to a massive round of applause and a standing ovation.

While I cannot be sure that my career path as a scholar of twentieth-century French literature originated in that precise moment of widespread energy and enthusiasm for an acclaimed writer, it certainly remains one of my fondest memories—which is why I have been surprised at the lecture's absence from any literary history of Perec and the Oulipo, including David Bellos's meticulous biography *Georges Perec: A Life in Words*. How could such a delightful event have been so thoroughly erased from the scholarly record? My father and I patiently waited in line for a signed copy of the English translation of *Life: A User's Manual*, a book that traveled with me later to college and graduate school, even as the English words on its spine became increasingly surrounded by French titles from my coursework. As I write now, the book still holds pride of place on my bookshelf, yellowing pages and all.

One reason this anecdote does not appear in the scholarship on Perec is that it is, of course, a fiction, as any scholar of Perec would know—but it is not an implausible tale. I would have been too young in the spring of 1980 to retain any memories of Perec (or really of anyone for that matter), but Perec had in fact recently spent a good deal of time in New York City conducting research and field work for his film *Récits d'Ellis Island* (*Ellis Island*), which aired on French television in 1980. Had Perec lived longer—he died prematurely of lung cancer, in 1982, at forty-five years old—he might have finally received the attention in the anglophone world that he had long hoped to earn, and that he once thought he might achieve with his 1975 book *W ou le souvenir d'enfance* (*W or The Memory of Childhood*).[4] Perec had longstanding literary "global ambitions," as Bellos suggests, with a particular eye towards the U.S.: he had studied English from a young age, he had a deep passion for American cinema, and his books routinely inscribed American friends, expressions, places, and culture.[5] Yet he had little success in English during his lifetime: *Les Choses*, winner of the 1965 Prix Renaudot in France, had unimpressive sales figures when Grove released the translation in 1968 (1,645 copies sold in the U.S. in its first year, compared to over 100,000 in France), and American publishers turned down the opportunity to publish *Life: A User's Manual* after it won the Prix Médicis in 1978, fearing that it would be difficult, if not impossible, to translate.⁶ During his lifetime, Perec did not earn the global recognition that he had sought in New York—but what if he had?

I begin this chapter with a counterfactual frame as a way of opening up a series of intersecting questions about global ambition, translation, and the notion of "potentiality" that has been core to the Oulipo since its inception in 1960, and that together help us to rethink the transatlantic dimensions of Perec's work and of Oulipian ideas more expansively. When the co-founders Raymond Queneau and François le Lionnais first convened a meeting with the earliest Oulipo members—fewer than a dozen writers, poets, mathematicians, and pataphysicians, all of whom shared a common love of games—they debated whether to signal the term "experimental" or "potential" in their group's title and mission. They ultimately abandoned their original name "Sélitex"—an acronym for Séminaire de Littérature Expérimentale (Seminar on Experimental Literature)—in favor of Oulipo, an acronym for Ouvroir de Littérature Potentielle (Workshop for Potential Literature) that registered ideas both of collective labor (an "ouvroir" typically refers to a workroom for women, nuns in particular, to make and mend clothing) and of potentiality.⁷ Le Lionnais described potentiality capaciously as "opening new possibilities previously unknown to authors," a definition that Jacques Bens later extended by calling "a potential work one which is not limited to its appearances, which contains secret riches, which willingly lends itself to exploration."⁸ This exploratory potential of Oulipian writing has converged around ideas of imposed constraint: the more daring and seemingly impossible the formal rule, the more exciting the literary work might be, which is why *La disparition* (*A Void*, 1969), Perec's 300-page lipogrammatic novel written without the letter "e" referenced already in this book, remains to this day the most emblematic and cited example of the Oulipo project at work.

While practitioners and scholars of Oulipian writing have tended to associate potential literature with this liberatory effect of aesthetic constraints, this chapter expands the framework of potentiality by taking its cue from other published and unpublished materials in Perec's corpus. The potentiality of literature, for Perec, was not a strictly formal or aesthetic question; it also presented an opportunity to imagine, often in hypothetical or counterfactual terms, his relation to potential worlds, communities of readers, or other interlocutors. What I will call "intimate potentialities," a concept tied to Giorgio Agamben's reflections on potentiality as an "ethical experience," connects Perec's writings in and around New York (both the *Récits d'Ellis Island* film and his unpublished notes while there) with his thinking about translation and potential readerships, which we find most explicitly in his correspondence and literary collaborations with his close friend and fellow Oulipian, the American writer Harry Mathews.[9] For the last decade of Perec's life, he engaged in a translation practice with Mathews in which they published translations of each other's works between France and New York, sent each other letters in and about translation, and strived to imagine, together, how to find new audiences for their work.

This chapter reimagines Perec through the prism of transatlantic translators—a perspective that also allows me to extend a recent scholarly interest in the Oulipo's relationship to translation and multilingualism.[10] Perec was deeply invested in French–English translation as an Oulipian exercise; as he told an interviewer shortly before he died, "Translating is to impose oneself, to produce a text through a constraint which is represented by the original text."[11] For as much as Perec thought about translation, and for as much as general translation theorists and Oulipian specialists have argued for re-envisioning translation as a creative practice (in the words of Hervé Le Tellier, the current president of the Oulipo, "all translations of an Oulipian work are in and of themselves Oulipian achievements"), the Pléiade edition of Perec's works does not include his multiple translations, published or unpublished.[12]

Perec was an accomplished and highly practiced translator, particularly of works by Mathews, and their collaborative process signals the ways in which translation operates as a constitutive condition of writing. Through archival materials that I have assembled from both Perec's and Mathews's collections, this chapter makes a case for reading translation not as an afterthought—as something that may occur once a text is completed, a symbol of literary achievement if a writer is lucky enough—but as a social and highly relational practice. I will trace this idea through Perec and Mathews's public and private translations that present a vision of translation as a form of intimate potentiality—a vision that reaches fruition in the collaborative film project *Récits d'Ellis Island* (1978–1980) that Perec made with filmmaker Robert Bober. My reading offers a response to recent critics who have accused conceptual writing, and the Oulipo in particular, of participating in a "cerebral avant-garde" that produces a "stonewalling of the affects."[13] As I hope to demonstrate, the Franco-American collaboration between Perec and Mathews instantiates, here through the figure of the translator, the broader claims of this book: how the high experimentalism of French literary productions in the postwar decades was not as formally detached, impersonal, or conceptual as it seemed, but was predicated on intimate social practices between writers and other cultural agents.

The Intimate Potentialities of Translation

Georges Perec and Harry Mathews's friendship began with an offer of translation. In July 1970, Geneviève Serreau, an actress and writer who assisted the publisher Maurice Nadeau at *Les Nouvelles littéraires*, told Perec about a novel that they would soon be publishing in French translation by an American writer. Serreau thought Perec would appreciate the wordplay and style of *Conversions*, and she was right: in their very first correspondence, an undated letter from late 1970, Perec wrote to Mathews in French to express the "intense jubilation" he experienced upon reading this novel about an enigmatic quest that takes the protagonist from a New York dinner party to the ocean floor near an unnamed French island. Perec noted the similarities between Mathews's style and his recently completed novel *La disparition*, which he offered to send to Mathews. He ended the letter with an idea for a future collaboration:

> Geneviève had the thought that I should suggest collaborating on the translation of your most recent book, and I would be happy to do it. (To tell you the truth, I use English quite poorly, but I suppose that my collaboration would come once we get down to the nitty gritty.)[14]

Though Mathews had not yet read Perec's work (he lied in his response to say he had), he knew of Perec's literary reputation through mutual friends and of his Renaudot prize a few years earlier for his novel *Les choses* (*Things*).[15] Mathews must have quickly responded to Perec's fan letter, and the two met shortly thereafter at the Bar du Pont-Royal in Paris, the first in-person meeting of what Mathews later called "the most exhilarating, hilarious, intense, and satisfying relationship I have ever known with a man."[16]

Perec and Mathews embarked on a journey of mutual translation that would continue for the rest of Perec's life. Perec went on to translate a collection of Mathews's poems and his novels *Tlooth* and *The Sinking of the Odradek Stadium*, and Mathews in turn translated into English Perec's *Ellis Island*, as well as several of his shorter texts, including the chapters titled "Rorschash" and "Lift Machinery" in *Life: A User's Manual*, the short story *"Still Life/Style Leaf"* and several texts in Oulipian publications.[17] Translation wasn't just a professional courtesy or obligation for these writers; the topic and practice of translation permeated all their letters over the next twelve years, and informal translations made their way into the marginalia of Perec's notebooks, in ways that signaled a consistent engagement with translation for the last decade of his life.

By his second letter, Perec was already addressing Mathews with the informal "tu," and he continued writing about translation. "I'm advancing word by word through your book, getting lost, finding myself again, frightened or fascinated. I think we will need to break it down sentence by sentence" ("J'avance mot à mot dans ton livre, m'y perdant, m'y retrouvant, effrayé ou fasciné. Je crois qu'il va falloir qu'on se mette à la décortiquer phrase à phrase") and proposes that they spend a few days together next time Mathews is in Paris.[18] This insight into Perec's experience of reading Mathews affirms the American writer and current Oulipo member Daniel Levin Becker's point that "thinking about Oulipians as writers is an incomplete enterprise without thinking about them as readers."[19] Perec read Mathews in English with a particular eye towards the eventual French translation he might create, and he proposed in this letter what would become their standard practice: dissecting each sentence and working on the text together, ideally in person. While they met frequently to collaborate on translations (often in Paris, sometimes in Lans-en-Vercors in southeastern France, where Mathews had a home), nearly every single letter Perec wrote was tinged with references to translation. In a letter from March 1972, as he was working on the French version of *Tlooth*, Perec asked Mathews his opinion on translating the English "tractors" for the French *"traiteurs,"* literally "caterers" in English. The translation would be inexact, as Perec readily admits—the French version would have metallic caterers instead of "genuine metallic tractors"—but he found the translation particularly funny because "it means only having to change the letter 'c'."[20]

As he worked on *Tlooth*, Perec wrote repeatedly to Mathews to walk him through his translation process and ideas. He particularly lingered on passages that relied on phonetic wordplay in English. For instance, one tricky phrase from Mathews's novel was "fur bowls," a phonetic rendering of a Russian woman saying the English words "four balls," changing both the vowel sounds, in reference to baseball; rather than offering a phonetic transcription, the opening line of Mathews's novel—"Mannish Madame Nevtaya slowly cried 'Fur bowls!'"—uses English words that are close enough to produce an absurd semantic effect. In his letter and then in the final translation, Perec proposes several possible translations, including "quartz bol" and "bol de quartz" (both of which use semantically legible French words but do not accurately represent a foreign accent speaking French) and "Cat Ballou" (a better phonetic transposition, which had the added benefit of alluding to Jane Fonda's 1965 film, though Perec feared the reference would escape most readers).[21] In the published version, Perec ends up with a different turn of phrase (*"Goitre à bal!"*) that cleverly integrates both the semantic and phonetic wordplay.[22] Perec's letters to Mathews show us the inner workings of the translation process, and just how much translation was the medium of their growing friendship.[23]

In fact, over the course of their entire twelve-year correspondence, there is almost no letter that *doesn't* mention translation in some form or another. Sometimes these include Perec's ideas about translation alternatives, as in the above examples. Other times they reference more practical details related to publishing, on either side of the Atlantic: delays in the publication timeline for *Tlooth* with *Les lettres nouvelles*; editorial discussions about whether to title Mathews's novel as *Tlooth, Dlame, Dentité, Dengue, Dhante,* or *Dhantès* before landing on *Les verts champs de moutarde de l'Afghanistan*; or mentions of a possible lead with New Directions for a translation of *W*.[24] In a postcard from 1980 that he wrote to Mathews in English, Perec registered excitement about the prospect of *La Vie mode d'emploi* finding an American press:

> Good news at last: good as gold. Mr. Budenholzer, from Anchor Press (Doubleday) would like to know if we are interested in an English translation of Life Instruction Manual. He wrote you too with this suggestion and asks me to please get in touch with you or myself with whatever ideas, requirements, or formats I think may be necessary in order to work towards this translation. So what I m'goin miself to respond this gentle man, I ask you in turn? Hein?[25]

The letter reveals Perec's growing comfort in English—not only in his choice of language for the postcard, but especially in the confidence of the last sentences, which play translingually with phonetics and spelling: one hears the accent of "miself" compared to the correctly spelled "myself" in the previous sentence, or the colloquial orality added by the apostrophe placement ("I m'goin") and the final turn to French ("hein" as a spoken interjection for "eh"). Moreover, the letter reveals just how much Mathews was Perec's main connection to the U.S. publishing world (hence the "we" who might be interested in the translation). Mathews had helped his friend find an American literary agent, Maxine Groffsky, when Perec visited New York in 1975, and Perec turned to Mathews for all advice about translating and publishing in the U.S.[26]

As this example makes plain, Perec often wrote to Mathews in English, especially in the late 1970s, in letters filled with bilingual puns and phonetic jokes. In an undated letter from New York City in 1979, Perec writes jokingly: "General Post O. Fizz: Here I am Ellisislanding a go-go / and would be very pleased to see / you. Do you plan to go to NYC / or would you like me to come / for a vicaine?" Both "Post O. Fizz" (*post office*) and "vicaine" (*weekend*) poke fun at a French pronunciation of English terms. Continuing the phonetic bilingual game, Perec appends his address at the Abbey Victoria hotel and his "faune" (read: *phone*) number.[27] Perec had studied English from a young age, but it's clear that his friendship and translation work with Mathews gave him confidence in his linguistic skills and an eagerness to push his writing in new directions.[28] The letters in that sense instantiate his widow Paulette Perec's claim, made many years later, that the process of translating Mathews allowed Perec to relearn English.[29] In one of Perec's very last letters to Mathews, written in French while in residence in Australia, he talks proudly of a text he had just written originally in English. The text itself isn't included, but the letter speaks to the pair's translation-oriented friendship and penchant for French–English neologisms: "I did it practically all alone, I swear, without a dictionary and in 2 hours! I'm astonishé. I've since found tons of words in the Webster dictionary. Thank you, Harry, for having helped me make such progress in English."[30] Perec is never far from a joke—*astonishé*, the neologism Perec uses in French, bends an English word to the rules of French grammar—but his excitement about English-language writing and appreciation for Mathews nonetheless come through as genuine.

Even when Perec was not writing in English, though, translation was always close at hand, a sign of his intimacy with Mathews. Their translation work was not a simple quid pro quo or transactional exchange, on the order of "I'll translate you if you translate me"; it was what spawned and indexed their closeness from beginning to end. A particularly poignant letter Perec wrote in 1980 consoles Mathews about his father's death: "And if the thought that I am your friend can bring you comfort, know that I am your friend, and I am happy that our paths crossed nearly eleven years ago" ("Et si l'idée que je suis ton ami peut te réconforter, sache que je suis ton ami et que je suis heureux que nos chemins se soient croisés il y aura bientôt onze ans"). The turn towards tenderness is slipped in between references to translation: the letter begins by announcing that he is sending four pages of his short story, "*Still Life/Style Leaf*," for Mathews to translate for *Yale French Studies*, and it ends with the announcement that Perec will soon be returning to his translation of *Odradek*, which he anticipates coming out in France in 1981.[31] Perec's affection and warmth are framed by the reciprocity of translation. The sentiment, meanwhile, is articulated as a hypothetical, a potential source of comfort only *if* Mathews finds it to be so. Perec's expression of affection takes the form of a potential intimacy, one that can be present, even if not actualized or formally received.

This is where Agamben's reflections on potentiality can be most instructive. He returns to Aristotle's analysis of potentiality in *Metaphysics* to suggest that potentiality should be understood conceptually not as that which disappears at the moment when an action occurs (as in, when something possible reaches fruition), but as "the *potential not to be*."[32] Potentiality, in that sense, is not annulled even as it becomes actualized, but maintains itself as a productive vulnerability. For Agamben, this is a distinctly human phenomenon tied to the ability to make art and produce knowledge ("human beings, insofar as they know and produce, are those beings who, more than any other, exist in the mode of potentiality"), and it is also a profoundly ethical experience that "expose[s] . . . in every form one's own amorphousness and in every act one's own inactuality."[33] The paradigmatic figure of potentiality, for Agamben, is Herman Melville's "*Bartleby, the Scrivener*," the literary character whose famous formulation—"I would prefer not to"—registers through the conditional tense his desire *not* to continue copying documents, while remaining perfectly capable of doing so. Bartleby's strength (his "*potentia*") lies in his willingness to face his own impotentiality—a model that can serve as both an ethical imperative and a "paradigm for literary writing."³⁴ Bartleby must stop copying, in Agamben's estimation, because such an act, in its "infinite repetition of what was abandons all its potential not to be."³⁵ Only by turning away from copying can Bartleby open himself up to the "experience of potentiality"—an experience that is "possible only if potentiality is always also potential not to (do or think something), if the writing tablet is capable of not being written on."³⁶ This willingness to expose oneself to the experience of potentiality, to recognize and accept one's own failings, and to see this as a fundamental condition of humanity and of being in the world is ultimately, for Agamben, "the most proper mode of human existence."³⁷ It is also a necessary precondition for writing: "only when we succeed in . . . experiencing our own impotentiality do we become capable of creating, truly becoming poets."³⁸

As foundational as the principle of potentiality has been to Oulipian practices, it has tended to refer less to the experience or positionality of the writer than to the formal possibilities of the text itself. In this respect, Oulipian potentiality evokes what the Académie française dictionary calls its "linguistic underpinnings," as in potential statements or sentences that "without being confirmed, are considered feasible according to the grammatical rules of a given language."³⁹ Agamben offers us a way in to seeing how potentiality can extend from literary experimentation to a subject's individual experience in the world, vis-à-vis themselves, others, and the act of writing.⁴⁰ Like Melville's Bartleby, Perec's literary experiment with Mathews is one that actively embraces an idea of potentiality as an ethical experience.⁴¹ Theirs is of a related but slightly different order, where intimacy and friendship are articulated in the form of a potential, and where the practice of shared translation—unlike copying—sparks the infinite potentialities of language.

In many ways, Mathews and Perec were articulating and enacting an idea of translation that was radically innovative. We could call this type of mutual translation an expression of intimate potentiality that few writers have ever practiced at all, let alone with such systematic and sustained intensity. Joseph Brodsky translated six poems by Czeslaw Milosz into Russian, in exchange for which Milosz translated one of Brodsky's poems into Polish.⁴² Mathews and Perec's translation practice, meanwhile, functioned as a literary expression of friendship. David Bellos gestures at this when he notes that Perec's "loving relationship with Harry" and his "interest in translation" together explained why "New York was coming to replace Saarbrücken as Perec's main foreign antenna."[43] Perec had been involved in other collaborative translation projects in the past, especially in his work with Eugen Helmle for German radio, but his increasing interest in New York as of the mid-1970s was, as Bellos suggests, an opportunity to spend more time with Mathews.[44] For Perec and Mathews, translation was never an activity to pay the bills, nor was it simply, as they sometimes expressed, a writing practice they could turn to in moments of writers' block; it offered, as their correspondence suggests, something that other forms of writing could not: a formal enactment of intimacy and friendship.[45]

This insight into the ways that translation served as a relational praxis offers another mode of thinking through the close connections between translation and the Oulipian project. Oulipo practitioners and scholars have examined this question in various ways, often highlighting the difficulty (if not sheer impossibility) of translating Oulipian constraints, and how Oulipian texts might help us problematize theories of translation more broadly.[46] Le Tellier's assertion that Oulipian translations constitute literary achievements in their own right seems justified, given that translators will inevitably need to make drastic changes to a text to maintain a formal constraint.[47] This perspective bears out in practice, too: the Englishman Ian Monk was so enthralled by Perec's *La disparition* that he set out to translate the entire novel into English, only to learn after the fact that the translation rights had already been sold to Gilbert Adair; though his efforts did not earn him a book deal, he was rewarded with a seat in the Oulipo.[48] Many Oulipo members, in addition to Monk, have been experienced translators, and it's quite usual, as Alison James has shown, to find interlingual play at the heart of Oulipian texts.[49] For both practitioners and scholars, the principles of the Oulipo present a distinct opportunity to theorize translation generally. As Rachel Galvin has succinctly put it: "to translate is always to write under constraints"—suggesting not only that every translator is, in a sense, an Oulipian, but also the degree to which all translation is, like Oulipian projects, ultimately an exercise in potentiality.[50]

Oulipian translation has helped to problematize simplistic (and widespread) perceptions of a strict dichotomy between writing and translating. It also, as I am suggesting here, can expand our thinking about translation as a collaborative and relational practice. In an essay on translation that Mathews wrote years after Perec's death, he envisions translation as a potential conversation. "When I translate," Mathews writes, "I imagine myself talking to a friend across the table."[51] For years, Mathews had indeed sat with a friend across the table (or in his absence sent letters) to work on translations together; even when they were not actually sitting across from each other, they always *might* have been, a potentiality, as Agamben writes, of that which "could have been, but never took place."[52]

Their translation practice—what I am calling here an example of intimate potentialities—followed the spirit of collaboration and exchange at the heart of the Oulipo and posited translation as a form of connection. This vision reanimates Gayatri Spivak's point that "translation is the most intimate act of reading." For Spivak, there can be no translation without intimacy—a fact borne out, as she demonstrates, through translators that may have linguistic expertise without adequate cultural awareness.[53] We see in Perec and Mathews's practice a revitalized version of intimate translation, the stakes of which were both personal and professional, and that hinged on reciprocal reading and two-way exchange. Like so much else within the Oulipian framework of potentiality, engaging deeply in another's work was more about the process than the product. Translation indexed the potentiality of friendship, the chance to be in full and complete conversation with another.

The Perec–Mathews correspondence encourages us to understand Oulipian translation through this wider lens. On the one hand, it offers another rejoinder to critiques about the Oulipo's cold conceptualism and refusal of human emotion, what Calvin Bedient has called a "new detachment from affects" that distinguishes newer avant-gardes (Oulipo, visual poetry, conceptual writing, etc.) from historical avant-gardes.[54] To join Alison James and Rachel Galvin's convincing defenses of Oulipo as producing "aesthetic effects" and embracing subjectivity, I'll add how this attention to the relational and intimate dimensions of translation, seen through the archival materials, supports a critical practice that, following the Oulipo itself, attends to process, not just product.[55] The letters also suggest that for Perec the hope of being published in English was not simply motivated by commercial ambition; his aspiration for a global reading public cannot be decoupled from the personal and professional opportunities that translation provided for his and Mathews's friendship. This is what we see in his affectionate appeal to Mathews—"So what I m'goin miself to respond . . . I ask you in turn?"—a question that imagines a potential translation and asks for a collaborative decision.

When Perec passed away in 1982, Mathews sent a short obituary to the *New York Times*, but his article was turned down and never printed—a small indicator of how little attention Perec's death received in the American press.[56] Two years later, Mathews published a tribute to his friend in *Le Monde* titled "Mon ami"—a French version that Mathews self-translated, not from the original obituary, but from a longer and more intimate account of Perec that he had written in English.[57] It opens with a description of the translations they had done for each other—from Perec's "generous act of translating *Tlooth*" to his own completed and promised translations of Perec's work—and turns to their mutual love and affection:

> Georges taught me what friendship might be—a true passion, as complete and unstinting and upsetting as love. It was in fact love. He quickly knew me better than I knew myself, and knew I was better than I would admit. Little by little he overcame my hesitation and showed me that loving a friend was not risking oneself, not exposing oneself to some danger, but discovering and realizing oneself in the other, in differences as well as similarities, in disagreement and disappointment as well as in reassurance and encouragement. He taught me that giving is the way to abundance and happiness.[58]

Mathews once again figures friendship through the language of potentiality—the possibilities of what *might be*—and as an intimate ethical encounter, the possibility of actualizing oneself through the other. The version that Mathews published in *Le Monde* condensed that description of friendship and insisted on their shared intimacy: "With Georges, friendship couldn't be anything but passionate, and if in our case the idea of a physical relationship never presented itself, sometimes I regret that."[59] The closest they came to consummating their relationship, as Mathews tells it, was to lay on the floor, listening to music together into the wee hours of the night.[60] The tribute, meanwhile, suggests that their mutual translations had provided a different kind of passionate consummation, one which rested less on the "genius of the translator" than on the fact that they would translate each other's works "without having read them before, simply because [each] was the author."[61]

One of the last translations between the two friends was Mathews's English translation of *Récits d'Ellis Island*, a film project that Perec had worked on in New York in 1978 and 1979. The filming itself had been an opportunity for Perec to spend time with Mathews, and Perec had other reasons for agreeing to work on the film, as I'll discuss in more detail below. I want to read the film as an apotheosis of intimate potentiality in practice, not just as an example of a collaborative translation between Mathews and Perec, which it was, but one in which Perec put into effect the principles of intimate potentialities that he had been developing, in tandem with his friend, throughout the 1970s.

Ellis Island: On Radical Listening and an Alternative New York

Like most of the literary projects that I have discussed throughout this book, *Récits d'Ellis Island* was a commissioned work. The filmmaker Robert Bober had been deeply moved by reading Perec's 1975 autobiographical book *W or the Memory of Childhood* and approached him soon after its publication with the idea of co-creating a film about Ellis Island. Perec was not interested. He was no stranger to literary commissions or to collaborative projects in a range of audiovisual modalities: he had long collaborated with colleagues in Germany on making French radio plays, had made a series of comedic episodes for listeners in the Ivory Coast following an offer from Radio-Abidjan, and had most recently written a television film for the BBC that aired in 1978.[62] His initial refusal to commit to the film, David Bellos reports, had to do with his reluctance to confront a "nostalgic and explicitly Jewish theme."[63] Perec changed his mind, though, when he learned that Ellis Island no longer functioned as a welcome station for immigrants, but was instead a site in ruins. As he ends up explaining it in the film and the book publication that accompanied it: "What I, Georges Perec, have come here to examine / is dispersion, wandering, diaspora. / To me Ellis Island is the ultimate place of exile, that is, / the place where place is absent, the non-place, / the nowhere."[64] Ellis Island, for him, signaled the potentiality of what could have been, and, with Agamben, of what might not be.

This declaration occurs in the first half of the two-part documentary film. Both parts were just under an hour long and, produced by the Institut National de l'Audiovisuel, aired on the channel TF1 in 1980.[65] The film opens with a reverse shot of Perec flipping through an album of old photographs taken at Ellis Island. Perec himself reads the voice-over narration, and it locates the filmmakers' point of view as a product of transnational encounters: "In Paris," the film begins:

When we said that we were going to make a film about Ellis Island, almost everyone asked us what it would be about. In New York, almost everyone asked us why. Not why a film about Ellis Island, but why us: how did it concern us, Robert Bober and Georges Perec? It would probably be a bit artificial to say that we made this film only with the goal of understanding why we had the desire or need to make it. It's essential, though, that the images that follow answer these two questions and describe not only this unique place but also the path that brought us here.

À Paris, quand nous disions que nous allions faire un film sur Ellis Island, presque tout le monde nous demandait de quoi il s'agissait. À New York, presque tout le monde nous demandait pourquoi. Non pas pourquoi un film à propos d'Ellis Island, mais pourquoi nous: en quoi cela nous concernait-il, nous, Robert Bober et Georges Perec? Il serait sans doute un peu artificiel de dire que nous avons réalisé ce film à seule fin de comprendre pourquoi nous avions le désir ou le besoin de le faire. Il faudra bien pourtant que les images qui vont suivre répondent à ces deux questions et décrivent non seulement ce lieu unique, mais le chemin qui nous y a conduit.[66]

The opening anchors the film in its geographical displacement between Paris and New York. Both an autobiographical undertaking and a product of transatlantic exchanges, *Récits d'Ellis Island* toggles between differing perspectives and stakes, both personal and collective. The first part of the film, "Traces," takes place mainly at Ellis Island: with Bober presumably behind the camera, we observe Perec as he walks with a tour group through the site, listens to a guide recount, in English, Ellis Island's history, and returns in French voice-over to reflect on the space. The second part, "Mémoires" (Memories), shifts Perec's position from observer and listener to speaker and interviewer: we see and hear him talking to nearly a dozen immigrants or descendants of immigrants, whose families came through Ellis Island. Most of the interviews take place in the interviewee's home or office and are conducted entirely in English, with one exception: the very last interview occurs back in Paris with a subject, Madame Rabinovici, who had been turned away at Ellis Island for being too young, and who eventually immigrated to France; her remarks, in response to Perec's question cited in this chapter's epigraph about whether life would have been better in New York rather than Paris, present a powerful closing argument for the film: "certainly yes ... I amounted to nothing here" ("absolument sûre ... je suis arrivée à rien").[67]

Since the film aired in 1980, there have been multiple and differing print versions of the Ellis Island project, in both French and English. The Éditions du Sorbier released the first French print edition in 1980. It includes Perec's written text that he read in voice-over narration for the film; a selection of photographs and film stills from Ellis Island; transcriptions of several interviews Perec had conducted in New York, translated into French (Mrs. Rabinovici's text is not included); and a short section called "Repérages" ("On Location") that lists the people, places, and foods that Perec encountered while in New York (more on this shortly).[68]

Perec's primary French publisher P.O.L. reissued a version of this original text fifteen years later, in a stunning large format edition that includes additional Ellis Island photographs in color and a couple of snapshots of Perec's handwritten manuscript.[69] When P.O.L. again reissued the publication in 2019, they opted for a more succinct title (*Ellis Island*) and included only Perec's written text from the voice-over narration, without any interview material or visual aids. The Pléiade edition of Perec's works, published in 2017, made a similar choice, including the text only from the first half of the film.[70] The first English edition, published by the New Press in 1995, closely resembles the P.O.L. edition from that same year, and it includes Harry Mathews's translations of Perec's text and Jessica Blatt's translations of the interviews; when New Directions released a reprint in 2021, it too was modeled on the more recent (2019) P.O.L. version, with a new afterword by Mónica de la Torre.[71]

All of the published texts shuffle around the narrative sequence from the film, jumping between personal reflections and historical details about immigration patterns to the United States. While the books' typography and layout reflect the poetic nature of Perec's writing, they substantially alter the versification, even between the two P.O.L. editions. They do not record the voice of the American tour guide who brings Perec's group around Ellis Island, though Perec's text translates and incorporates many of the guide's anecdotes and words into the French narrative. (There is no citation in the book, so one would know this only by comparing the text to the film.) The interviews that take center stage in the film's second half are translated into English from the French text, itself a translation from interviews that Perec conducted in English. In short, no individual version of the Ellis Island project looks exactly like any other. The sheer number and variety of differing editions speak to the multiple potentialities of this work—as if any story that Perec were to make about Ellis Island exceeded a single, definitive version.

I want to pause on the interviews for a minute, not only because of their absence from the most recent print editions, but because of what they reveal about Perec's approach to the project. There is something uncanny in hearing Perec's voice as he asks his subjects about their families' experiences of immigration and lives in New York. Part of that effect comes from the fact that this is one of the last and longest audiovisual recordings of Perec, made shortly before he passed away. But it comes as well from the ways that he listens attentively, draws out his subjects' memories through carefully crafted questions, and validates their point of view with nods and audible "yesses." The camera, for instance, gives us a close-up profile of Perec nodding his head in affirmation as he listens to Nathan Solomon talk about his personal journal and hometown in Poland (29:28); as Semyon Shimin describes his ancestors through old photos, we watch Perec point out different family members and hear his frequent "uh-huh's," affirming and repeating Shimin's words aloud (13:35 to 14:04); and as Mrs. Croce talks about her life in Italy before immigrating to the U.S., Perec consistently validates her statements and improvises with detailed follow-up questions, even as she veers towards anti-communist political discourse (38:00 to 43:44). Perec's careful listening and improvised questions do not make it into the published transcriptions of the interviews—which seem to include pre-prepared questions only—but they register his interviewing style and listening skills. We can call this a kind of active, affirmative listening, a version of what Joe Kincheloe first dubbed "critical listening" and that recent calls for anti-racist and restorative justice practices refer to as "radical listening."[72] A pedagogical practice with real-world applications, radical listening involves an openness, as we see with Perec, to intimate exchange and to active listening across linguistic, cultural, socioeconomic, and political differences without imposing a worldview.[73]

We can understand Perec's interviewing style and contribution to the *Ellis Island* project as an extension of his translation practice. His translation work with Mathews prepared him to conduct interviews confidently in English—to work, as it were, *in translation*—and it also modeled a mode of intimate exchange and relational listening, like a conversation across a table with a friend. There is an irony in the fact that the English-language interviews, which would not require any translation whatsoever had they been transcribed from the film, were translated back into English from the French edition when they appeared in print in 1995. Readers and viewers in French can nonetheless access an English-language Perec, who bridges linguistic and cultural divides, acknowledging and echoing back what he hears. The camera is careful to switch between interviewer and interviewee, showing Perec in a pose of active listening and reinforcing a sense that the film is about both the immigrants' stories and their mutual exchanges. For Perec, this personal element was a critical component of a film about Ellis Island; what he found unsuccessful in PBS' documentary *Destination America* about Ellis Island, as he wrote in his journal, was its "lifeless energy for TV: people are there only to say something, without silences; it's not about filming *them* but about showing a representative sample" ("esprit télé assez plat: les gens ne sont là que pour dire qqc, pas de silence, ce ne sont pas *eux* qu'on filme mais un échantillon").[74] To avoid the deadening effect of documentaries, a successful film about Ellis Island would need to center the personal voices of immigrants in direct and full conversation with the interviewer, interactive silences and all.

This reading of the film diverges from most scholarly engagements with the project that focus on how the film returns to themes (memory, history, Jewishness, islands) that resonate across Perec's oeuvre.[75] The context of Perec's extensive engagement with Franco-American translation is, as I have been suggesting, a critical lens through which to understand why and what this project is doing in his corpus. *Récits d'Ellis Island* is an unusual object in Perec's body of works, but it does also align itself with a general vision of Oulipian potentiality. "How can you grasp what isn't shown, what wasn't photographed or catalogued or restored or staged?" Perec asks rhetorically in the film, a question that signals his personal investment in pursuing the Ellis Island project.[76] His answer comes a bit later in the text (though earlier in the film): ". . . this place / belongs to a memory potentially / our own, / to a probable autobiography. / our parents or grandparents might have been here."[77] For Perec, the child of Polish Jewish immigrants in France who both died during World War II (his father as a volunteer in 1940, his mother in the concentration camps), the potentiality of Ellis Island as an alternative family story holds particular narrative and emotional resonance. Bober's personal motivation was similar: his great-grandfather was one of roughly 250,000 immigrants to have been turned away from Ellis Island, in his case because he had contracted conjunctivitis on the voyage over. How might their family histories have been different had the Bobers or Perecs ended up not in Paris but New York? It makes sense that Bober would turn to a writer whose literary project circled around the absence of his Jewish parents and the potential of literature to imagine an alternative history.[78]

The private notebooks and documents that Perec kept from his two trips to New York to work on the film, in 1978 and 1979, suggest in fact a potential personal history that runs parallel to, and in many respects escapes, the making of the Ellis Island project. His notebooks and papers at the Bibliothèque de l'Arsenal in Paris are filled with names, addresses, doodles, drawings of his family tree, crosswords, and reactions to what he is experiencing—much of which has little relation to the film production itself. The "On Location" section of the original 1980 print edition, mentioned earlier, provides some insight into the kinds of documentation that Perec kept during his trip: lists of people he met with or would have liked to meet; names of the sites that he visited, including museums, libraries, neighborhoods, streets, shops, and restaurants; concerts and events that he attended; and foods that he ate. These details give a sense of Perec's multilayered exploration of New York and the scope of the city that he traversed, across all boroughs. The published lists condense his journal entries and comments into a kind of Oulipian form (Perec was a lover of lists), gesturing at the fact that the trip was not simply about the Ellis Island project.

These documents allow us to toggle between two versions of New York—between Perec's archival New York and the one visible in the film. In his notebooks, Perec records his observations about the city in short clips—"Traversée de Central Park en bus" or "Magnifique découverte de la skyline" ("Crossing Central Park by bus"; "Magnificent discovery of the skyline")—as well as information about his meetings with friends, publishers, literary agents, translators, and professors. The notebooks abound with hundreds of addresses and phone numbers and notes to himself, often in English ("Ask Maxine for Richard HOWARD, Edmund WHITE"), and with short journal-style entries, in French, about his daily activities that include places and people that never make it into one of his lists: on June 9th, "Passé chez Knopf voir Nancy Nicholas" ("Went to the Knopf offices to see [the editor] Nancy Nicholas").[79] One contact leads to another (Perec includes the name and contact information, for instance, of another literary agent, John Ware, whom, as he notes, he contacts at Nancy Nicholas's recommendation), tracing lines of connection across the pages of the notebook and through the city. The notebooks, in that sense, reflect how Perec crisscrosses the city by bus, on foot, and by subway to cultivate a literary network:

> Sunday June 11th
> Woke up close to 11:00
> Walked to the Frick Collection
> Crossed Central Park
> Returned downtown to Greenwich Village by bus
> Ate a tuna salad in an Italian café . . .
> Drink with Kate
> Spent a few moments in Washington Square
> Vodka at Maxine's house
> Dinner at 1/5 (melon prosciutto and fettuccine!!)
> Met Tom Bishop, director of the French dept at NYU)
>
> Dimanche 11 juin
> Levé vers 11 heures
> monté à pied jusqu'à la Frick Collection
> traversé Central Park
> descendu en bus à Greenwich Village
> mangé une salade de thon dans un café italien . . .
> pot avec Kate
> passé quelques instants à Washington Square
> vodka chez Maxine
> dîner au 1/5 (melon prosciutto et fettucine!!)
> rencontré Tom Bishop, direct du dept français au NYU[80]

The clipped, straightforward style of the notebooks closely resembles Perec's *An Attempt at Exhausting a Place in Paris* (*Tentative d'épuisement d'un lieu parisien*, 1975), a short text that he had recently published and that records his observations over the course of three days as he sits in the same café in Paris's Saint-Sulpice neighborhood. Perec relishes recording the mundane parts of life (what he eats, who and what he sees), while he also attends here, in the notebooks, to his physical movement through New York. There is a sense of energy and dynamism of travel in the brisk prose, as he moves from one cultural encounter to the next. Perec is building a literary community for himself in New York, actualizing an idea of what a potential life in New York might, in fact, have been like had he ended up there. Between addresses and drawings, he notes to himself in English: "America was safety valve and haven, place for renewal and a source of support," a statement that, in the context of its placement in the notebooks seems every bit as much about Perec as it was about his interview subjects.[81]

In insisting on this alternative view into the Ellis Island film through the notebooks, I am responding to the project's two epistemological imperatives: first, Perec and Bober's articulation of the film as one that emerges from, and must respond to, the geographical and hermeneutic discrepancies between Paris and New York, and next, the call to attend to obscured or counterfactual traces, to grasp what *isn't shown, what wasn't photographed or catalogued or restored or staged*. The notebooks provide a sense for this potential history, the invisible traces of the project, and what might have been had New York been Perec's home. The film spends most of its time indoors, not just in an abandoned Ellis Island, but in the homes of people whose families passed through there—homes, the film suggests through its camera shots of Perec gazing at family photos and comfortably sitting in family room armchairs, that might have belonged to him. By centering our attention on these intimate encounters—in translational exchanges where Perec listens, asks questions, and responds in English—the film stages an imagined potential history for Perec, one that could have existed had history been otherwise.

In October 1983, a year after Perec's death, the French Department at NYU invited Mathews to give a talk about Perec's work and legacy. Mathews accepted the invitation but opened his lecture with a reflection on the challenges of doing so. "I feel that I should point out to you that there are two difficulties for me in speaking to you about Georges Perec," he said. One of those difficulties, as he goes on to explain, has to do with his interest in talking more about Perec the person than his literary work. But the primary one, Mathews shares,

> is the result of the unimaginable discrepancy between his reputation in this country and his reputation in France. In America, he is an unknown; in France he was famous. When he died last year, not a word about his death appeared in the American press, but in France national television programs were interrupted to announce it.[82]

It is the lecture's particular situatedness in New York—a place where Perec did not enjoy the same literary reputation as in France—that unsettles Mathews. And we can understand his lecture as an attempt to bridge the divide between those two Perecs, to make Perec's literary legacy in France meaningful for a U.S. audience, as any translator would do. Mathews's translation of *Ellis Island* in the years after his friend's death—the last translation he would ever publish—extends the work of the film: it is a project that opens up, through the work of translation, the potentiality of other readers, encounters, or legacies that Perec might have had in New York.

The framing of Mathews's lecture and the Ellis Island film together remind us—to return to the opening frame of this chapter—that it is always worth imagining what might have happened had Perec found during his lifetime the global recognition that he had sought in New York. By way of conclusion, I offer, in lieu of a counterfactual, precisely a *factual* account, the story of a later Oulipian text that reveals how Perec's legacy did actually reach the U.S. We see in that novel, Hervé Le Tellier's *L'anomalie,* just how much Oulipian writing has actively drawn energy from Perec's example, in which the (fictional) narrative stakes and (actual) literary history stage the potentialities of transatlantic translators, even today, in a Paris–New York literary circuit.

Coda: Transatlantic Translators After Perec

In his 2020 novel *L'anomalie* (*The Anomaly*), Hervé Le Tellier—a member of Oulipo since 1992 and its president since 2019—tells the story of an Air France flight traveling from Paris to New York that meets with a strange and unusual fate after undergoing extreme turbulence: the plane lands in the U.S. twice, once on March 10, 2021, and then again on June 24, 2021. The passengers on board each flight are identical, down to their DNA and their most private and intimate memories, and those who land in June do not realize how much time has elapsed since they left Paris. The only difference between the two groups lies in the fact that those who arrive in June lack any awareness of the experiences that have comprised the lives of their "doubles" in the previous three months.

Scientists offer competing rationales for this "anomaly," social workers are on the scene to understand the psychosocial effects of coming face-to-face with one's clone, and FBI agents prepare alternative identities for those who wish to start their life anew as someone else. The novel dials in on about a dozen characters, most of them French or American, and all of whom must confront varying personal stakes when encountering their double: a successful lawyer who is pregnant, madly in love, and jealous of her March self; a criminal mastermind who travels under false identities, commits murder for exorbitant sums, and cannot access his passwords; the pilot of the plane who ends up dying of pancreatic cancer, twice; a Nigerian singer who rises to international fame between flights. At the heart of the novel, though, is Victor Miesel, a middling French writer who earns a living through his translation work, mainly of American bestsellers that "reduce literature to the status of minor art for minors. This work has opened doors to reputable if not powerful publishers, not that this has helped his own manuscripts cross any of their thresholds."[83] As it turns out, Victor June does not need to confront his March double: after feverishly writing a book called *L'anomalie* and sending it off to his Paris-based editor, Victor March dies by suicide in April. His book, meanwhile, becomes an instantaneous bestseller and turns its author into a global cult phenomenon.

In its final act of literary doubling, Hervé le Tellier's actual novel *L'anomalie,* like Miesel's fictional one, achieved global literary acclaim. The French novel Le Tellier published in 2020 won France's highest literary award, the Prix Goncourt, and sold well over a million copies in its first year.[84] The American release of *The Anomaly,* the fifth Le Tellier novel that Adriana Hunter translated into English, became an immediate *New York Times* bestseller when published by Other Press in 2021. This was Le Tellier's first bestselling novel, on either side of the Atlantic, and the first international Oulipo bestseller. Whether a stroke of dumb luck, a sign of Le Tellier's literary genius, or a boldfaced challenge to his readers, this coincidence between fiction and publishing history is almost too good to be true. The novel's popularity confounded Le Tellier most of all: "I am surprised by the book's success, given that it's so experimental, bizarre, and a little crazy."[85] His reaction was not all that dissimilar from Victor June, who reads *L'anomalie* and finds that "the enthusiasm generated by this book is beyond him" ("l'enthousiasme que ce livre a soulevé lui échappe").[86]

The reception of Le Tellier's novel challenges yet again a perceived tension between avant-garde poetics and commercial success, a point that has been a throughline in this book. Just like Robbe-Grillet and the project of the New Novel actively benefited from the lucrative college textbook industry, as the last chapter argued, we see here, following Andreas Huyssen, just how dramatically some of the most ambitious art and literature in the second half of the twentieth century have blended an attention to avant-garde techniques and mass cultural concerns, even if unintentionally.[87] Book sales in France also suggest, despite Le Tellier's perceptions to the contrary, that mainstream readers gravitate towards experimental books, and especially those that win coveted literary prizes: before *L'anomalie*, the novel that had sold the greatest number of copies in France had been Marguerite Duras's 1984 autobiographical novel *L'amant* (*The Lover*), another Goncourt prizewinner by an assuredly experimental writer.[88]

Le Tellier's novel and his literary success should also be read as a distinctly Oulipian story—and one that concretely engages questions about global ambition, Franco-American literary exchange, and the potentialities of translation at the heart of Perec's life and work. When writing *L'anomalie*, Le Tellier (and his character Victor Miesel) clearly had Perec in mind. The novel abounds with references to his Oulipian predecessor: one of the novel's closing words, "Ulcérations," is a direct tribute to Perec's heterogrammatic poem by that name, and Victor June, contemplating ideas for his next literary project, expresses the anxiety of Perec's literary influence: "Why walk in Perec's shadow?" ("Pourquoi marcher à l'ombre de Perec?"),[89] he asks himself, before sketching out a novel that, in a *mise en abyme*, has the shape of *L'anomalie*.[90]

Le Tellier's novel almost seems to respond to the note that Perec scribbled in the margins of his unfinished final novel *53 Days* and that serves as one of the epigraphs in this chapter—"Without a plane how can you travel from NY to France on Friday and return on the same Friday?"—while bending that question playfully into fictional form. The novel stages a transatlantic passage (of people, goods, ideas) from Paris to New York and back again. Miesel travels to New York primarily as a translator: he has won a translation prize for a thriller, and a celebration has been planned in his honor at Manhattan's Albertine bookstore—an actual bookstore on the Upper East Side whose mission, as its website currently attests, is "to make French literature available to American audiences from coast to coast."[91] Victor Miesel's literary vision for what turns out to be his great novel is, quite dramatically, born out of this cross-cultural encounter. The collaboration between Victor Miesel and his double, as translators and writers both, achieves that potential for literary success in New York to which Perec had aspired, here actualized through another Oulipian writer's text. It is easy to imagine that, for Perec, there could have been no better literary legacy than that.

Conclusion
New York and the Twenty-First-Century Global Francophone Novel

ON JANUARY 31, 2017, readers of the Francofil listserv received a call for papers with an impressive list of confirmed speakers: the Winthrop-King Institute for Contemporary French and Francophone Studies at Florida State University would be hosting an international conference in October on the subject of French-language fiction and its ties to the U.S., and the conveners aimed to put francophone writers and academics into conversation with one another. The call noted that American fiction had long influenced French novels, but it pinpointed a definitive shift "beginning around 2010" after which "the American presence in French writing has taken a markedly different turn." The call noted a variety of ways in which this turn had manifested itself in contemporary novels: through their setting in the United States; through plots modeled on American road novels; by invoking iconic American singers, actors, or writers as titular characters; in blatant or veiled critiques of globalization and U.S. foreign policy; or via the incorporation of American slang or popular culture references. Peeking through the staid academic prose of the call, one could almost sense the urgency of the CFP's question: "Why is all this happening, and why now?"[1]

As this book has argued throughout, the idea that the U.S. played a considerable role in the conceptualization and production of French-language fiction is far from a new phenomenon. From the postwar period onwards, as each chapter has demonstrated, French fiction has been shaped by connections, ideas, and contacts with American cultural agents—whether that was through editors who took a risk on creative publishing ventures, producers and publishers who saw experimental theater as a new avenue for television, professors who connected writers to American college campuses and the lucrative business of textbook publishing, or fellow writers who saw in translation renewed opportunities for personal and professional ambitions. The American presence in French writing has been around for a long while and, as the case studies in this book emphasize, has exceeded a traditional framing that perceives American influence through a lens of intertextuality or representation.

The FSU conference organizers were nonetheless onto something: there *is* something new and strange that started to happen in the contemporary francophone novel in the twenty-first century. We can identify it in part, as the CFP pointed out, through the proliferation of references to American icons, place names, and historical figures—often blatantly on display in the titles of books like *Bye-Bye Elvis* (2014), *Le ravissement de Britney Spears* (2011), or *Oona & Salinger* (2014).[2] But what characterizes this "turn" most notably, I suggest by way of conclusion, is a dramatic attunement to the stakes of global publishing in francophone texts. In its twenty-first-century iteration, a heightened anxiety about U.S. publishing networks and readership has not only dictated the titles and content of recent books but has seeped into the prose of prizewinning novels.

The examples that I will briefly highlight serve as a reminder of just how much American audiences, real and potential, have mattered, and continue to matter, for French literary production. Perceived by writers, editors, and other cultural agents as crucial consumers of works produced *in French*, U.S.-based audiences have catalyzed and shaped French literature. This untold literary history, as I have argued, reorients our understanding of post-1945 francophone literary production and still resonates in today's publishing world. There are important lessons to draw from this literary history as it continues to unfold—ones that I hope will be particularly relevant for other scholars who, like me, teach foreign languages and literatures in a U.S. context and find themselves ever more urgently called upon to make a case for the relevancy of our disciplines to our students and institutions. The texts themselves offer a renewed opportunity to reflect critically on the practice of teaching foreign literatures in the U.S. academy today and on the ways in which students might catalyze new revolutionary projects.

The success of a novel like Le Tellier's *The Anomaly*, as we saw in the last chapter, reveals the international appeal in the twenty-first century of a French novel that positions itself, quite literally, in the transatlantic space between Paris and New York. Of course, not all writers will go on, as Le Tellier did, to win coveted literary prizes or to have their novels translated into multiple languages. Yet we can look to a novel like *The Anomaly* to identify a broader literary trend in recent years: the ubiquity of contemporary novels that thematize just how much American audiences and consumers of culture have catalyzed, bolstered, and supported francophone literary production. Just like Victor Miesel's novel *The Anomaly,* the global bestseller that emerges out of the protagonist's travels from Paris to New York to promote his translation with American booksellers, francophone novels have attended metanarratively to the literary ecosystem through which close contacts in the American university, publishing world, or media industries might spawn a literary masterpiece. In that sense, the contemporary francophone novel is well aware of the literary dynamics that have been at play for decades. What this suggests is that while the American influences I have been tracing have mostly not been noticed by literary historians, novelists seem to have intuited or observed these dynamics at work and have taken them as central to their understandings of what it means to be a writer of French-language fiction. In short, these francophone writers, who have come of age in the past few decades, have taken it as a given that a novel written in French is intimately American. While the examples that I'll sketch out are far from exhaustive, they point specifically to the ways that contemporary francophone writers engage with American college campuses, publishing networks, and new media in their fiction.

The Swiss writer Joël Dicker won multiple literary accolades in Switzerland and France, including the *Grand prix de l'Académie française* and the *Prix Goncourt des Lycéens,* for his 2012 novel *La Vérité sur l'Affaire Harry Quebert*, and when Penguin released the English translation (*The Truth About the Harry Quebert Affair*) in 2014, it immediately became a *New York Times* bestseller and an Amazon "book of the month."[3] The novel centers on the writer Marcus Goldman, a former student and close friend of his famous literature professor Harry Quebert, after he has published a massively successful first novel and now struggles to figure out the subject of his next work. Harry encourages Marcus to take space from his fancy New York City life and invites him in October

2008 to spend time at his home in Aurora, New Hampshire, in search of literary inspiration. Marcus's stay does indeed prove fruitful for his writing career: he discovers in Harry's private papers a collection of love letters from a teenage girl, Nola Kellergan, who had gone missing decades earlier, in 1975, and whose disappearance had remained unsolved. Unsettled by his discovery and determined to figure out the truth, especially after Nola's remains are uncovered on Harry's property, Marcus assumes the dual role of sleuth and writer: he searches for clues, all while writing down his findings and selling pieces of this new book to a riveted audience of readers and news consumers across the country.

As a novel, *The Truth About the Harry Quebert Affair* models itself on the tradition of the sensationalized news story, or what in French is dubbed the "fait divers." It has been common practice in U.S. fiction since at least Theodore Dreiser's *An American Tragedy* (1925), and popularized by books like Truman Capote's *In Cold Blood* (1967), for novelists to draw inspiration from shocking stories circulating in the news. In France, the *fait divers* tradition was popularized in the nineteenth century by writers like Victor Hugo, Guy de Maupassant, and Paul Bourget and remained throughout the twentieth century and into today, as Minh Tran Huy argues, an integral feature of the francophone literary landscape.[4] What makes a *fait divers* so appealing, as Roland Barthes once assessed it, is what he called its characteristic "immanence," the fact that it can be easily consumed and understood without having any outside information.[5] This attribute of the *fait divers* features prominently in Dicker's novel, with its frequent mentions of readers transfixed by the news: "All anyone was talking about was this news story happening in Aurora" ("on n'y parlait que de ce fait divers survenu à Aurora"), as one character reports while reading a newspaper.[6] Dicker's novel is not based on a specific news story—there was no Nola Kellergan possibly murdered by a popular college professor in New Hampshire who had been her lover—but it figures a *fait divers* as its driving plot and registers within the novel's pages the genre's spectacular appeal and mass consumption among readers.

In fact, Dicker's novel seems acutely concerned with representing reading practices—not only through the widespread obsession with the news story, but in the popularity of Marcus Goldman's books. The prologue of *The Truth About the Harry Quebert Affair* opens with Marcus's self-proclaimed notoriety:

> My book was the talk of the town. I could no longer walk the streets of Manhattan in peace. I could no longer go jogging without passersby recognizing me and calling out, "Look, it's Goldman! It's that writer!"[7]

> Tout le monde parlait du livre. Je ne pouvais plus déambuler en paix dans Manhattan, je ne pouvais plus faire mon jogging sans que des promeneurs me reconnaissent et s'exclament: "Hé, c'est Goldman! C'est l'écrivain!"[8]

Never has a writer seemed more popular than in Dicker's novel. And it's not just in Manhattan: the novel insists in dozens of references that Marcus's books, like Harry Quebert's novels before him, have captivated not just "all of New York," but "all of America" and "the whole country" ("toute l'Amérique" and "tout le pays").[9] Everyone across the U.S., regardless of social class or location, is reading Marcus's books: he's read and recognized as a literary celebrity by police agents in New Hampshire and pastors in Alabama.[10] Books serve a democratizing and redemptive function: because they are read by all, "a book is probably the only way to prove to America that Harry is not a monster" ("un livre est probablement la seule façon de prouver à l'Amérique que Harry n'est pas un monstre"), Marcus determines.[11] The novel frequently presents Marcus in conversations with his literary agent and editor, both eager to have him write a bestselling book that, if successful, could turn Nola Kellergan into "a registered trademark" for the fictional publishing company, Schmid & Hanson.[12] Dicker's novel is just as much about the literary and commercial stakes of publishing as it is about solving an unsolved murder. It allegorizes the desire and aspiration to write and sell a bestseller, a book whose achievement will be measured by its circulation in America.

Dicker's novel offers a meta-reflection on the mechanisms and anxieties of global publishing in the twenty-first century and literalizes a dilemma facing francophone writers today: is it possible to write a successful novel that *does not*, in some way, rely on U.S. connections? It is no coincidence that Dicker situates his novel in the U.S. literary world: the way to attain success, the novel repeatedly tells us, is with the support from U.S. editors and literary agents who can turn a book into a commercially viable product. The real-world success of Dicker's novel affirms Gisèle Sapiro's analysis of the world system of translation in the early twenty-first century: while the percentage of translations from French into English has fallen considerably since the 1980s, the books most likely to achieve global success have been bestsellers and mass market genres like mystery thrillers.[13]

We can situate books like Dicker's *The Truth About the Harry Quebert Affair* and Le Tellier's *The Anomaly* alongside French-Moroccan writer Leïla Slimani's *Chanson Douce* (*The Perfect Nanny*), all of them part of a similar phenomenon of post-2010 international success stories. In all cases, thriller-like novels first won highly coveted literary prizes in France (Slimani's book was awarded the 2016 Prix Goncourt), became bestsellers in the U.S. and elsewhere when they were released in translation (in the case of Dicker and Slimani, even by the same English translator), and narrativized the stakes of a literary culture that mediates between Paris and New York.[14] This is a particularly French set of examples that underscore Dan Sinykin's recent point that U.S. publishing conglomerates have "generated the incentives for literary genre fiction."[15] Slimani's novel originated in an actual New York-based *fait divers* from 2012, when two children, only six and two years old, were stabbed to death in a Manhattan apartment by their nanny, who then attempted, unsuccessfully, to take her own life. *The Perfect Nanny* tracks the highly publicized case from New York, even while relocating the story to Paris.[16] Slimani's characters, Mila and Adam Massé, are the same ages the New York children were at their deaths and are similarly discovered by their mother in the bathtub, with a kitchen knife in the hands of the nanny. Slimani's descriptions of the mother's "scream from deep within" ("un cri des profondeurs") echo the initial news reports of the case.[17] In New York, the children's father was met at JFK airport by the police to break the news of the murder, just as, in the novel's closing pages, Lieutenant Verdier awaits Paul Massé at the Eurostar section of the Gare du Nord. It is astonishing how closely Slimani's novel hews to the news.

The question at the heart of *The Perfect Nanny* is one that journalists reporting on that crime also sought to answer: what could possibly motivate a caregiver to kill the children in her charge? After opening with a scene of the murders, the novel flashes back in time, to the moment when Myriam and Paul Massé hire Louise to watch their children, and then charts their path back to the present. A wonder-nanny, Louise cooks like a first-rate chef and brings order and calm to the couple's chaotic work lives, but her troubled past is glimpsed in snatches, suggesting a basis—if not a motive—for the crime she will commit. References to Louise's increasingly unhealthy physical appearance, troubles with her landlord, and history of mental illness all echo news coverage of the New York nanny. One article describes how the nanny had "continued hearing voices, male and female, speaking in Spanish but still unintelligible to her save for when they urged her to hurt others."[18] Likewise, in the novel, a voice speaks to Louise:

> *Someone has to die. Someone has to die for us to be happy.* Morbid refrains echo inside Louise's head when she walks. Phrases that she didn't invent—and whose meaning she is not sure she fully grasps—fill her mind.[19]
>
> *Il faut que quelqu'un meure. Il faut que quelqu'un meure pour que nous soyons heureux.* Des refrains morbides bercent Louise quand elle marche. Des phrases, qu'elle n'a pas inventées et dont elle n'est pas certaine de comprendre le sens, habitent son esprit.[20]

In its transformation from news story to novel, *The Perfect Nancy* borrows and cribs from news sources, offering us a record of Slimani's consumption of American news. The novel brims over with visual references to media technologies and texts: Louise leaves the television on all day long, watching "apocalyptic news reports" with the children "in rapt silence" by her side.[21] The novel describes photographs of the crime scene and of the children taken before their deaths—photos matching those that appeared in newspapers and magazines in the wake of the New York case (such as one of the "bouquets of flowers and children's drawings" littering the entrance to the couple's apartment building).[22] Slimani even references pictures from the New York family's personal blog. "Just uploaded photos from my iPhone," the New York mother wrote in one of her last blog posts before the murders, and some of the images of her children—wearing a white dress, lying on the ground half-naked, visiting a friend's farm—emerge in the novel, recast as Massé family snapshots taken on Myriam's iPhone.[23] All of Slimani's characters, in the end, are stuck behind screens, and if Louise's crime is figured, at least in part, as a result of our apocalypse-focused news culture, so too does Slimani register her own position as a media consumer who clicks on blogs, googles, and binges on news websites; transfixed by images of the event, she molds them into literary form.

In staying so very close to its New York source material—not just with the crime itself, but in references that recycle text and images from New York media outlets and blogs—Slimani betrays anxieties (and realities) about writing a francophone novel today. In their introduction to a 2016 issue of *Expressions maghrébines*, Olivia Harrison and Teresa Villa-Ignacio suggest that it may be "impossible to write or read Maghrebi literature without taking into account the context of its eventual translation for a global and hegemonically Anglophone audience," noting as well that "the authors who are most often translated into English have usually been consecrated in Europe first."[24] This certainly applies to Slimani, even though her novel's success postdated their observation. Slimani's novel betrays a keen awareness of the mechanics of cultural translation, positioned, as it is, on both sides of the translation border: it is, at once, a clear-cut example of cultural transposition from a U.S. source text, and a literary source text whose sensationalized topic and claims to universality (as the back cover of the Gallimard edition puts it, this is a book in which "our era is revealed to us"—"C'est notre époque qui se révèle"), makes it a prime contender for the global translation market. Slimani's firm commitment to the source material is both a strategy and a hindrance, suggestive of the difficulty of freeing oneself from the obligatory constraints imposed by New York's centrality in the publishing sphere. Her novel wears on its sleeves the ambivalences and limitations of fiction writing for the twenty-first-century francophone author—as if to make sure its readers cannot forget that the whole enterprise, from a book's conception to its marketing strategies, required a solid footing in New York.

Recognizing those literary dynamics, some recent novels have taken a direct, even cynical approach. The narrator of Tanguy Viel's 2013 novel *La disparition de Jim Sullivan* (*The Disappearance of Jim Sullivan*, 2021), a French author with grand literary ambitions, is determined to write an international bestseller. The narrator's aspirations might indeed reflect Viel's own: while an accomplished writer in France who had been publishing with the Minuit imprint since 1998, Viel had yet to write a globally successful breakout novel.[25] Glancing at his bookshelf, the narrator of *The Disappearance of Jim Sullivan* notes the outsized percentage of American novels translated into French—a sign, he determines, that to write a globally successful work, translated into "every language" ("toutes les langues du monde") and sold in "almost every bookstore" ("beaucoup de librairies"), his novel will need to look to the U.S. for a model.[26]

> I'm not saying that every international novel is an American novel.... Americans have a disturbing advantage over us: even when they set the action in Kentucky, among chicken farms and corn fields, they manage to make a novel international ... [the kind of books that] sell just as many copies in Paris as in New York.[27]

> Je ne dis pas que tous les romans internationaux sont des romans américains. ... [L]es Américains ont un avantage troublant sur nous: même quand ils placent l'action dans le Kentucky, au milieu des élevages de poulets et des champs de maïs, ils parviennent à faire un roman international ... des romans qu'on achète aussi bien à Paris qu'à New York.[28]

This realization prompts the narrator to pick up a map and randomly select a good ol'-fashioned American city (his choice is Detroit) as the setting for his next novel—that novel, of course, is *La disparition de Jim Sullivan*.

Alternating between fictional and metafictional frames, Viel's novel adopts a tongue-in-cheek attitude to recognize the literary forces, and particularly the weight of the American academy, on contemporary francophone authorship. In his aspiration to write a bestseller, the narrator elects not just a U.S. setting but a university professor as a protagonist: "I also noticed that in American novels, one of the main characters was always a university professor, often at Yale or Princeton, but whatever the case, a college with a name revered throughout the world" ("J'ai remarqué cela aussi dans les romans américains, que toujours un des personnages principaux est professeur d'université, souvent à Yale ou à Princeton, en tout cas un nom qui résonne à travers le monde entier");[29] in deciding that his character Dwayne Koster should be a literature professor at the University of Michigan, the narrator notes that it too is "an excellent university, although not quite as prestigious as Berkeley or UCLA" ("laquelle est aussi une excellente université, même si elle est moins prestigieuse que Berkeley ou UCLA").[30]

Viel's book makes the case that these features are typical of American novels, but they're actually quite typical of *French* novels in this period, too. In its self-conscious selection of setting and characters, *The Disappearance of Jim Sullivan* joins many other recent francophone novels situated on American college campuses. Catherine Cusset's 2016 novel *L'autre qu'on adorait* (*The Other Man We Loved*), a finalist for the Goncourt prize that Slimani's novel ended up winning, recounts the life (and demise) of a French professor on the faculty at Columbia. The novel echoes Cusset's 1999 book, *Le problème avec Jane* (*The Problem with Jane*), which offers an unflattering take on French departments on elite U.S. campuses, in that case a thinly veiled version of Yale (called "Devayne"), where Cusset (sibling of François Cusset, whose reflections on French in American higher education we've seen from a different angle) had once served on the faculty.[31]

Other francophone authors have similarly drawn on their experiences of teaching in American colleges as fodder for their fiction. Abdourahman A. Waberi's most recent book, *Dis-moi pour qui j'existe?* (2022), is a transatlantic epistolary novel between a Djiboutian professor of Romance languages at George Washington University (where Waberi serves on the faculty and teaches creative writing in French) and his young daughter, who has fallen ill in Paris. Haitian novelist Louis-Philippe Dalembert, a former visiting professor at the University of Wisconsin, Milwaukee, wrote *Milwaukee Blues*, a Goncourt finalist in 2021, as a broad exploration of race relations in the U.S. The novel fictionalizes the murder of George Floyd with references to other incidents of race-based violence and police brutality in the United States—here through a character Emmett, a former college football player, killed by a police officer in Milwaukee. Dalembert signals the importance of college institutions through the many characters who remember Emmett and plan a mass demonstration in his honor: his football coach at an unnamed state university in the Southwest, his former girlfriend who becomes a professor of Africana studies at NYU, two graduate students of history and comparative literature at the University of Wisconsin, Milwaukee, who lead protests after Emmett's death.[32] Unlike Dalembert, Waberi, and Cusset, Viel never seems to have taught at an American university, but his novel indirectly registers the fact that contemporary francophone novels take place on American college campuses, while recognizing, to comic effect, the close imbrication between U.S. universities and literary success.

For Russell Williams, contemporary novels such as Viel's suggest prevalent anxieties among French writers in the face of U.S. cultural hegemony. Williams finds in recent Franco-American novels insecurities about the

French novel's "waning influence on the global stage" and the different strategies that authors have deployed, from "quiet recognition" to "informed resistance," to respond to that reality.[33] There is truth in this assessment, though I would frame the issue somewhat differently: the long history of twentieth-century literary projects born out of transatlantic collaborations between French writers and U.S. cultural figures has now become axiomatic within the twenty-first-century novel itself, in ways that both expose the literary dynamics that have been at play for decades and that constrain contemporary fiction writing. Novels published in the past ten years or so must emphatically be understood in light of that literary history. It is of course important not to underestimate the significance of very real changes in global publishing at the turn of the twenty-first century, from shifting power relations away from France's previously hegemonic position, to the industry's increasing corporatization that favors the publication of readable bestsellers. While these factors help to explain why contemporary francophone novels might be particularly attuned to Franco-U.S. literary power relations, they do not fully account for the deeply embedded continuities over time that have only intensified in the present day. The story I have been telling throughout this book, while unacknowledged by literary historians, has been thoroughly assimilated into the projects of contemporary novelists—so much so that what previously functioned as revolutionary and experimental now reads as formulaic. Francophone novelists know the recipe for global success, and their ingredients are mostly American. But whereas in Ionesco's and Duras's time the results were radical, now they feel predictable in their sameness, as if they've lost their critical edge.[34]

In other words, in a return of the repressed, contemporary francophone novels remind us of what French literary history might have preferred to ignore: the history of French literature in the postwar period could not escape the American publishing world. What we discover in the archives and untold publication stories, and now in the novels themselves, is how American audiences, again and again, shaped the French literary texts that came to exist. For those of us who teach French language and literature in a U.S. context, this history has vital implications for how we teach what we teach. Our students need to know the complicated role they play in the making of French literature. At a time when it is easy to despair about the irrelevance of foreign language instruction in U.S. higher education, this literary history offers an object lesson: not just a clear rationale for why French literature matters here, in the past and present, but the surprising likelihood that what happens in our American college classrooms might inspire even the most unexpected, revolutionary French literary projects of the future.

Notes

Introduction

1. Jacques Lacan, "Hommage fait à Marguerite Duras du *Ravissement de Lol V. Stein*," *Cahiers Renaud-Barrault*, no. 52 (December 1965): 7–15.

2. These statistics on sales come from Laure Adler, *Marguerite Duras: A Life*, trans. Anne-Marie Glasheen (Chicago: University of Chicago Press, 2000), 253.

3. While far from an exhaustive list, some of the excellent scholarship on the novel can be found in Julia Kristeva, *Black Sun: Depression and Melancholia* (New York: Columbia University Press, 1989); Elisabeth Lyon, "The Cinema of Lol V. Stein," in *Feminism and Film Theory*, ed. Constance Penley (New York: Routledge, 1988), 244–273; Pierre St. Amand, "The Sorrow of Lol V. Stein," trans. Jennifer Curtiss Gage, *Paragraph* 19, no. 1 (March 1996): 21–35; Susan Rubin Suleiman, *Subversive Intent: Gender, Politics, and the Avant-Garde* (Cambridge: Harvard University Press, 1990); and Sharon Willis, *Marguerite Duras: Writing on the Body* (Urbana: University of Illinois Press, 1987).

4. Marguerite Duras, *Le Livre dit: Entretiens de "Duras filme,"* ed. Joëlle Pagès-Pindon (Paris: Gallimard, 2014), 114.

5. Borchardt's letter, addressed to Grove's administrative assistant, reads as follows: "Under separate cover, a copy of Gallimard's edition of the new novel by Marguerite Duras, *Le Ravissement de Lol V. Stein*. I believe Barney and Dick already read this in manuscript form. I look forward to your offer." Letter from Georges Borchardt to Judith Schmidt, 23 April 1964 (Grove Press Records, Special Collections Research Center, Syracuse University Libraries, Box 237).

6. Duras won the *Prix de Mai* for her novel *Moderato Cantabile* (Paris: Gallimard, 1958). The comparison between Duras and Beauvoir comes from a sales pitch when Grove Press decided to buy the translation rights for *Le Ravissement* (Undated Notecard in Grove Press Records, Special Collections Research Center, Syracuse University Libraries, Box 237).

7. In French, Jacqueline Piatier calls this "l'allure louche d'une ville imaginaire, voire symbolique"; see her article, "Projet pour une révolution à New York," *Le Monde* (30 October 1970): 18.

8. "... à quoi New-York ressemble comme un building ressemble à une assiette de corn-flakes," in Pierre Bourgeade, "Un projet douteux," *Le Monde* (30 October 1970): 18. Interestingly, Bourgeade had himself just published a fairly dubious novel about New York, in which a young French woman encounters a host of perverse characters; see Pierre Bourgeade, *New York Party* (Paris: Gallimard, 1969).

9. Alain Robbe-Grillet, *Projet pour une révolution à New York* (Paris: Minuit, 1970), 77; *Projects for a Revolution in New York*, trans. Richard Howard (New York: Grove Press, 1972), 61. In a strange twist, a character in the novel admits later on to making a mistake about the name of the subway—as if a proofreader had pointed this out to Robbe-Grillet: "One other thing: you mention West Greenwich or the Madison subway station—any American would say 'the West Village' or 'Madison Avenue'" (160). The funny correction nonetheless does not fix the mistake about subways on Madison.

10. The most compelling reading of the novel remains a chapter in Susan Suleiman's *Subversive Intent*, in which she argues that "*Projet*'s 'murderous mythology,' consisting in the repeated violation of the maternal organs, can indeed be seen as a metaphor of the modern writer's activity"; see Susan Rubin Suleiman, "Reading Robbe-Grillet: Sadism and Text in *Projet pour une révolution à New York*," in *Subversive Intent: Gender, Politics, and the Avant-Garde* (Cambridge: Harvard University Press, 1990), 51–71, esp. 70.

11. As Casanova puts it in 1999, "It may be that we find ourselves today in a transitional phase, passing from a world dominated by Paris to a polycentric and plural world in which London and New York, chiefly, but also to a lesser degree Rome, Barcelona, and Frankfurt, among other centers, contend with Paris for hegemony." Pascale Casanova, *The World Republic of Letters*, trans. M. B. DeBevoise (Cambridge: Harvard University Press, 2004 [1999]), 164.

12. Lafayette's quote comes from a private letter in 1777 to his wife Adrienne, while the origin of Jefferson's quote is unknown. For more on the early political intersection between France and the United States, see James W. Ceaser, *Reconstructing America: The Symbol of America in Modern Thought* (New Haven: Yale University Press, 1997), particularly ch. 3.

13. Andrew Moore, "The American Farmer as French Diplomat: J. Hector St. John de Crèvecoeur in New York After 1783," *Journal of the Western Society for French History* 39 (2011): 133–143.

14. Gisèle Sapiro, "French Literature in the World System of Translation," in *French

Global: A New Approach to Literary History, eds. Christie McDonald and Susan Rubin Suleiman (New York: Columbia University Press, 2010), 301.

15. For an in-depth analysis of the international translation market between 1932 and 1977, see Daniel Milo, "La bourse mondiale de la traduction: un baromètre culturel?," *Annales: Histoires, Sciences Sociales* 39e année, no. 1 (February 1984): 92–115.

16. For a select sampling, see, in addition to Ceaser's *Reconstructing America*, Frank Costigliola, *France and the United States: The Cold Alliance Since World War II* (New York: Twayne, 1992); Julian G. Hurstfield, *America and the French Nation, 1935–1945* (Chapel Hill: University of North Carolina Press, 2012 [1986]); Richard F. Kuisel, *Seducing the French: The Dilemma of Americanization: A Century of French Perceptions*, trans. Gerry Turner (Berkeley: University of California Press, 1993); Denis Lacorne, Jacques Rupnik, and Marie-France Toi, eds., *The Rise and Fall of Anti-Americanism* (New York: St. Martin's, 1990); Jean-Philippe Mathy, *French Resistance: The French-American Culture Wars* (Minneapolis: University of Minnesota Press, 2000); Michel Winock, "'US Go Home': l'antiaméricanisme français," *L'Histoire* 50 (November 1982): 7–20.

17. See Brooke L. Blower, *Becoming Americans in Paris: Transatlantic Politics and Culture Between the World Wars* (New York: Oxford University Press, 2011); Charles Glass, *Americans in Paris: Life and Death Under Nazi Occupation* (New York: Penguin, 2009); Adam Gopnik, ed., *Americans in Paris: A Literary Anthology* (New York: Literary Classics of the United States, 2004); Lynn Gumpert and Debra Bricker Balken, eds., *Americans in Paris: Artists Working in Postwar France, 1946–1952* (Munich: Hirmer Publishers, 2022); and David McCullough, *The Greater Journey: Americans in Paris* (New York: Simon & Schuster, 2012).

18. Some notable examples include Jean-Philippe Mathy, *Extrême-Occident: French Intellectuals and America* (Chicago: University of Chicago Press, 1993), Brent Hayes Edwards, *The Practice of Diaspora: Literature, Translation, and the Rise of Black Internationalism* (Cambridge: Harvard University Press, 2013); Louis Menand, "The Promise of Freedom, the Friend of Authority: American Culture in Postwar France," in *Americanism: New Perspectives on the History of an Ideal*, eds. Michael Kazin and Joseph A. McCartin (Chapel Hill: University of North Carolina Press, 2006), 205–220; and Yan Hamel, *L'Amérique selon Sartre: littérature, philosophie, politique* (Montreal: Presses universitaires de Montréal, 2013).

19. Claude-Edmonde Magny, *L'âge du roman américain* (Paris: Seuil, 1948); William Cloonan, *The French in American Literature, Americans in French Literature* (Liverpool: Liverpool University Press, 2018). See also Mathy, *Extrême-Occident* and the podcast *L'Amérique des écrivains français*, especially episodes 1 ("Amérique, je t'aime, je te hais"), 2 ("Après la guerre la modernité"), and 3 ("Écrire à l'américaine"), which trace the literary origin of the French verb "américaniser" to Baudelaire's writings on Poe and discuss literary influences in poetry, dime novels, and crime fiction (*France Culture*, 2–4 November 2020).

20. Rebecca Walkowitz, *Born Translated: The Contemporary Novel in an Age of World Literature* (New York: Columbia University Press, 2015).

21. Christie McDonald and Susan Rubin Suleiman, eds., *French Global: A New Approach to Literary History* (New York: Columbia University Press, 2010).

22. François Cusset, *French Theory: How Foucault, Deleuze, Derrida, & Co. Transformed the Intellectual Life of the United States*, trans. Jeff Fort (Minneapolis: University of Minnesota Press, 2008), 5.

23. Cusset, *French Theory*, 87. One could see this, for example, in Foucault's choice of register when his translator Mark Seem asked him to write the introduction to the English version of *Anti-Oedipus*: "Foucault, with great awareness of the displacements involved, chose a programmatic tone and the imperative mood in order to invite the Americans to use this 'great book' as a 'guide to everyday life'" (89).

24. A critique of the misguided application of French philosophy-as-theory is a throughline across Cusset's book but is especially trenchant in chapters 4, 6, 7, and 9. As Cusset phrases the critique rhetorically, in reference to Derrida's rise as a cultural phenomenon in the U.S., "How is it that this thought was able to become the most bankable product ever to emerge on the market of academic discourses? How did this obscure trajectory find itself taken hold of, domesticated, digested, and served in individual doses in an American literary field . . . ? How is [it] that for every French reader of a book by Derrida in the land of obligatory high school philosophy courses, ten Americans have already looked it over, despite their meager philosophical formation?" (107).

25. David Damrosch, *What Is World Literature?* (Princeton: Princeton University Press, 2003); see 281 and 297, as well as 5, where Damrosch first articulates "a mode of circulation and of reading." As a work anchored more in intellectual history than literary studies, Cusset's book attends specifically to a U.S. context and is less interested in exploring how the emergence of theory in the U.S. returns to France and transforms discourses and disciplines there.

26. Sapiro, "French Literature in the World System of Translation," 304.

27. In a French context, I am thinking especially of works like Bernard Lahire's *La condition littéraire: la double vie des écrivains* (Paris: Éditions la Découverte, 2006) and Gisèle Sapiro's *La sociologie de la littérature* (2014), recently translated into English as *The Sociology of Literature*, trans. Madeline Bedecarré and Ben Libman (Stanford: Stanford University Press, 2023).

28. Jordan S. Carroll, *Reading the Obscene: Transgressive Editors and the Class Politics of US Literature* (Stanford: Stanford University Press, 2021) and Loren Glass, *Counter-Culture Colophon: Grove Press, "the Evergreen Review," and the Incorporation of the Avant-Garde* (Stanford: Stanford University Press, 2013), 10.

29. Mark McGurl, *The Program Era: Postwar Fiction and the Rise of Creative Writing* (Cambridge: Harvard University Press, 2011), 281. Such was the case, for instance, with Gordon Lish's heavy hand in editing Raymond Carver's short stories, which McGurl credits as instrumental in creating "literary minimalism" as a "singular aesthetic triumph" in American letters in the 1960s and 1970s (293).

30. See Dan Sinykin, *Big Fiction: How Conglomeration Changed the Publishing In-*

dustry and American Literature (New York: Columbia University Press, 2023); Laura McGrath, "Literary Agency," *American Literary History* 33, no. 2 (Summer 2021): 350–370; and Kinohi Nishikawa, *Street Players: Black Pulp Fiction and the Making of a Literary Underground* (Chicago: University of Chicago Press, 2018), as well as Josh Lambert's *The Literary Mafia: Jews, Publishing, and American Literature* (New Haven: Yale University Press, 2022).

31. Alice Kaplan, *Looking for "The Stranger": Albert Camus and the Life of a Literary Classic* (Chicago: University of Chicago Press, 2016), 176, 179–181, and 191–198. Sarah Bakewell adds that, alongside Knopf, periodicals like the *New Yorker*, *Time*, and the *New York Post* worked hard to advertise French existentialism as intellectually sophisticated and cutting-edge; see *At the Existentialist Café: Freedom, Being, and Apricot Cocktails* (New York: Other Press, 2016), 172–173. For more on the intellectual links between French existentialism and U.S. culture, of which there has been a considerable amount of scholarship, see Cusset, *French Theory* (24–25) and Louis Menand, "The Promise of Freedom, the Friend of Authority: American Culture in Postwar France," in *Americanism: New Perspectives on the History of an Ideal*, eds. Michael Kazin and Joseph A. McCartin (Chapel Hill: University of North Carolina Press, 2006), 205–220.

32. Cécile Cottenet, *Literary Agents in the Transatlantic Book Trade: American Fiction, French Rights, and the Hoffman Agency* (New York: Routledge, 2017); Laurence Cossu-Beaumont, *Deux agents littéraires dans le siècle américain: William et Jenny Bradley, passeurs culturels transatlantiques* (Lyon: ENS Éditions, 2023); and Laura Claridge, *The Lady with the Borzoi: Blanche Knopf, Literary Tastemaker Extraordinaire* (New York: Farrar, Straus and Giroux, 2016).

33. Hannah Sullivan, *The Work of Revision* (Cambridge: Harvard University Press, 2013).

34. "Il s'agit d'ouvrir de nouvelles possibilités inconnues des anciens auteurs," writes Le Lionnais in this foundational definition of "la grande mission de l'Oulipo." See Jacques Bens, "Queneau oulipien," in the Oulipo's *Atlas de littérature potentielle* (Paris: Gallimard, 1981), 22.

35. See Alain Robbe-Grillet's collection of essays in *Pour un nouveau roman* (Paris: Éditions de Minuit, 1963), esp. "Sur quelques notions périmées" (1957), 25–44.

36. For more on the playwrights that fell under the umbrella term of "theater of the absurd," see Martin Esslin, *The Theatre of the Absurd* (New York: Anchor Doubleday, 1961).

37. Pierre Bourdieu, "The Market of Symbolic Goods," in *The Field of Cultural Production: Essays on Art and Literature*, ed. Randal Johnson (New York: Columbia University Press, 1993), ch. 3.

38. Merve Emre, *Paraliterary: The Making of Bad Readers in Postwar America* (Chicago: University of Chicago Press, 2017).

39. Emre's reading of the American Express brand is particularly sharp on this point, showing how it functioned as an institution that aided tourism and international travel, but also as one whose registered literary presence (in works such as James

Baldwin's *Giovanni's Room* or Erica Jong's *Fear of Flying*) could challenge heteronormative ideas of family and travel (*Paraliterary*, 103). By internally reconciling with such brands, literature could, on the one hand, call attention to commercial forces and serve as a site of resistance. Yet the power of branding could paradoxically *also* subvert attempts at literary resistance, as evidenced, Emre suggests, when a work like *Fear of Flying* becomes itself "read too widely across the dominant sphere... branded as 'mainstream,' 'popular,' or 'too familiar' to encode a culturally subversive mode of discourse" (*Paraliterary*, 122).

40. Lawrence Rainey, *Institutions of Modernism: Literary Elites & Public Culture* (New Haven: Yale University Press, 1998), 3.

41. Rainey, *Institutions of Modernism*, 73.

42. Andreas Huyssen, *After the Great Divide: Modernism, Mass Culture, Postmodernism* (Bloomington: Indiana University Press, 1986), 198; also see 144 for the point about Adorno in the United States.

43. Kristin Ross, *Fast Cars, Clean Bodies: Decolonization and the Reordering of French Culture* (Cambridge: MIT Press, 1996), 183 and 13.

44. Ross, *Fast Cars, Clean Bodies*, 75–77.

45. Robbe-Grillet, *Project*, 160 (English) and *Projet*, 189 (French).

46. Paul Morand, *New York*, trans. Hamish Miles (London: Heinemann, 1931), 295–296.

47. Simone de Beauvoir, *America Day by Day*, trans. Carol Cosman (Berkeley: University of California Press, 1999), 8.

48. Jean-Paul Sartre, "Individualism and Conformism in the United States," in *Literary and Philosophical Essays*, trans. Annette Michelson (New York: Collier Books, 1955), 110.

49. Nathalie Sarraute, *Lettres d'Amérique* (Paris: Gallimard, 2017), 48; my translation. Unless specified otherwise, all translations are my own.

50. Hélène Cixous, *Manhattan: Lettres de la préhistoire* (Paris: Galilée, 2002), Prière d'insérer and 65.

51. Mathy, *Extrême-Occident*, 90–103.

52. Beth Luey, "The Organization of the Book Publishing Industry," in *The Enduring Book: Print Culture in Postwar America*, eds. David Paul Nord et al. (Chapel Hill: University of North Carolina Press, 2009), 29–54.

53. Other examples one might consider in this broader narrative of Franco-American literary entanglement include (but are not limited to): Michel Butor's prize-winning travel narrative of the U.S., *Mobile* (Paris: Gallimard, 1962), which Butor wrote while a visiting faculty member at Bryn Mawr; Mohammed Dib's poetic novel *L.A. Trip* (Paris: Éditions de la Différence, 2003), which was created for the purposes of translation and was simultaneously released in French and in a bilingual edition translated by Paul Vangelisti (Los Angeles: Green Integer, 2003); Assia Djebar's thesis project, *Le roman maghrébin francophone entre les langues, entre les cultures: quarante ans d'un parcours: Assia Djebar 1957–1997* (Université Paul Valéry-Montpellier,

1999), which Djebar published under her given name, Fatima-Zohra Imalhayène, and undertook largely for pragmatic purposes, as she was advised that a doctorate would give her greater access to teaching in the American university system; Nathalie Sarraute's posthumously published *Lettres d'Amérique* (Paris: Gallimard, 2017), which show the author's firsthand engagement with American universities and cultural figures; Monique Wittig's many professional, personal, and literary affiliations with the U.S., including her long-term teaching position at the University of Arizona and her cowritten book with her American partner Sande Zeig, *Brouillon pour un dictionnaire des amantes* (Paris: Grasset, 1976) / *Lesbian Peoples: Material for a Dictionary* (New York: Avon Books, 1979); and Marguerite Yourcenar's lifelong relationship with the American Grace Frick, the sole authorized translator of Yourcenar's work into English.

Chapter 1

1. Paule d'Oncin, *Plympton House* (New York: Brentano's Books, 1943), 188: "Or, un livre français, publié en Amérique, en ce moment . . . quelle classe de lecteurs ce genre de livre pourra-t-il intéresser? Atteindra-t-il le grand public?"

2. See, for example, Gisèle Sapiro, *La guerre des écrivains 1940–1953* (Paris: Fayard, 1999); Jacques Cantier, *Lire sous l'Occupation* (Paris: CNRS, 2019); and Jacques Debû-Bridel, *Les Éditions de Minuit: historique* (Paris: Éditions de Minuit, 1945).

3. Emmanuelle Loyer, *Paris à New York: Intellectuels et artistes français en exil (1940–1947)* (Paris: Grasset, 2005); Jeffrey Mehlman, *Émigré New York: French Intellectuals in Wartime Manhattan, 1940–1944* (Baltimore: Johns Hopkins University Press, 2000); and Colin W. Nettelbeck, *Forever French: Exile in the United States 1939–1945* (New York: Berg, 1991).

4. Joanna Russ, *How to Suppress Women's Writing* (Austin: University of Texas Press, 2018 [1983]).

5. John B. Hench, *Books as Weapons: Propaganda, Publishing, and the Battle for Global Markets in the Era of World War II* (Ithaca: Cornell University Press, 2010).

6. Susan Rubin Suleiman, *The Némirovsky Question: The Life, Death, and Legacy of a Jewish Writer in 20th-Century France* (New Haven: Yale University Press, 2016), 58.

7. That the first woman awarded a Goncourt would also be Jewish and foreign is additionally worthy of note. See, for example, Julia Elsky, *Writing Occupation: Jewish Émigré Voices in Wartime France* (Stanford: Stanford University Press, 2020), ch. 4.

8. Angela Kershaw, *Forgotten Engagements: Women, Literature and the Left in 1930s France* (Amsterdam: Rodopi, 2007); Jennifer E. Milligan, *The Forgotten Generation: French Women Writers of the Interwar Period* (Oxford: Berg, 1997).

9. Paul Nizan, quoted in Angela Kershaw, *Forgotten Engagements*, 39; originally published as "Littérature feminine," *L'Humanité* (20 March 1937). See also Milligan, *The Forgotten Generation*.

10. A graph of this "Top 100 List" is illustrated in Cantier, *Lire sous l'Occupation*, 25–28.

11. See Sapiro, *La guerre des écrivains 1940–1953*, 34.

12. Cantier, *Lire sous l'Occupation*, 51–52.

13. Cantier, *Lire sous l'Occupation*, 86–104.

14. Cantier, *Lire sous l'Occupation*, 143–169.

15. Cantier, *Lire sous l'Occupation*, 152.

16. Cantier, *Lire sous l'Occupation*, 206–208.

17. Cantier, *Lire sous l'Occupation*, 227.

18. Edith Thomas, "Christine de Pisan," in *Messages: Domaine français. Un manifeste des lettres d'aujourd'hui*, ed. Jean Lescure (Geneva: Éditions des trois collines, 1943), 265–273.

19. For more on Elsa Triolet's wartime publications, see Elsky, *Writing Occupation*, esp. 147–148.

20. Debû-Bridel, *Les Éditions de Minuit*, 49.

21. Debû-Bridel, *Les Éditions de Minuit*, 61–62, 46.

22. Thomas's stories were recently reprinted and translated in a bilingual edition published by the MLA. See Edith Thomas, *Résistance: Contes de la Seconde Guerre Mondiale en France* (New York: Modern Language Association of America, 2022), with an excellent introduction by Michelle Chilcoat and Lori J. Jarso, and a foreword by Dorothy Kaufmann.

23. Debû-Bridel, *Les Éditions de Minuit*, 82.

24. Hench, *Books as Weapons*, 4–5.

25. Hench, *Books as Weapons*, 45–46.

26. Hench, *Books as Weapons*, 86, 96.

27. Charles Cestre, "The Literary Scene in Paris," *New York Times* (21 January 1940): 8, 22.

28. Woods reviewed multiple titles, including Pierre de Lanux's *France de ce monde*; Jules Romains's *Message aux Français*, and André Morize's *France, été 1940*. Katherine Woods, "New Books in French in America," *New York Times* (10 August 1941): 8, 18.

29. There was, of course, also a considerable market for books in French in Quebec, whose book industry before the 1940s had been vastly dominated by imports from France. Their book market expanded rapidly after World War II, in large part because of Parisian publishers who opened new firms there. See Jacques Michon, "Book Publishing in Quebec," in *History of the Book in Canada, vol. III: 1918–1980*, eds. Carole Gerson and Jacques Michon (Toronto: University of Toronto Press, 2007), 199–207.

30. Census data from 1940 estimates about 359,520 foreign-born native French speakers living in the U.S. See https://www.census.gov/history/pdf/1910mothertongue.pdf.

31. See Hench, *Books as Weapons*, 75–79. According to Hench, "The highest priority was to secure books to be used in France and Belgium, nearest the planned invasion landings. OWI [the Office of War Information] asked the French-language publishers that had established operations in New York before or after the fall of France to recommend titles 'they feel valuable in the way of showing democracy in action and as an example of American thought and writing'" (79).

32. See Loyer, *Paris à New York*; Mehlman, *Émigré New York*; and Nettelbeck, *Forever French*.

33. Nettelbeck, *Forever French*, 63.

34. For more on Schiffrin's biography and literary trajectory, see Amos Reichman, *Jacques Schiffrin: A Publisher in Exile, from Pléiade to Pantheon*, trans. Sandra Smith (New York: Columbia University Press, 2019).

35. Loyer, *Paris à New York*, 265.

36. Loyer, *Paris à New York*, 96.

37. Loyer, *Paris à New York*, 98.

38. A. Bon, *Livres français parus en Amérique de 1940 à 1944: documents bibliographiques* (Rio de Janeiro: Institut franco-brésilien de haute culture, 1944). While many of the titles are reprints of classics, Bon's list invites further study on a considerable number of lesser-known writers published across the Americas.

39. Stanton Griffis, *Lying in State* (New York: Doubleday, 1952), 63.

40. See https://web.archive.org/web/20090126022958/http:/brentanos.fr/pages/who arewe/historyANG.htm.

41. Jeffrey Mehlman, *Émigré New York*, 66. A photograph, taken by Arturo Schwarz, can be seen here: https://www.toutfait.com/issues/volume2/issue_5/articles/schleif/popup_05.html.

42. Margaret Hughes, *Les Lauriers sont coupés . . . Journal d'une volontaire américaine en France (Avril–Septembre, 1940)* (New York: Brentano's Books, 1941), 11.

43. William Thayer's review of Hughes's book from March 7, 2021, can be found here: https://penelope.uchicago.edu/Thayer/E/Gazetteer/Places/Europe/France/_Texts/HUGLAU/home.html.

44. Hughes, *Les Lauriers sont coupés*, 140.

45. Joan Cook, "Margaret Hughes, Helped French," *New York Times* (23 July 1980): 27 (obituaries): https://timesmachine.nytimes.com/timesmachine/1980/07/23/113949 235.html?pageNumber=27.

46. This according to the copyright pages of *Les lauriers sont coupés*: "Les bénéfices de l'auteur provenant de la vente de cet ouvrage sont remis à l'*American Friends of France* pour les prisonniers de guerre français" ("All of the author's profits from book sales will be given to the *American Friends of France* for French war prisoners").

47. Louis le François, *J'ai faim! . . . Journal d'un Français en France depuis l'armistice* (New York: Brentano's Books, 1942).

48. Louis le François, *J'ai faim!*, 7.

49. Louis le François, *J'ai faim!*, 8.

50. Tryphosa Bates-Batcheller, *La France au soleil et à l'ombre* (New York: Brentano's Books, 1944), 11.

51. Bates-Batcheller, *La France au soleil et à l'ombre*, 211.

52. Florence Conrad, *Camarades de combat* (New York: Brentano's Books, 1942), 317, 7.

53. Conrad, *Camarades de combat*, 327.

54. Conrad, *Camarades de combat*, 325.

55. Robert Tenger, "Au service de la langue et de la culture françaises en Amérique," *Pour la Victoire* 28 (14 July 1945): 8.

56. Helen Mackay's *La France que j'aime* was listed as a Brentano's publication but was ultimately printed in Canada.

57. These awards are printed in the cover pages of the 1942 edition of *La France que j'aime*, in a list of Mackay's previously published books with Plon but cannot be corroborated elsewhere. In fact, the 1929 edition of *Patte Blanche* was published by the *Éditions des Portiques*, not by Plon, which may have been confused with the award.

58. Margaret Higonnet, "Helen Mackay, American Modernist: Finding a Form for the Great War," *First World War Studies* 12, no. 3 (2021): 203–218, quote on 215.

59. Helen Mackay, *La France que j'aime* (Montreal: Les Éditions Variétés, 1942), 147.

60. Antoine de Saint Exupéry, "Préface," in *La France que j'aime*.

61. Helen Mackay, *Sainte terre de France* (New York: Brentano's Books, 1944), 137.

62. Hench, *Books as Weapons*, 79.

63. Brentano's is mainly referenced for its Paris bookstore branch that reopened after the liberation of France (Hench, *Books as Weapons*, 155).

64. See Hench, *Books as Weapons*, 97.

65. Hench, *Books as Weapons*, 100.

66. This according to the list of Overseas Editions and Transatlantic Editions books that Hench compiles in Appendix A (270–274). Many of the French-language books sent overseas were published by American trade publishers—such as Little, Brown; Harper & Brothers; or Knopf—and translated from English-language originals. Of the over ninety titles listed, only two women writers were included (Catherine Drinker Bowen and Constance Rourke).

67. As Loyer puts it, the EMF was established to address "the shortage of available books for recently arrived French readers" ("la pénurie de livres disponibles pour les nouveaux lecteurs français récemment arrivés"), *Paris à New York*, 97.

68. Robert Tenger, "Note de l'Éditeur," in *La garde montante*, eds. Françoise Perrier and Claude Lebel (New York: Brentano's Books, 1944).

69. Robert Tenger, "Note de l'Éditeur," in Helen Mackay's *Sainte Terre de France* (New York: Brentano's Books, 1944).

70. Tenger, in "Au service de la langue et de la culture françaises en Amérique," 8.

71. Merve Emre, *Paraliterary: The Making of Bad Readers in Postwar America* (Chicago: University of Chicago Press, 2017), 11.

72. Emre, *Paraliterary*, 3.

73. Emre, *Paraliterary*, chs. 1 and 2.

74. Antoine de Saint Exupéry and Consuelo de Saint Exupéry, *Correspondance 1930–1944* (Paris: Gallimard, 2021), 97n1.

75. See the reprint of the Manifesto on pp. 69–71: https://www.abbaye-saint-hilaire-vaucluse.com/Groupe_d%27Oppede_1940-1945.pdf.

76. Geneviève Le Hir, "A propos d'Oppède," *Études littéraires* 33, no. 2 (Summer 2001): 129.

77. See Jean-Lucien Bonillo and Christelle Juskiwieski, "Les ateliers de la guerre: Marseille et Oppède, 1940–1945," *Hypothèses* (20 May 2019): https://chmcc.hypotheses .org/8833; Le Hir, "A propos d'Oppède," 125–144; François Otchakovsky-Laurens, "Les dernières années du peintre Zelman en Provence (1939–1944)," *Provence historique* 73, no. 274 (July–December 2023): 469–486; Valérie-Anne Sircoulomb, *Le groupe d'Oppède pendant la seconde guerre mondiale: mémoire de DEA sous la direction de Mady Menier* (Université Lyon II-Lumière, 1990); and Bernard Zehrfuss, "Oppède, essai de renaissance," *Cahiers du Sud*, no. 232 (February 1941): 67–74.

78. Consuelo's biographers have linked the influence of Hidalgo's rallying cry to Consuelo's years studying and painting in Mexico; see Marie-Hélène Carbonel and Martine Fransioli Martínez, *Consuelo de Saint Exupéry: Une mariée vêtue de noir* (Monaco: Éditions du Rocher, 2010), 49.

79. Consuelo de Saint Exupéry, *Oppède* (New York: Brentano's Books, 1945), 47. All English translations corresponding to this edition are my own.

80. Consuelo de Saint Exupéry, *Oppède*, 60.

81. Consuelo de Saint Exupéry, *Oppède*, 143.

82. Consuelo de Saint Exupéry, *Oppède*, 41.

83. Consuelo de Saint Exupéry, *Oppède*, 73.

84. Consuelo de Saint Exupéry, *Oppède*, 109.

85. Consuelo de Saint Exupéry, *Oppède*, 126.

86. Consuelo de Saint Exupéry, *Oppède*, 240, 150.

87. Consuelo de Saint Exupéry, *Oppède*, 48.

88. Antoine de Saint Exupéry and Consuelo de Saint Exupéry, *Correspondance 1930–1944*, 52.

89. Antoine de Saint Exupéry and Consuelo de Saint Exupéry, *Correspondance 1930–1944*, 129.

90. Antoine de Saint Exupéry and Consuelo de Saint Exupéry, *Correspondance 1930–1944*, 173.

91. Antoine de Saint Exupéry and Consuelo de Saint Exupéry, *Correspondance 1930–1944*, 256 and 276–277.

92. Consuelo de Saint Exupéry, *The Tale of the Rose: The Love Story Behind "The Little Prince,"* trans. Esther Allen (New York: Random House, 2003), 252.

93. Consuelo de Saint Exupéry, *The Tale of the Rose*, 252, 259.

94. Reprinted on p. 69: https://www.abbaye-saint-hilaire-vaucluse.com/Groupe_d %27Oppede_1940-1945.pdf.

95. Reprinted on p. 70: https://www.abbaye-saint-hilaire-vaucluse.com/Groupe_d %27Oppede_1940-1945.pdf.

96. Christian Megret, "Un village abandonné a retrouvé la vie," *Le Jour l'Écho de Paris: édition de Marseille* (15 December 1940).

97. See documents collected on https://www.abbaye-saint-hilaire-vaucluse.com/ Groupe_d%27Oppede_1940-1945.pdf, particularly 19, 28–29, 81, 84, 136, 141, 147–148, 151–153, and 221.

98. Robert Tenger, "Note de l'éditeur," in Consuelo de Saint Exupéry's *Oppède* (New York: Brentano's Books, 1945).

99. Consuelo de Saint Exupéry, *Kingdom of the Rocks: Memories of "Oppède,"* trans. Katherine Woods (New York: Random House, 1946), 12; compared with *Oppède* (Brentano's Books), 19.

100. In "Kingdom of the Rocks," Random House Records, 1925–1999, Rare Book and Manuscript Library, Columbia University, Box 103.

101. Alice Langellier, "Review of *Oppède*," *Modern Language Journal* 30, no. 3 (March 1946): 168–169.

102. See reviews from *Kirkus* (1 September 1946), by Albert Guerard in the *New York Times* (15 December 1946): 87, and in *Book Review Digest* (1946): https://archive.org/details/bookreviewdigest029766mbp/page/710/mode/2up?q=the.

103. Kirkus review of *Kingdom of the Rocks* (1 September 1946) and Rose Feld, "Review of *Kingdom of the Rocks*," *Weekly Book Review* (29 December 1946): 2.

104. Russ, *How to Suppress Women's Writing*, 39 and 45.

105. Russ, *How to Suppress Women's Writing*, 63–64.

106. This according to Consuelo's private notes, Consuelo de Saint Exupéry, *Lettres du dimanche* (Paris: Plon, 2001), 77–78. See also Antoine de Saint Exupéry and Consuelo de Saint Exupéry, *Correspondance 1930–1944*, 112–113n2 for information about her American visa.

107. A recent exhibition about the genesis of *Le Petit Prince* at the *Musée des arts décoratifs* in Paris featured a striking wall-to-wall display of dozens of translations of the novel. According to the catalogue copy for the exhibit: "A worldwide publishing phenomenon for the last 75 years, *The Little Prince* has sold 200 million copies, in nearly 500 languages or dialects. Every year some five million copies are sold throughout the world, and the number of musical, theatrical, and audiovisual adaptations keeps growing" ("Phénomène mondial de l'édition depuis 75 ans, *Le Petit Prince* a été vendu à deux cents millions d'exemplaires, dans presque 500 langues ou dialectes. Chaque année, quelque cinq millions d'exemplaires se vendent dans le monde et les adaptations musicales, théâtrales et audiovisuelles se multiplient"), *A la rencontre du petit prince*, 17 February–26 June 2022.

108. Esther Allen, "Introduction," in Consuelo de Saint Exupéry, *The Tale of the Rose*, xii.

109. Russ, *How to Suppress Women's Writing*, 158.

110. Charles Peignot, "Market for French Books Maintained in America," *Publishers Weekly* (9 June 1945): 2278–2279.

111. Oncin, *Plympton House*, 176.

112. Oncin, *Plympton House*, 188.

Chapter 2

1. Judith Schlanger, *Présence des oeuvres perdues* (Paris: Hermann, 2010), 30–31: "Les oeuvres retrouvées nous plongent dans l'inverse de l'irrémédiable: non plus l'ab-

sence, le dommage et le manque, mais au contraire le supplément de présence . . . le nouvel arrivant retrouvé nous donne la joie de recevoir le vieux comme neuf."

2. Jean Vallier, *C'était Marguerite Duras, tome II, 1946–1996* (Paris: Fayard, 2010), 424; and Gilles Philippe et al., *Marguerite Duras: Oeuvres complètes II* (Paris: Gallimard [Pléiade], 2011), 1688.

3. Rebecca L. Walkowitz, *Born Translated: The Contemporary Novel in an Age of World Literature* (New York: Columbia University Press, 2015).

4. Barney Rosset, "On Beckett's *Film*," *Tin House* (Hollywood Issue), no. 6 (Winter 2000), reposted 23 February 2012: https://tinhouse.com/barney-rosset-on-beckets-film/.

5. T. W. Adorno, "Television and the Patterns of Mass Culture" [1954], in *Mass Culture: The Popular Arts in America*, eds. Bernard Rosenberg and David Manning White (Glencoe: Free Press, 1957), 478.

6. Tamara Chaplin, *Turning on the Mind: French Philosophers on Television* (Chicago: University of Chicago Press, 2007), 30.

7. Jérôme Bourdon, *Histoire de la télévision sous de Gaulle* (Paris: Anthropos/INA, 1990), 117.

8. Jean Boniface, *Arts de masse et grand public: la consommation culturelle en France* (Paris: Éditions ouvrières, 1961), 116.

9. Loren Glass, *Counter-Culture Colophon: Grove Press, the Evergreen Review, and the Incorporation of the Avant-Garde* (Stanford: Stanford University Press, 2013), 10.

10. Press release (1963) cited in Ed Halter and Barney Rosset, eds., *From the Third Eye: The Evergreen Review Film Reader* (New York: Seven Stories Press, 2018), 12.

11. A letter from Pamela Jones to Barney Rosset on September 6, 1960, states the following: "CBS has inquired about the availability of live and taped television rights in Samuel Beckett's ALL THAT FALL. The inquiry came from Louise Spring in the Story Department." Grove Press Records, Special Collections Research Center, Syracuse University Libraries, Box 87.

12. Ionesco confirmed his participation in a 1962 unpublished letter to his publisher (letter from Eugène Ionesco to Barney Rosset, 29 November 1962, Grove Press Records, Special Collections Research Center, Syracuse University Libraries, Box 371). A February 1963 letter from Richard Seaver to Samuel Beckett confirms both Beckett and Duras's participation: "I gather now all is set for a modified form of Barney's initial proposal" (letter from Richard Seaver to Samuel Beckett, 19 February 1963, Barney Rosset Papers, Box 48, Folder 3, Rare Book and Manuscript Library, Columbia University Library).

13. Edward D. Berkowitz, *Mass Appeal: The Formative Age of the Movies, Radio, and TV* (New York: Cambridge University Press, 2010), 124.

14. Christopher Anderson, *Hollywood TV: The Studio System in the Fifties* (Austin: University of Texas Press, 1994), 65–67 and 220.

15. Anderson, *Hollywood TV*, 12.

16. Anderson, *Hollywood TV*, 261–262.

17. Gary R. Edgerton, *The Columbia History of American Television* (New York: Columbia University Press, 2007), 192–193.

18. Lynn Spigel, *TV by Design: Modern Art and the Rise of Network Television* (Chicago: University of Chicago Press, 2008), 6, 213–232.

19. Spigel, *TV by Design*, 231.

20. Yves Portier-Réthoré, *La TV de 1964: de la RTF à l'ORTF, la naissance de la 2e chaîne* (Orléans: Corsaire Éditions, 2014), 9–10.

21. Jérôme Bourdon, *Histoire de la télévision sous de Gaulle* (Paris: Anthropos/INA, 1990), 117.

22. Bourdon, *Histoire de la télévision sous de Gaulle*, 117; and Jérôme Bourdon, *Du service public à la télé-réalité: Une histoire culturelle des télévisions européennes 1950–2010* (Bry-sur-Marne: INA Éditions, 2011), 101–106.

23. See Chaplin, *Turning on the Mind*, 113–115.

24. Bourdon, *Histoire de la télévision sous de Gaulle*, 128.

25. Chaplin, *Turning on the Mind*, 42.

26. This accords with Peter Bürger's *Theory of the Avant-Garde* (Minneapolis: University of Minnesota Press, 1987) or Susan Rubin Suleiman's *Subversive Intent: Gender, Politics, and the Avant-Garde* (Cambridge: Harvard University Press, 1990), esp. 12. While Andreas Huyssen distinguishes between the historical avant-garde in early twentieth-century Europe, and forms of postmodernism that emerged in the 1960s in America, he also sees them as part of a transatlantic continuum, similar "on the levels of formal experimentation and of a critique of the 'institution art.'" See *After the Great Divide: Modernism, Mass Culture, Postmodernism* (Bloomington: Indiana University Press, 1986), 168.

27. Jean-Louis Jeannelle, *Films sans images: une histoire des scénarios non réalisés de "La Condition humaine"* (Paris: Seuil, 2015), 19.

28. Lynn A. Higgins, *New Novel, New Wave, New Politics: Fiction and the Representation of History in Postwar France* (Lincoln: University of Nebraska Press, 1996), 11 and 15.

29. Alain Robbe-Grillet, *L'année dernière à Marienbad: ciné-roman* (Paris: Éditions de Minuit, 1961), 8–9.

30. Maurice Harmon, ed., *No Author Better Served: The Correspondence of Samuel Beckett and Alan Schneider* (Cambridge: Harvard University Press, 1998), 136.

31. Beckett (27 April 1958), quoted in Harmon, *No Author Better Served*, 45.

32. It is worth noting that, in a later letter to Schneider, dated February 6, 1963, Beckett expressed his disapproval of the Mitrani production: "*All That Fall* was done on French TV. Badly I thought—but well received." Harmon, *No Author Better Served*, 135.

33. Alan Schneider, "On Directing *Film*," in *"Film" by Samuel Beckett: Complete Scenario, Illustrations, Production Shots* (New York: Grove Press, 1969), 73.

34. Beckett, quoted in Olga Beloborodova, *The Making of Samuel Beckett's "Play / Comédie" and "Film"* (Antwerp: Bloomsbury, 2019), 236.

35. Gilles Deleuze, "The Greatest Irish Film (Beckett's "Film")," in *Essays Critical and Clinical*, trans. Daniel W. Smith and Michael A. Greco (Minneapolis: University of Minnesota Press, 1997), 23–26.

36. Gilles Deleuze, *L'image-mouvement, Cinéma 1* (Paris: Éditions de Minuit, 1983), 100 and 103.

37. Gilles Deleuze, *Cinema 1: The Movement-Image*, trans. Hugh Tomlinson and Barbara Habberjam (London: Continuum, 1986), 68.

38. Alain Robbe-Grillet, "Project III: Frank's Return: An Original Motion Picture Script," Grove Press Records, Special Collections Research Center, Syracuse University Libraries, Box 596.

39. Gilles Deleuze, *L'Image-temps. Cinéma 2* (Paris: Éditions de Minuit, 1985), ch. 5.

40. We can recall that in *Marienbad*, the character A, when presented with a photograph of herself, cannot recall a purported past relationship with the character X, who the film suggests may have abused her. In *Film*, we observe O ripping up old photos—an act that can be read as a direct nod to *Marienbad* as well as to André Bazin's seminal essay on photography and cinema ("The Ontology of the Photographic Image," trans. Hugh Gray, *Film Quarterly* 13, no. 4 (Summer 1960): 4–9). In rejecting the ostensible indexicality and legitimacy of the photographic image, E offers an alternative path to A, who cannot assert control over her memory and her past.

41. Beckett, quoted in Beloborodova, *The Making of Samuel Beckett's "Play / Comédie" and "Film,"* 317.

42. Graley Herren, *Samuel Beckett's Plays on Film and Television* (New York: Palgrave, 2007), 40.

43. Herren, *Samuel Beckett's Plays on Film and Television*, 40.

44. Colin Gardner, *Beckett, Deleuze and the Televisual Event* (New York: Palgrave, 2012), 48. Gardner convincingly reads O's temporary disappearance from the screen as one of the film's paradoxes, for it would seem that in those moments O effectively achieves imperceptibility.

45. See Linda Ben-Zvi, "Samuel Beckett's Media Plays," *Modern Drama* 28, no. 1 (Spring 1985): 22–37, esp. 30; and Jonathan Kalb, "The Mediated Quixote: The Radio and Television Plays, and Film," in *The Cambridge Companion to Beckett*, ed. John Pilling (New York: Cambridge University Press, 1994), 124–144.

46. Beloborodova, *The Making of Samuel Beckett's "Play / Comédie" and "Film,"* 265.

47. For more on this history, see Ross Lipman's documentary *Not Film*, produced by Amy Heller and Dennis Doros (Milestone Films, DVD, 2015).

48. Lynn Spigel, *Make Room for TV: Television and the Family Ideal in Postwar America* (Chicago: University of Chicago Press, 1992), 118.

49. Even after Dick Powell's death, Beckett corresponded with Grove about the "TV project" and agreed—in a telegraph (dated 8 March 1963) and filed as "Beckett TV"—that the actor Zero Mostel should be asked to play the role of O (a part for which Mostel was ultimately unavailable). Rare Book and Manuscript Library, Columbia University Library, Barney Rosset Papers, Box 48.

50. For more on these productions, see Herren, *Samuel Beckett's Plays on Film and Television*; Gardner, *Beckett, Deleuze and the Televisual Event*; and Jonathan Bignell,

Beckett on Screen: The Television Plays (Manchester: Manchester University Press, 2009).

51. See *Peephole Art: Beckett for Television*, produced and directed by John Reilly (Global Village, VHS, 1994). Information indicated at minute 27.

52. Letter dated 29 September 1964, in Harmon, *No Author Better Served*, 166.

53. See "Chronologie," in Eugène Ionesco, *Théâtre complet*, ed. Emmanuel Jacquart (Paris: Gallimard NRF [Pléiade], 1991), LXVII–CVI.

54. See, for instance, Emmanuel Jacquart, "Préface," in Ionesco's *Théâtre complet*, lii.

55. Julia Elsky, "Rethinking Ionesco's Absurd: *The Bald Soprano* in the Interlingual Context of Vichy and Postwar France," *PMLA* 133, no. 2 (March 2018): 353–354.

56. Advertisement for Ionesco, *Variety*, 2 January 1963, Grove Press Records, Special Collections Research Center, Syracuse University Libraries, Box 371.

57. Letter from Eugène Ionesco to Barney Rosset, 10 December 1962, Grove Press Records, Special Collections Research Center, Syracuse University Libraries, Box 371.

58. Eugène Ionesco, "*Samedi dernier au hammam-bad*," sketch proposal, Fonds Ionesco, Bibliothèque nationale de France, 4.COL.166 (1273).

59. Eugène Ionesco, "*L'oeuf dur*," proposal, Fonds Ionesco, Bibliothèque nationale de France, 4.COL.166 (1272).

60. Richard Seaver, Telegram, undated (circa 1963), Fonds Ionesco, Bibliothèque nationale de France, 4.COL.166 (904.2).

61. Eugène Ionesco, *Notes et contre-notes* (Paris: Gallimard [Folio], 1966), 60.

62. Thomas Bransten, "Ionesco Turns Talents to Film Sketch," *Herald Tribune* (24–25 February 1962): 3.

63. Eugène Ionesco, *La colère*, in *Les Sept Péchés capitaux*, dir. Sylvain Dhome (Pathé, 1962).

64. Spigel, *Make Room for TV*, 34–35, 89–91.

65. Eugène Ionesco, *La colère*, annotated screenplay, Fonds Ionesco, Bibliothèque nationale de France, 4.COL.166 (1264).

66. Letter from Eugène Ionesco to Joseph Bercholz, 12 December 1961, Fonds Ionesco, Bibliothèque nationale de France, 4.COL.166 (1261).

67. Letter from Eugène Ionesco to Barney Rosset, 29 November 1962, Grove Press Records, Special Collections Research Center, Syracuse University Libraries, Box 371.

68. Eugène Ionesco, "*L'oeuf dur*," French screenplay, Fonds Ionesco, Bibliothèque nationale de France, 4.COL.166 (1272), 3.

69. The archival record does not make clear to what extent Seaver, as Ionesco's editor and translator, suggested these cuts, though it is reasonable to expect that his opinions would have influenced Ionesco.

70. "The Hard-Boiled Egg," unpublished screenplay, Barney Rosset Papers, Rare Book and Manuscript Library, Columbia University Library, Box 48; quotes on 6, 6, 10, and 11.

71. "The Hard-Boiled Egg," unpublished screenplay, 5.

72. "The Hard-Boiled Egg," unpublished screenplay, 13–14.
73. "The Hard-Boiled Egg," unpublished screenplay, 14.
74. Marsha F. Cassidy, *What Women Watched: Daytime Television in the 1950s* (Austin: University of Texas Press, 2005), 29.
75. "Omelette norvégienne," *Art et Magie de la Cuisine*, with Raymond Oliver and Catherine Langeais, ORTF, 24 September 1962, Bibliothèque nationale de France, Inathèque.
76. Oliver launched episodes on egg preparations on 3 December 1956, with "Des oeufs," in which he provides instructions for cooking baked eggs, soft-boiled eggs, eggs *en cocotte*, poached eggs, fried eggs, and eggs Benedict. Subsequent egg episodes aired on 1 January 1957 ("Les omelettes"), 22 April 1957 ("Oeufs de Pâques"), 9 May 1957 ("Omelette norvégienne"), 17 August 1959 ("Omelette camping"), and two more episodes on the popular Norwegian omelette, on 24 September 1962 and 17 December 1965.
77. Dana Polan, *Julia Child's "The French Chef"* (Durham: Duke University Press, 2011), 122–123.
78. Polan, *Julia Child's "The French Chef,"* 129.
79. "The Hard-Boiled Egg," unpublished screenplay, 21–23.
80. Cassidy, *What Women Watched*, 28. For a fuller survey of postwar American cooking shows, see Polan, *The French Chef*, 45–77.
81. "The Hard-Boiled Egg," unpublished screenplay, 6.
82. Laura Mulvey, "Visual Pleasure and Narrative Cinema" [1975], in *Issues in Feminist Film Criticism*, ed. Patricia Erens (Bloomington: Indiana University Press, 1990), 62.
83. "The Hard-Boiled Egg," unpublished screenplay, 27.
84. "The Hard-Boiled Egg," unpublished screenplay, 29.
85. Eugène Ionesco, *L'avenir est dans les oeufs* [1951], in *Théâtre complet*, ed. Emmanuel Jacquart (Paris: Gallimard [Pléiade], 1991), 38.
86. "The Hard-Boiled Egg," unpublished screenplay, 27–28.
87. Patricia A. Turner, *Ceramic Uncles and Celluloid Mammies: Black Images and Their Influence on Culture* (New York: Anchor Books, 1994), 52.
88. Lauren Berlant, *The Female Complaint: The Unfinished Business of American Sentimentality in American Culture* (Durham: Duke University Press, 2008), 125 and 128.
89. See Donald Bogle, *Primetime Blues: African Americans on Network Television* (New York: Farrar, Straus and Giroux, 2001), 94.
90. In this context, Étienne Lalou's *reportage* on racism that aired on RTF in 1961 made a powerful appeal to viewers to rethink the racist assumptions that undergirded French society. See Igor Barrère and Étienne Lalou, "Le racisme: 1ère partie," *Faire Face*, RTF (11 September 1961): https://www.ina.fr/video/CPF86614340/le-racisme-1ere-partie-video.html.
91. "The Hard-Boiled Egg," unpublished screenplay, 17.
92. Melissa Thackway notes that "African characters were either entirely absent or visually marginalized in French film productions" in *Africa Shoots Back: Alternative*

Perspectives in Sub-Saharan Francophone African Film (Bloomington: Indiana University Press, 2003), 121.

93. See Julia Kristeva, *Black Sun: Depression and Melancholia* (New York: Columbia University Press, 1989), 246 and 257; Pierre St. Amand, "The Sorrow of Lol V. Stein," trans. Jennifer Curtiss Gage, *Paragraph* 19, no. 1 (March 1996): 21–35; Sharon Willis, *Marguerite Duras: Writing on the Body* (Champaign–Urbana: University of Illinois Press, 1987), 71; Susan Rubin Suleiman, "Duras/Lacan: Not Knowing as Entanglement," in *Subversive Intent: Gender, Politics, and the Avant-Garde* (Cambridge: Harvard University Press, 1990), 110–118.

94. Duras went on to rehearse and revise the Lol / Anne-Marie Stretter narrative in increasingly experimental and elliptical ways in the novels *Le Vice-Consul* (1966) and *L'amour* (1971), in the film *La Femme du Gange* (1974), and in the play-turned-film *India Song* (1973/1975).

95. Gilles Philippe et al., eds., *Marguerite Duras: Oeuvres complètes II* (Paris: Gallimard [Pléiade], 2011), 1688.

96. Judith Schlanger, *Présence des oeuvres perdues* (Paris: Hermann, 2010), 31.

97. Duras's biographer Jean Vallier refers to this "script perdu" in his discussion of *Le Ravissement*; see Jean Vallier, *C'était Marguerite Duras, tome II, 1946–1996* (Paris: Fayard, 2010), 424.

98. This according to Marguerite Duras, "Travailler pour le cinéma," *France-Observateur* (31 July 1958); reprinted in Philippe et al., *Marguerite Duras: Oeuvres complètes II*, 114. For more on Resnais's decision to select Duras, see Philippe et al., *Marguerite Duras: Oeuvres complètes II*, 1632.

99. "J'ai été ravi de vous voir à Paris et je suis très heureux que vous vouliez bien nous permettre de tenter de monter ce qui serait, si nous parvenions à ce qu'il se réalise, le programme de télévision américaine le plus excitant qui soit" (quoted in Vallier, *C'était Marguerite Duras*, 1030–1031).

100. While I suspect that there might also have been a compelling financial incentive to write a script for Rosset, the archival records do not indicate any promise of remuneration. Additionally, it is worth noting that, with the end of the French ban after the Algerian War (1962), and with the creation of the ORTF (1964), Duras would soon have her first opportunity to write an original production for French television: *Sans merveille*, co-written with Gérard Jarlot and directed by Michel Mitrani (1964).

101. A reference to this contract, with the date, appears in a letter from Jean Rossignol to Barney Rosset, 16 January 1968, Grove Press Records, Special Collections Research Center, Syracuse University Libraries, Box 237.

102. "Le Ravissement—Script Grove Press: manuscrit," *IMEC* 76 DRS 28.16.

103. Annalisa Bertoni, "Finitude et infinitude dans la gènese du *Ravissement de Lol V. Stein*," in *Les archives de Marguerite Duras*, ed. Sylvie Loignon (Grenoble: UGA Éditions, 2012): 213–225.

104. Marguerite Duras, "Dialogues: Tatiana Moukhine—Loley Bellon," Fonds Duras, *Le Ravissement*, IMEC 76, DRS 28.15.

105. Duras's choice of names for her characters—and her particular fascination with anglophone and Jewish names such as Blair and Stein—has been a compelling topic for many Duras interviewers and scholars. While I do not have the space to develop the question of naming at length here, readers should consider Duras's remarks on names such as Stein, Steiner, and Stretter in the collection *Marguerite Duras et le cinéma: Les yeux verts* (Paris: Cahiers du Cinéma, 2014), 123; and Laurent Camerini, *La Judéité dans l'oeuvre de Marguerite Duras: un imaginaire entre éthique et poétique* (Paris: Garnier, 2016).

106. "Je trouverais de beaucoup préférable que tu me demandes un script original, écrit spécialement pour toi. . . . Lol V. Stein a ici un retentissement très grand—je m'excuse de parler comme ça, mais on doit se dire la vérité—surtout dans la couche la plus littéraire des lecteurs. Et ces gens me disent qu'il ne faut pas y toucher, qu'il faut laisser la lecture avec la lecture et faire du cinéma à côté." Letter from Marguerite Duras to Joseph Losey, cited in Vallier, *C'était Marguerite Duras*, 1044.

107. Marguerite Duras, "Projet de film avec Joseph Losey: scénario," Fonds Duras, *Le Ravissement*, IMEC 76, DRS 28.19.

108. Marguerite Duras, "Projet de film avec Joseph Losey: 3 fragments," Fonds Duras, *Le Ravissement*, IMEC 76, DRS 28.20.

109. Marguerite Duras, "Manuscrit version n. 2. Fonds Duras," *Le Ravissement*, IMEC 76, DRS 28.2.

110. Marguerite Duras, "Lol Blair: manuscrit. Fonds Duras," *Le Ravissement*, IMEC 76, DRS 28.4.

111. Vallier misses this crucial point when he posits an explanation for the cardstock dividers; see Vallier, *C'était Marguerite Duras*, 1042.

112. These can be seen in the file labeled "Projet de film avec Joseph Losey: scénario," Fonds Duras, *Le Ravissement*, IMEC 76, DRS 28.19.

113. See Jean Cléder, *Entre littérature et cinéma: les affinités électives* (Paris: Armand Colin, 2012), 128; and Maïté Snauwaert, "Le Cinéma de Lol V. Stein," *Dalhousie French Studies* 95 (Summer 2011): 73–90.

114. Marguerite Duras, *The Ravishing of Lol Stein*, trans. Richard Seaver (New York: Grove Press, 1966), 6. The English translation removed the middle initial "V" from the title.

115. See Jean Cléder, "Anatomie d'un modèle, Duras / Godard—Cinéma / Littérature: 'une question d'envers et d'endroit,' *Revue critique de fixxion française contemporaine* 7 (2013): 1–22, esp. 8 for a reference to "cinémato-graphie"; and Julie Beaulieu, *L'entrécriture de Marguerite Duras: Du texte au film en passant par la scène* (Montreal: Les Presses de l'Université de Montréal, 2018).

116. Marguerite Duras, "Original Film Script by Marguerite Duras. Working Title: *Lol Blair*," Grove Press Records, Special Collections Research Center, Syracuse University Libraries, Box 944, 31.

117. Duras, *The Ravishing*, 55. The French version of this scene of the novel reads as follows: "Tatiana Karl, à son tour, nue dans sa chevelure noire, traverse la scène de lumière, lentement. C'est peut-être dans le rectangle de vision de Lol qu'elle s'arrête. Elle

se tourne vers le fond où l'homme doit être. La fenêtre est petite et Lol ne doit voir des amants que le buste coupé à la hauteur du ventre. Ainsi ne voit-elle pas la fin de la chevelure de Tatiana." Duras, *Le Ravissement de Lol V. Stein* (Paris: Gallimard, 1964), 64.

118. Duras, "Original Film Script," 61.

119. Duras, "Original Film Script," 61.

120. Duras, "Original Film Script," 87.

121. Duras, "Original Film Script," 86.

122. Suleiman, *Subversive Intent*, 116.

123. Martin Jay, *Downcast Eyes: The Denigration of Vision in Twentieth-Century French Thought* (Berkeley: University of California Press, 1993), 526. For Jay's specific references to the *nouveau roman*, the literary movement to which Duras was somewhat reluctantly affiliated, see 436 and 463.

124. Jay, *Downcast Eyes*, 432.

125. Anne Brancky, *The Crimes of Marguerite Duras: Literature and the Media in Twentieth-Century France* (Cambridge: Cambridge University Press, 2020), 44–45.

126. Marguerite Duras, *La vie matérielle* (Paris: P.O.L., 1987), 127–130.

127. Duras, *The Ravishing*, 181. "Le soir tombait lorsque je suis arrivé à l'Hôtel des Bois. Lol nous avait précédés. Elle dormait dans le champ de seigle, fatiguée, fatiguée par notre voyage" (*Le Ravissement*, 191).

128. Duras, "Original Film Script," 139.

129. Duras, *The Ravishing*, 54. "Les yeux rivés à la fenêtre éclairée, une femme entend le vide—se nourrir, dévorer ce spectacle inexistant, invisible, la lumière d'une chambre où d'autres sont" (*Le Ravissement*, 63).

130. We find this pairing of psychoanalysis and figurative cinema in Madeleine Borgomano, *L'écriture filmique de Marguerite Duras* (Paris: Albatros, 1985); and Elisabeth Lyon, "The Cinema of Lol V. Stein," in *Feminism and Film Theory*, ed. Constance Penley (New York: Routledge, 1988), 244–273; see also Florence de Chalonge's discussion of the "regard à la fenêtre" in *Espace et récit de fiction: le cycle indien de Marguerite Duras* (Villeneuve-D'Ascq: Presses Universitaires du Septentrion, 2005), 145–170.

131. Spigel, *Make Room for TV*, 118.

132. Duras, *The Ravishing*, 39 and *Le Ravissement*, 49.

133. Marguerite Duras, "Le Cinéma de Lol V. Stein," *Art Press International* 24 (January 1979) : 5.

134. Duras, "Original Film Script," 16.

135. Duras, *La vie matérielle*, 36.

136. Schlanger, *Présence des oeuvres perdues*, 30–31.

137. Schlanger, *Présence des oeuvres perdues*, 66.

138. Schlanger, *Présence des oeuvres perdues*, 226.

Chapter 3

1. Alain Robbe-Grillet, *For a New Novel: Essays on Fiction,* trans. Richard Howard (Evanston: Northwestern University Press, 1989), 13.

2. Loren Glass, *Counterculture Colophon: Grove Press, the "Evergreen Review," and the Incorporation of the Avant-Garde* (Stanford: Stanford University Press, 2013), 47.

3. François Cusset, *French Theory: How Foucault, Deleuze, Derrida, & Co. Transformed the Intellectual Life of the United States*, trans. Jeff Fort (Minneapolis: University of Minnesota Press, 2008), 66 and 76–77.

4. Alain Robbe-Grillet and Yvone Lenard, *Le rendez-vous* (New York: Holt, Rinehart and Winston, 1981), 151.

5. Jean Ricardou, *Pour une théorie du nouveau roman* (Paris: Seuil, 1971), 212–216.

6. Anne Simonin, *Les Éditions de Minuit 1942–55: Le devoir d'insoumission* (Paris: IMEC, 2008), 453–454.

7. Robbe-Grillet, *For a New Novel*, 32.

8. Robbe-Grillet, *For a New Novel*, 136.

9. Mark McGurl, *The Program Era: Postwar Fiction and the Rise of Creative Writing* (Cambridge: Harvard University Press, 2009), ix and 281.

10. Jonathan Zimmerman, "Where the Textbook Is King: The Textbook in American Culture," in *The Enduring Book: Print Culture in Postwar America*, vol. 5 of *A History of the Book in America*, eds. David Paul Nord et al. (Chapel Hill: University of North Carolina Press, 2009), 304–324; see 306.

11. Eugene Exman, *The House of Harper: One Hundred and Fifty Years of Publishing* (New York: Harper and Row, 1967), 297; and James R. Squire and Richard T. Morgan, "The Elementary and High School Textbook Market Today," in *Textbooks and Schooling in the United States*, eds. David L. Elliott and Arthur Woodward (Chicago: National Society for the Study of Education, 1990); 107–126; see 108.

12. Beth Luey, "The Organization of the Book Publishing Industry," in *The Enduring Book: Print Culture in Postwar America*, vol. 5 of *A History of the Book in America*, eds. David Paul Nord et al. (Chapel Hill: University of North Carolina Press, 2009): 29–54; see 37–38.

13. Ursula Vils, "A Good Teacher's Anthem: All You Need Is Love," *Los Angeles Times* (14 May 1970): D1.

14. Benjamin Ebling II, "Review of *Parole et pensée*, by Yvone Lenard," *French Review* 56, no. 5 (May 1983): 966–968; see 966.

15. Exman, *The House of Harper*, 297.

16. Letter from Mark Sabin to Yvone Lenard, 1 December 1971, and letter from George E. McSpadden to Yvone Lenard, 9 September 1971, both in personal files of Yvone Lenard.

17. "A l'honneur," *Le Californien* (11 December 1970).

18. Luey, "The Organization of the Book Publishing Industry," 40.

19. Macmillan advertisement for the Modern French Literature Series, *The French Review* (December 1968 and March 1969): front matter.

20. Dell advertisement for the Laurel French Series Language Library, *The French Review* 42, no. 3 (February 1969): front matter.

21. Germaine Brée and Carlos Lynes Jr., "Introduction" to Marcel Proust, *Combray*,

eds. Germaine Brée and Carlos Lynes Jr. (New York: Appleton-Century-Crofts, 1952), viii.

22. Richard Boswell, "Review of *Mise en train: première année de français*, by Michel Benamou and Eugène Ionesco," *Modern Language Journal* 54, no. 3 (March 1970): 217.

23. For more on this pedagogical shift, see Jack C. Richards and Theodore S. Rodgers, *Approaches and Methods in Language Teaching*, 3rd ed. (New York: Cambridge University Press, 2014), 65.

24. Michel Benamou, *Pour une nouvelle pédagogie du texte littéraire* (Paris: Librairies Hachette et Larousse, 1971), 9.

25. Benamou, *Pour une nouvelle pédagogie du texte littéraire*, 10; emphasis in original.

26. Michel Benamou and Eugène Ionesco, *Mise en train: Première année de français* (New York: Macmillan, 1969), 48.

27. Benamou, "Introduction," in *Mise en Train*, vi–vii.

28. Benamou explains, "I asked Eugène Ionesco to write the dialogues for this book because I wished to attack the psychological and pedagogical problems of learning French outside France from the vantage point of the theatre" ("Introduction," in *Mise en train*, vii).

29. Eugène Ionesco, "*The Bald Soprano*: The Tragedy of Language," in *The Grove Press Reader, 1951–2001*, ed. S. E. Gonstarski, trans. Donald Watson (New York: Grove Press, 2001), 49.

30. Julia Elsky identifies earlier influences on *La cantatrice chauve*, from Ionesco's pedagogical formation in Romania to his work as a diplomat in wartime France ("Rethinking Ionesco's Absurd: *The Bald Soprano* in the Interlingual Context of Vichy and Postwar France," *PMLA* 133, no. 2 (March 2018): 347–363). Ionesco's debt to the English-language primer may nonetheless run deeper than even Elsky has recognized. While her essay largely debunks Martin Esslin's reading of Ionesco, Elsky echoes Esslin to suggest that the title *La cantatrice chauve* refers to an actor's fortuitous mistake during rehearsals (Elsky 361n10). We find in *L'anglais sans peine*, however, a bald soprano mentioned explicitly in the dialogues; see A Chérel, *L'anglais sans peine* (Paris: Assimil, 1945), 179.

31. Letter from Michel Benamou to Eugène Ionesco, 10 March 1964, Fonds Ionesco, Bibliothèque nationale de France, 4-COL-166 (170).

32. In a letter to Benamou in January 1966, the Macmillan editor Eric Schoenfeld wrote that he had "just returned from the MLA Conference in Chicago where the people to whom I mentioned your project with M. Ionesco expressed their delight and anticipation." Letter from Eric Schoenfeld to Michel Benamou, 3 January 1966, Exercices de conversation, Correspondance 1965–1968, Bibliothèque Nationale de France, Fonds Ionesco, 4-COL-166 (171).

33. See Roman Koropeckyj, "Another Ionesco Joke," *New York Times* (15 April 1994): A30. Other institutions include Harvard University (Cynthia Verba and Richard Crawford, *The Ph.D. and Your Career: A Guide for Musicologists*, Office of Career

Services of Harvard University for the American Musicological Society, 1980: cdn.ymaws.com/www.amsmusicology.org/resource/resmgr/files/resources/ams-career-guide.pdf, 28–29); University of Michigan, Ann Arbor (Benamou, "Introduction," in *Mise en train*, vi); University of Wisconsin, Milwaukee ("Memorial Resolution for Professor Michel Benamou" (14 September 1978): apps.uwm.edu/secu-policies/storage/faculty/1112.pdf); University of Victoria (*University of Victoria Calendar, 1983–84*: archive.org/details/universityofvict1983univ, 74); and Phillips Academy (*1973–74 Catalog*: archive.org/details/catalogcourseofs00phil, 243–244).

34. Language Enrollment Database, 1958–2016, *Modern Language Association*, 2020: apps.mla.org/flsurvey_search

35. Roland Barthes, "Préface," in Bruce Morrissette, *Les romans de Robbe-Grillet* (Paris: Éditions de Minuit, 1963), 7–16; quotes on 10 and 8.

36. Roland Barthes, "Littérature littérale," *Critique*, nos. 100–101 (September–October 1955): 820–826, and "Littérature objective," *Critique*, nos. 86–87 (July–August 1954): 581–591. Maurice Blanchot, "Notes sur un roman," *Nouvelle Nouvelle Revue Française* 3, no. 31 (July 1955): 105–112.

37. Alain Robbe-Grillet, *Ghosts in the Mirror*, trans. Jo Levy (New York: Grove Weidenfeld, 1988), 149. Robbe-Grillet reprised this legend on the radio decades later, transcribed and printed in his book *Préface à une vie d'écrivain* (Paris: Seuil, 2005), 179–187.

38. Letter from Barney Rosset to Renee Spodheim, 29 June 1956, Grove Press Records, Special Collections Research Center, Syracuse University Libraries, Box 600.

39. Letter from Georges Borchardt to Barney Rosset, 13 May 1957, Grove Press Records, Special Collections Research Center, Syracuse University Libraries, Box 600.

40. Barney Rosset, Guggenheim Fellowship recommendation letter, Grove Press Records, Special Collections Research Center, Syracuse University Libraries, Box 600.

41. Robbe-Grillet, *Ghosts in the Mirror*, 149–150.

42. For a helpful chronology of the New Novelists' visits to the United States, see Lison Noël, *The French New Novel: Réception du nouveau roman par le milieu artistique américain: 1963–1981* (Université de Paris Ouest Nanterre-La Défense, PhD dissertation, 2014), 322–355.

43. Letter from Alain Robbe-Grillet to Barney Rosset, 22 May 1958, Grove Press Records, Special Collections Research Center, Syracuse University Libraries, Box 594.

44. Letter from Alain Robbe-Grillet to Barney Rosset, 3 June 1978, Barney Rosset Papers, Columbia University, Rare Book and Manuscript Library, Box 40.

45. Glass, *Counter-Culture Colophon*, 12; see 37.

46. Alain Robbe-Grillet, Syllabus for Le Nouveau Nouveau Roman, NYU course G45.2731, Fonds Alain Robbe-Grillet, IMEC, dossier 22 ARG/141/2 (1971–1976).

47. Letter from Jérôme Lindon to Alain Robbe-Grillet, 22 November 1982, Fonds Robbe-Grillet, IMEC, Correspondance Lindon.

48. Alain Robbe-Grillet, "Order and Disorder in Film and Fiction," trans. Bruce Morrissette, *Critical Inquiry* 4, no. 1 (Autumn 1977): 1–20; see 3.

49. Robbe-Grillet, "Order and Disorder in Film and Fiction," 5.

50. See Robbe-Grillet, *Préface à une vie d'écrivain*, 121, and Letter to Catherine Robbe-Grillet, 14 May 1978, in Alain Robbe-Grillet and Catherine Robbe-Grillet, *Correspondance, 1951–1990*, ed. Emmanuelle Lambert (Paris: Fayard, 2012), 463.

51. Letter from Alain Robbe-Grillet to Catherine Robbe-Grillet, 9 June 1978, in Alain Robbe-Grillet and Catherine Robbe-Grillet, *Correspondance*, 485.

52. Robbe-Grillet and Lenard, *Le rendez-vous*, ix.

53. Robbe-Grillet and Lenard, *Le rendez-vous*, ix.

54. In this classic lipogram that avoids the letter "*e*" over the course of nearly 300 pages, Perec dramatizes the idea of loss conceptually and formally in the characters' search for missing people. Such was the aim of the Oulipian movement from its inception in 1960: to produce narrative innovation through an imposed set of formal constraints.

55. Robbe-Grillet and Lenard, *Le rendez-vous*, xi.

56. Emmanuelle Lambert, *Mon grand écrivain* (Paris: Les impressions nouvelles, 2009), 43.

57. Robbe-Grillet and Lenard, *Le rendez-vous*, 84.

58. Robbe-Grillet and Lenard, *Le rendez-vous*, 11.

59. Alain Robbe-Grillet, Brouillons: *Djinn*, Fonds Alain Robbe-Grillet, IMEC, dossier 22 ARG/56/21.

60. Alain Robbe-Grillet, Epreuves corrigées: *Djinn*, Fonds Alain Robbe-Grillet, IMEC, dossier 22 ARG/57/10.

61. Alain Robbe-Grillet, Galleys: *Le rendez-vous*, Fonds Alain Robbe-Grillet, IMEC, dossier 22 ARG/56/26, 112.

62. Robbe-Grillet and Lenard, *Le rendez-vous*, 83.

63. In the final page proofs to the grammar exercises at the end of chapter 4 (Épreuves corrigées: *Djinn*. Fonds Alain Robbe-Grillet, IMEC, dossier 22 ARG/57/4), for example, Robbe-Grillet changes the instructions to say "Les verbes en –re" ("–re verbs") as opposed to "–ir" (76), corrects "révolver" to "revolver" ("revolver" 77), and changes "Djinn qui announce" to "Djinn qui annonce" ("Djinn who announces" 90).

64. Yvone Lenard, Guidelines for Robbe-Grillet, Fonds Alain Robbe-Grillet, IMEC, dossier 22 ARG/57/10.

65. Alain Robbe-Grillet, Brouillons: *Djinn*, Fonds Alain Robbe-Grillet, IMEC, dossier 22 ARG/56/23. The bolded passages, my emphasis, show where Robbe-Grillet was responding to grammatical instructions. The English comes from the subsequently published American translation of *Djinn*, trans. Yvone Lenard and Walter Wells (New York: Grove Press, 1982), 70–71.

66. Phone interview with Yvone Lenard, 5 July 2016.

67. Yvone Lenard, Proposal to Robbe-Grillet, Fonds Alain Robbe-Grillet, IMEC, dossier 22 ARG/57/9.

68. Robbe-Grillet and Lenard, *Le rendez-vous*, 83.

69. Alain Robbe-Grillet, *Djinn: Un trou rouge entre les pavés disjoints* (Paris: Éditions de Minuit, 2013 [1981]), 8. In addition to personal notes, Bishop sent Robbe-

Grillet annual letters on stationery from NYU Paris, inviting him to the lunches of the Association New York University en France (Tom Bishop, Correspondance: 1980–89, Fonds Alain Robbe-Grillet, IMEC, dossier 22 ARG/141/4).

70. Robbe-Grillet and Lenard, *Le rendez-vous*, 56, 92–93, 134–135, 138.

71. Robbe-Grillet and Lenard, *Le rendez-vous*, 134.

72. Robbe-Grillet and Lenard, *Djinn*, 107.

73. Robbe-Grillet and Lenard, *Le rendez-vous*, 135.

74. Robbe-Grillet and Lenard, *Djinn*, 109.

75. Robbe-Grillet, *Djinn*, 10.

76. See letter from Alain Robbe-Grillet to Catherine Robbe-Grillet, 1979, in Alain Robbe-Grillet and Catherine Robbe-Grillet, *Correspondance*, 502, and letter from Georges Borchardt to Barney Rosset, 13 May 1957, Grove Press Records, Special Collections Research Center, Syracuse University Libraries, Box 600.

77. See scholarship on *Djinn* such as Mariette Ball, "The Language Game in *Djinn*," *Romance Studies* 2 (Summer 1983): 1–17; Abbes Maazaoui, "Représentation et altérité dans les romans de Robbe-Grillet," *The French Review* 68, no. 3 (February 1995): 477–486; Ben Stolzfus, "Robbe-Grillet's *Djinn*: The Grammar of Subversion," *Degree Second: Studies in French Literature* 8 (July 1984): 19–26; and Anna Whiteside, "Believe It or Not: On Reading the Fantastic and Robbe-Grillet's *Djinn*," *L'Esprit Créateur* 28, no. 3 (Fall 1988): 79–87.

78. Alain Robbe-Grillet, Brouillons: *Djinn*, Fonds Alain Robbe-Grillet, IMEC, dossier 22 ARG/56/20.

79. See Michel Grodent, "Alain Robbe-Grillet: 'Pour écrire *Djinn*, j'ai songé à Jane Birkin,'" *Le soir Bruxelles* (4 April 1981), Livres-Arts-Culture and Francis Matthys, "Rencontré Alain Robbe-Grillet," *La Libre Belgique* (9 April 1981).

80. Jeanyves Guérin, "Review of *Djinn*, by Alain Robbe-Grillet," *Esprit: nouvelle série* 55–56, nos. 7–8 (July–August 1981): 125–126.

81. Jacqueline Piatier, "Robbe-Grillet ensorcelle la grammaire," *Le monde des livres* (20 March 1981): 15; Jean-François Josselin, "Rendez-vous au manège," *Le nouvel observateur*, no. 856 (6–12 April 1981): 70–71; and Jean-Jacques Brochier, "La Chronique du Capricorne: Oedipe à Cologne," *Magazine littéraire*, no. 171 (April 1981): 53.

82. Guérin, "Review of *Djinn*," 126.

83. Anne Pons, "Robbe-Grillet: Le troisième clone," *Le Point* (25 May 1981): 149.

84. See, respectively, Jean-François Vilar, "Review of *Djinn*, by Alain Robbe-Grillet," *Rouge*, no. 976 (3–9 July 1981): 21; G. D., "Alain Robbe-Grillet recidive . . . ," *Canalmanach* (March 1981); and Michel Nuridsany, "Robbe-Grillet: Humour et science-fiction," *Le Figaro* (6 March 1981).

85. Quoted in Grodent, "Alain Robbe-Grillet: 'Pour écrire *Djinn*.'"

86. Mireille Calle-Gruber, "Survivre à sa mode: Entretien avec Robbe-Grillet," *Micromégas* 7, no. 1 (1981): 7–15.

87. Susan Rubin Suleiman, *Subversive Intent: Gender, Politics, and the Avant-Garde* (Cambridge: Harvard University Press, 1990), 42; emphasis in the original.

88. Roland Barthes, *Le plaisir du texte* (Paris: Seuil, 1973), 35, 44.

89. Roland Barthes, *S/Z* (Paris: Seuil, 1970), 10.

90. Letter from Barney Rosset to Yvone Lenard, 19 May 1981, Grove Press Records, Special Collections Research Center, Syracuse University Libraries, Box 599.

91. Letter from Barney Rosset to Yvone Lenard, 13 August 1981, Grove Press Records, Special Collections Research Center, Syracuse University Libraries, Box 599.

92. "Le Palmarès: Les meilleurs livres des dix dernières années," *Le monde des livres* (21 March 1986).

93. In a series of interviews conducted while writing *La reprise*, Robbe-Grillet explains the Kierkegaardian origin of the title and describes the novel as a reprisal of *Les gommes*; see Alain Robbe-Grillet, *Entretiens complices*, ed. Roger-Michel Allemand (Paris: EHESS, 2018), 159–162.

94. Robbe-Grillet, *For a New Novel*, 13.

95. Rachel Sagner Buurma and Laura Heffernan, *The Teaching Archive: A New History for Literary Study* (Chicago: University of Chicago Press, 2021), 5.

96. Mark McGurl has described creative writing programs as on their way to becoming a "global Anglophone phenomenon" (*The Program Era*, 364) but limits his discussion exclusively to English-language departments. The number of francophone writers, past and present, who held short- and long-term professorial appointments on American college campuses is too vast to cite exhaustively but includes the following: Michel Butor at Bryn Mawr and Middlebury Colleges (1960) and at the University of Buffalo (1962); Assia Djebar at NYU (from 2001–2015); Louis-Philippe Dalembert at the University of Wisconsin, Milwaukee (2013); Alain Mabanckou at the University of Michigan (2002–2005) and UCLA (2006–present); and Abdourahman A. Waberi (2014–present).

97. Michel Butor, *Mobile: études pour une représentation des États-Unis* (Paris: Gallimard, 1962); Louis-Philippe Dalembert, *Milwaukee Blues* (Paris: Sabine Wespeiser, 2021); Maylis de Kerangal, *Canoës* (Paris: Gallimard, 2023) and *Je marche sous un ciel de traîne* (Paris: Verticales, 2000); and Abdourahman A. Waberi, *Dis-moi pour qui j'existe?* (Paris: JC Lattès, 2022). Maylis de Kerangal discusses her experience of coming to writing while living on a Colorado campus in the podcast *L'Amérique des écrivains français*, episode 3: "Écrire à l'américaine," *France Culture* (4 November 2020).

98. Raylene Ramsay reflects the perspective of many who claimed that the *nouveau roman* had become "no longer novel or subversive" by the time that Robbe-Grillet embarked on his autobiographical trilogy; see Ramsay's article, "Writing on the Ruins in *Les Derniers Jours de Corinthe*: From Reassemblage to Reassessment in Robbe-Grillet," *French Review* 70, no. 2 (December 1996): 231–244, esp. 241. On the flip side, when Tom Bishop organized a colloquium on the French New Novel at NYU in 1982, he declared it in his opening remarks still "alive and kicking"; see Tom Bishop, "Opening Remarks," in *Three Decades of the French New Novel*, ed. Lois Oppenheim (Urbana: University of Illinois Press, 1986), 18.

Chapter 4

1. Perec poses this question to Mme Rabinovici in the second half of his film *Récits d'Ellis Island*, the only interview in the film that takes place in French: "Mais vous pensez que vous auriez mieux réussi aux États-Unis, à New York, qu'en Roumanie ou en France?" Robert Bober and Georges Perec, *Récits d'Ellis Island [1978–1980]*, DVD video (France: INA, 2007), 113 minutes; quote in "Deuxième Partie: *Mémoires*," minute 58:05.

2. Perec drafted his French novel *53 Jours* (*53 Days*) in 1981 as a writer-in-residence at the University of Queensland in Brisbane, Australia. The novel was unfinished and published posthumously in 1989. This quote, part of Perec's marginalia, was written in English. See Harry Mathews Papers, University of Pennsylvania, Kislak Center for Special Collections, Rare Books and Manuscripts, Box 15, Folder 15.

3. Georges Perec, *Espèces d'espaces* (Paris: Seuil, 2022 [Galilée, 1974]), 76.

4. See David Bellos, *Georges Perec: A Life in Words* (London: Harvill, 1994), 569.

5. Bellos roots this aspiration towards global recognition in the earliest phases of Perec's career, before he had even published a novel, and traces it through to his later works. See Bellos, *Georges Perec*, 162 and 610.

6. Grove released the English translation as *Les Choses: A Story of the Sixties*, trans. Helen Lane (New York: Grove Press, 1968); it was later retranslated by David Bellos and Andrew Leak as *Things* (Boston: David R. Godine, 1990). For sales figures, see Jean-Jacques Thomas, *Perec en Amérique: la traversée identitaire* (Brussels: Les Impressions Nouvelles, 2019), 104. The first edition of *Life A User's Manual* appeared with Collins Harvill in London and David Godine in Boston, both in 1987, translated by David Bellos. Knopf had considered publishing *Life: A User's Manual* in the late 1970s and had the translator Richard Howard consider it before turning down the book. See Bellos, *Georges Perec*, 646.

7. On this selection of a name, see Hervé Le Tellier, *Esthétique de l'Oulipo* (Montreuil: Le Castor Astral, 2006), 22.

8. Both of these original quotations in French—"Il s'agit d'ouvrir de nouvelles possibilités inconnues des anciens auteurs" (Le Lionnais) and "une oeuvre potentielle est une oeuvre qui ne se limite pas à ses apparences, qui contient des richesses secrètes, qui se prête volontiers à l'exploration" (Bens)—can be found in Jacques Bens, "Queneau Oulipian," *Atlas de littérature potentielle* (Paris: Gallimard, 1981), 22–23; translation in Warren Motte, ed. and trans., *Oulipo: A Primer of Potential Literature* (Normal: Dalkey Archive Press, 2015), 65.

9. Agamben's discussion of potentiality as ethical can be found in Giorgio Agamben, *The Coming Community*, trans. Michael Hardt (Minneapolis: University of Minnesota Press, 1993), 43.

10. See most notably the *Modern Language Notes* special issue dedicated to this topic: Camille Bloomfield and Derek Schilling, eds., "Translating Constrained Literature / Traduire la littérature à contraintes," *MLN* 131, no. 4 (September 2016).

11. Georges Perec and Kaye Morley, "The Doing of Fiction," Extracts from an interview in August 1981, *Review of Contemporary Fiction* 29, no. 1 (Spring 2009): 101.

12. "Toute traduction d'une œuvre oulipienne est un exploit et une œuvre oulipienne en soi," in Le Tellier, *Esthétique de l'Oulipo*, 247. While the vast scholarship on the imbalances between originality and translation is too extensive to cite in full, Karen Emmerich's *Literary Translations and the Making of Originals* (New York: Bloomsbury, 2017) provides an excellent overview and analysis of the literary, ethical, and political stakes of these too-often opposed categories.

13. Calvin Bedient, "Against Conceptualism: Defending the Poetry of Affect," *Boston Review* (24 July 2013): https://www.bostonreview.net/articles/against-conceptualism/.

14. "Geneviève m'a suggéré de vous proposer de collaborer à la traduction de votre dernier livre et je serais heureux de le faire. (À vrai dire, je manipule très mal l'anglais mais je suppose que ma collaboration viendrait après un premier débroussaillage.)" Letter from Georges Perec to Harry Mathews, undated, in Harry Mathews Papers, University of Pennsylvania, Kislak Center for Special Collections, Rare Books and Manuscripts, Box 37, Folder 5.

15. Mathews admits to this lie in his autobiographical text *The Orchard: A Remembrance of Georges Perec* (Flint: Bamberger Press, 1988), 13.

16. From Harry Mathews's "Autobiography" in *The Way Home*, cited in Bellos, *Georges Perec: A Life in Words*, 448.

17. Perec's translations of Mathews's novels include *Les verts champs de moutarde de l'Afghanistan* (*Tlooth*]) (Paris: Les Lettres Nouvelles Denoël, 1975) and *Le naufrage du stade Odradek* (Paris: Hachette, 1981). Perec's archives at the Bibliothèque de l'Arsenal in Paris also include handwritten drafts and typed final versions of his French translations of Mathews's short story "The Bratislava Spiccato" ("Spiccato de Bratislava") and several poems (dated 1974), most of which remain unpublished in French; these include Mathews's poems, "The Scruple Shop" ("La boutique à scrupules"), "The Battle" ("La Bataille"), "The Swimmer" ("Le nageur"), "Poems After Robert Reignier" ("Poèmes à la Manière de Robert Reignier"), and "Deathless, Lifeless" ("Sans mort, sans vie"), in Fonds Perec, Cote 30: Harry Mathews, Bibliothèque de l'Arsenal, Paris, France. Meanwhile, Mathews's translations of Perec include chapters 27 ("Rorschash") and 74 ("Lift Machinery") in *Life: A User's Manual*, trans. David Bellos (Boston: David Godine, 1987); three of Perec's "Epithalames" originally published in French in *La Bibliothèque oulipienne* 19 (1982): "Sentimental Tales 1 & 2"; "Histoires de Coeur 1"; and "Histoires de Coeur 2" (in *New Observations*: No. 99 Oulipo/Oupeinpo, eds. Harry Mathews and Lynn Crawford [New York: 1994]); "Still Life/Style Leaf," *Yale French Studies* 61 (1981): 299–305; and *Ellis Island* (New York: New Press, 1995).

18. Letter from Georges Perec to Harry Mathews, 14 November 1970, in Harry Mathews Papers, University of Pennsylvania, Kislak Center for Special Collections, Rare Books and Manuscripts, Box 37, Folder 5.

19. Daniel Levin Becker, *Many Subtle Channels: In Praise of Potential Literature* (Cambridge: Harvard University Press, 2012), 247.

20. "Que diras-tu de traduire 'tractors' par 'traiteurs' ('les authentiques traiteurs métalliques . . .'). Je trouve que ça fait très drôle et il n'y a qu'un c à changer." Letter

from Georges Perec to Harry Mathews, 14 March 1972, in Harry Mathews Papers, University of Pennsylvania, Kislak Center for Special Collections, Rare Books and Manuscripts, Box 37, Folder 5. Of course, Perec is not totally precise about this: "tractors" would also require changing the "eu" into "o," but the spelling change in English would have no effect on the pronunciation of the vowels (while the consonant change, from "t" to "c," would).

21. Here's Perec's thought process more fully: "J'essaie de traduire 'fur bowls.' Pour dire 'Quatre balles,' une russe, même hommasse, ne saurait dire 'quartz bol' ni 'Bol de quartz' mais plus vraisemblablement 'Cat Ballou' (plus médiocre, et allusion peu perceptible) ou 'Bal des quat'za(rts),' qui me semble pas trop mauvais." ("I'm trying to translate 'fur bowls.' To say 'four balls,' a Russian woman, even mannish, wouldn't say 'quartz bol' or 'bol de quartz,' but more likely 'Cat Ballou' [it's not great, and the allusion isn't obvious], or 'Bal des quat'za(rts),' which strikes me as not bad.") Letter from Georges Perec to Harry Mathews, 4 January 1971, in Harry Mathews Papers, University of Pennsylvania, Kislak Center for Special Collections, Rare Books and Manuscripts, Box 37, Folder 5.

22. Harry Mathews, *Les Verts Champs de moutarde de l'Afghanistan*, trans. Georges Perec (Paris: P.O.L., 1998 [Denoël, 1974]), 9.

23. It would be fair to note, too, how in this particular instance their homosocial bonding relied on deriding a Russian woman's gender expression and accent. "Hommasse" (the French equivalent for "mannish" from Mathews's novel and evoked in Perec's letter) is a word used pejoratively, as the Académie française dictionary reminds us, "only for a woman who has something coarse and ill-mannered in her appearance, size, or behavior, and who has nothing of the delicateness of her sex" ("Il ne se dit que d'une femme qui a quelque chose de grossier dans son air, dans sa taille, dans ses manières, & qui n'a rien de la délicatesse de son sexe"). *Dictionnaire de l'Académie française*: https://www.dictionnaire-academie.fr/article/A1H0121-03.

24. These letters are dated, respectively, 30 September 1974, 18 September 1974, and 1 December 1975, all in Harry Mathews Papers, University of Pennsylvania, Kislak Center for Special Collections, Rare Books and Manuscripts, Box 37, Folder 5.

25. Letter from Georges Perec to Harry Mathews, 22 August 1980, in Harry Mathews Papers, University of Pennsylvania, Kislak Center for Special Collections, Rare Books and Manuscripts, Box 37, Folder 5.

26. Thomas, *Perec en Amérique*, 132–133.

27. Letter from Georges Perec to Harry Mathews, undated (1979), in Harry Mathews Papers, University of Pennsylvania, Kislak Center for Special Collections, Rare Books and Manuscripts, Box 37, Folder 5.

28. For more on Perec's English skills, see Bellos, *Georges Perec*, 104, 107–111, 131, and 195. Perec, according to Bellos, "did not like making mistakes in English" (692).

29. Paulette Perec, ed., *Portrait(s) de Georges Perec* (Paris: Bibliothèque nationale de France, 2001), 31.

30. "J'ai fait pratiquement tout seul, promis juré, sans dictionnaire et en 2 heures!

En suis astonishé. Depuis trouvé des dizaines de mots dans le Webster. Je te remercie, Harry, de m'avoir fait faire de tels progrès en anglais." Letter from Georges Perec to Harry Mathews, 21 September 1981, in Harry Mathews Papers, University of Pennsylvania, Kislak Center for Special Collections, Rare Books and Manuscripts, Box 37, Folder 5.

31. Letter from Georges Perec to Harry Mathews, 31 March 1980, in Harry Mathews Papers, University of Pennsylvania, Kislak Center for Special Collections, Rare Books and Manuscripts, Box 37, Folder 5.

32. Giorgio Agamben, *Potentialities: Collected Essays in Philosophy*, ed. and trans. Daniel Heller-Roazen (Stanford: Stanford University Press, 1999), 182; emphasis in original.

33. The first quote comes from Agamben's *Potentialities*, 182, and the second from *The Coming Community*, 43.

34. Agamben, *Potentialities*, 260.

35. Agamben, *Potentialities*, 268.

36. Agamben, *Potentialities*, 250.

37. Agamben, *The Coming Community*, 43.

38. Agamben, *Potentialities*, 253.

39. "Potentiel, potentielle," in *Dictionnaire de l'Académie française*: https://www.dictionnaire-academie.fr/article/A9P3676?history=0. The adjective refers generally in French to the idea of being "likely to exist" ("susceptible d'exister") and defined here in its linguistic capacity ("sans être attestés, sont considérés comme réalisables selon les règles grammaticales d'une langue donnée").

40. Chris Andrews has recently turned to Agamben's work in his discussion of potentiality but sees it as exclusively tied to the idea of literary constraint. See Chris Andrews, *How to Do Things with Forms: The Oulipo and Its Inventions* (Montreal and Kingston: McGill-Queen's University Press, 2022), particularly 221–224.

41. Perec had great admiration for "*Bartleby, the Scrivener*," even going so far as to express a wish to "rewrite" Melville's short story, as if it had been his own; see Perec's remarks, quoted in Patrick Fortin-Tillard, "L'effet Bartleby: répétitions et nouveautés dans *Un homme qui dort* de Georges Perec," *Études littéraires* 42, no. 2 (Summer 2011): 181–193; quote on 185.

42. See Jascha Hoffman, "An Approximate Timeline of Twisted Translations," *The Believer* 57 (October 2008): https://www.thebeliever.net/a-timeline-of-twisted-translations/.

43. Bellos, *Georges Perec*, 611.

44. Bellos, *Georges Perec*, esp. 381–384.

45. On the notion that translation could help in moments of writer's block, see Bellos, *Georges Perec*, 465. In an unpublished paper in his files, Mathews writes about how Perec worked on the translation of *Tlooth* when he was "going through a dry period" in his writing. In Untitled, Typed manuscript, Harry Mathews Papers, University of Pennsylvania, Kislak Center for Special Collections, Rare Books and Manuscripts, Box 11, Folder 3.

46. Alison James makes this point well through a comparison of different English translations of *La disparition*; see her article, "The Maltese and the Mustard Fields: Oulipian Translation," *SubStance* 37, no. 1 (2008): 134–147.

47. Le Tellier, *Esthétique de l'Oulipo*, 247.

48. Becker, *Many Subtle Channels*, 91.

49. Alison James, "Interlingual Oulipo," in "Translating Constrained Literature / Traduire la littérature à contraintes," *MLN* 131, no. 4 (September 2016): 964–976.

50. Rachel Galvin, "Form Has Its Reasons: Translation and 'Copia'" in "Translating Constrained Literature / Traduire la littérature à contraintes," *MLN* 131, no. 4 (September 2016): 855.

51. Harry Mathews, "Translation and the Oulipo: The Case of the Persevering Maltese" [1997], in *The Case of the Persevering Maltese: Collected Essays* (Normal: Dalkey Archive Press, 2003), 77–78.

52. Agamben, *Potentialities*, 269.

53. Gayatri Spivak, "The Politics of Translation," in *Outside in the Teaching Machine* (New York: Routledge, 1993), 179–200.

54. Bedient, "Against Conceptualism."

55. Rachel Galvin, "Lyric Backlash," *Boston Review* (11 February 2014): https://www.bostonreview.net/articles/rachel-galvin-lyric-backlash/, and Alison James, "Oulipian Feelings: On the Emotional Effects of Constraints," *Contemporary French and Francophone Studies* 25, no. 5 (2021): 557–565.

56. The typed, one-page obituary in Harry Mathews's papers has a scrawled note at the top of the page: "Obit written f NYT, not published." Harry Mathews Papers, University of Pennsylvania, Kislak Center for Special Collections, Rare Books and Manuscripts, Box 11, Folder 3.

57. Harry Mathews, "Mon ami," *Le Monde* (27 July 1984): 14.

58. Harry Mathews, "About Georges Perec" folder, in Harry Mathews Papers, University of Pennsylvania, Kislak Center for Special Collections, Rare Books and Manuscripts, Box 11, Folder 3.

59. "Avec Georges, l'amitié ne pouvait être que passionnelle, et si dans notre cas la question d'une relation physique ne s'est jamais posée, j'en viens parfois à le regretter." Harry Mathews, "Mon ami," *Le Monde* (27 July 1984): 14.

60. Mathews returns to this idea in his book-length tribute to Perec, *The Orchard*, 16. Across the book, Mathews recalls his friend in intimate terms, in many cases connected to language and translation: "I remember that GP loved *Peanuts* and that he had learned from it most of the English he knew when he began translating *Tlooth*" (21), or "I remember Georges Perec's enthusiasm when I did good work writing in French and his gentle suggestions to abandon work that was of doubtful quality" (9).

61. "L'essentiel pour moi dans la collaboration de Georges ne fut point tant son génie de traducteur ni son désintéressement (il traduisit un de mes romans sans aucune garantie de publication) que le fait qu'il acceptât de traduire des livres sans les avoir lus auparavant, uniquement parce que j'en étais l'auteur" ("The essential part for me in Georges's collaboration wasn't so much his genius as a translator or his dis-

interest [he translated one of my novels without any promise of publication] but the fact that he accepted to translate my books without having read them before, simply because I was the author"). Mathews, "Mon ami."

62. See, for example, Bellos, *Georges Perec*, 391, 445, 511, and 641.

63. Bellos, *Georges Perec*, 616.

64. The English translation maintains the poetic style of the French original, even as it breaks verses differently: "ce que moi, Georges Perec, je suis venu / questionner ici, c'est l'errance, la dispersion, / la diaspora. / Ellis Island est pour moi le lieu même de / l'exil, / c'est-à-dire / le lieu de l'absence de lieu, le non-lieu, le / nulle part." See Georges Perec, *Ellis Island* (Paris: P.O.L., 2019), 60, and Georges Perec, *Ellis Island*, trans. Harry Mathews (New York: New Directions, 2021), 43.

65. *Récits d'Ellis Island*, DVD video. The quote in the above paragraph can be found at 40:43 in "Première Partie: Traces."

66. *Récits d'Ellis Island*, "Première Partie: Traces," minute 0:36 to 1:30.

67. *Récits d'Ellis Island*, "Deuxième Partie: Mémoires," minute 58:13 to 58:26.

68. Georges Perec and Robert Bober, *Récits d'Ellis Island* (Paris: Éditions du Sorbier, 1980).

69. Georges Perec avec Robert Bober, *Récits d'Ellis Island: histoires d'errance et d'espoir* (Paris: P.O.L., 1995).

70. Georges Perec, *Oeuvres: tome II*, eds. Christelle Reggiani et al. (Paris: Bibliothèque de la Pléiade, 2017).

71. Georges Perec and Robert Bober, *Ellis Island*, trans. Harry Mathews and Jessica Blatt (New York: New Press, 1995). Georges Perec, *Ellis Island*, trans. Harry Mathews with an afterword by Mónica de la Torre (New York: New Directions, 2021).

72. Joe L. Kincheloe, *Knowledge and Critical Pedagogy: An Introduction* (Dordrecht: Springer, 2008), 230.

73. As scholars of critical pedagogy have defined it, "radical listening involves consciously valuing others by attempting to hear what the speaker is saying for the meaning he or she intends, rather than the meaning the listener interprets through his/her own view of the world." See Melissa Winchell, Tricia M. Kress, and Ken Tobin, "Teaching/Learning Radical Listening: Joe's Legacy Among Three Generations of Practitioners," in *Practicing Critical Pedagogy*, eds. Mary Frances Agnello and William Martin Reynolds (Cham: Springer, 2016), 101.

74. Georges Perec, Cahiers, Cote 42: Oeuvres: Récits d'Ellis Island, Fonds Perec, Bibliothèque de l'Arsenal, Paris, France; emphasis added.

75. While the secondary literature on *Récits d'Ellis Island* has not been as extensive as other works by Perec, some notable exceptions include Peter Wagstaff, "The Dark Side of Utopia: Word, Image, and Memory in Georges Perec's *Récits d'Ellis Island: histoires d'errance et d'espoir*," in *The Seeing Century: Film, Vision, and Identity*, ed. Wendy Everett (Amsterdam: Rodopi, 2000), 36–48; Amanda Crawley Jackson, "Islands, Camps, Zones: Towards a Nissological reading of Perec," in *Georges Perec's Geographies: Material, Performative and Textual Spaces*, eds. Charles Forsdick, Andrew

Leak, and Richard Phillips (London: UCL Press, 2019), 95–110; *"Récits d'Ellis Island": de Georges Perec et Robert Bober au miroir contemporain*, ed. Julien Roumette (Paris: Lettres modernes Minard, 2019); and Alison James, *Constraining Chance: Georges Perec and the Oulipo* (Evanston: Northwestern University Press, 2009), 64–65.

76. Perec, *Ellis Island*, 29. "Comment saisir ce qui n'est pas montré, ce qui n'a pas été photographié, archivé, restauré, mis en scène?" (43). Unless noted otherwise, page numbers correspond to the 2021 New Directions edition in English and the 2019 P.O.L edition in French.

77. Perec, *Ellis Island*, 42. "Ce lieu fait pour nous partie d'une mémoire potentielle, d'une autobiographie probable, nos parents ou nos grands-parents auraient pu s'y trouver" (59).

78. Perec's most direct literary work about his absent parents can be found in *W or the Memory of Childhood*, a hybrid autobiographical text that interweaves personal memories and fictional narratives. The book's dedication, "À E"—literally to the letter "E," whose pronunciation in French is identical to "eux," the word for "them"—makes plain the project of *La disparition*, where the missing letter "e" (a linguistic substitute for "them," his parents) signals a broader engagement with tropes of disappearance and loss.

79. Georges Perec, Cahiers, Cote 42: Oeuvres: Récits d'Ellis Island, Fonds Perec, Bibliothèque de l'Arsenal, Paris, France.

80. Georges Perec, Cahiers, Cote 42: Oeuvres: Récits d'Ellis Island, Fonds Perec, Bibliothèque de l'Arsenal, Paris, France, 52, 2, 23.

81. Georges Perec, Cahiers, Cote 42: Oeuvres: Récits d'Ellis Island, Fonds Perec, Bibliothèque de l'Arsenal, Paris, France, 52, 2, 10.

82. Harry Mathews, "Georges Perec," NYU lecture (25 October 1983), Harry Mathews Papers, University of Pennsylvania, Kislak Center for Special Collections, Rare Books and Manuscripts, Box 11, Folder 3.

83. Hervé Le Tellier, *The Anomaly*, trans. Adriana Hunter (New York: Other Press, 2021), 21. In French: "qui donnent à la littérature un statut d'art mineur pour des mineurs. Sa profession lui a ouvert les portes d'éditeurs réputés, sinon puissants, sans que ses propres manuscrits d'auteur en franchissent pour autant le seuil" (Hervé Le Tellier, *L'anomalie* [Paris: Gallimard, 2020], 26).

84. Roger Cohen, "The Novel That Riveted France During Lockdown Arrives in the U.S.," *New York Times* (21 November 2021): https://www.nytimes.com/2021/11/23/books/anomaly-herve-le-tellier.html.

85. Interview in Cohen, "The Novel That Riveted France."

86. Le Tellier, *The Anomaly*, 319; *L'anomalie*, 269.

87. Andreas Huyssen, *After the Great Divide: Modernism, Mass Culture, Postmodernism* (Bloomington: Indiana University Press, 1986), in particular chs. 2 and 10.

88. Cited in Cohen, "The Novel That Riveted France."

89. Le Tellier, *The Anomaly*, 200; Le Tellier, *L'anomalie*, 171.

90. Georges Perec wrote "Ulcérations" at the end of 1973 and distributed copies to

friends at a New Year's Eve gathering. Each of the 400 verses, including the title, has the same 11 letters, in different orders, and the constraint required Perec to reuse each letter once before moving on to the next verse. Miraculously, the sequence of letters succeeds in creating a legible poem, with many references to "art/artist," the light of the moon ("la lune"), and darkness ("le noir"). See Georges Perec, *Ulcérations* (Paris: Bibliothèque oulipienne, 1974). *L'anomalie* closes with the words "Ulcérations / et / sable / fin" typographically displayed as a disintegrating poem, ostensibly to reflect the characters' disappearance into the void, as another duplicate plane is found and destroyed.

91. See the Albertine Bookstore website: https://www.albertine.com/about-us/.

Conclusion

1. The three-day conference, titled "Stars and Strife: Writing America in Recent French and Francophone Literature," was held on October 24–26, 2017. It featured five keynote speakers that included writers and academics (Salim Bachi, Antoine Bello, Felicia McCarren, Jean-Marc Moura, and Abdourahman Waberi), and the program offered a couple dozen talks from scholars, including myself, based in the U.S., Europe, Canada, and North Africa. For more on the CFP and conference program, see https://winthropking.fsu.edu/event/stars-and-strife-conference.

2. Some examples include Frédéric Beigbeder's *Oona & Salinger* (2014) (*Manhattan's Babe*, 2016), Caroline de Mulder's *Bye-Bye Elvis* (2014), Jean Rolin's *Le ravissement de Britney Spears* (2011), Simon Liberati's *Jayne Mansfield 1967* (2011), Lakdar Belaïd's *World Trade Cimeterre* (2011), Kettly Mars and Leslie Péan's *Le Prince noir de Lillian Russell* (2011), and Hubert Catherine Mavrikakis's *Les derniers jours de Smokey Nelson* (2011).

3. Joël Dicker, *La Vérité sur l'Affaire Harry Quebert* (Geneva: Éditions Rosie & Wolfe, 2012); *The Truth About the Harry Quebert Affair*, trans. Sam Taylor (New York: Penguin, 2014).

4. Minh Tran Huy, *Les écrivains et le fait divers: Une autre histoire de la littérature* (Paris: Flammarion, 2017).

5. Roland Barthes, "Structures du fait divers," in *Essais critiques* (Paris: Seuil, 1964): 188–197.

6. Dicker, *La Vérité sur l'Affaire Harry Quebert*, 549. The English translation is mine; the published English version translated by Sam Taylor— "The biggest story was the incident with the young girl in Somerset," 393—besides changing the name of the New Hampshire town, does not accurately reflect the tone of the original.

7. Dicker, *The Truth About the Harry Quebert Affair*, 15.

8. Dicker, *La Vérité sur l'Affaire Harry Quebert*, 13.

9. For a selection of examples, see Dicker, *La Vérité sur l'Affaire Harry Quebert*, 14, 170, 469, 510, 555, 673, 706.

10. See Dicker, *La Vérité sur l'Affaire Harry Quebert*, 136 and 744.

11. Dicker, *La Vérité sur l'Affaire Harry Quebert*. 214. The English version substi-

tutes "the world" for "America"—"a book is probably the only way to prove to the world that Harry is not a monster" (153)—a translation choice that both deemphasizes the book's broad insistence on the U.S. and implicitly reinforces the idea that being read in the U.S. is akin to global success.

12. "Si on est les premiers à sortir un livre, Nola Kellergan pourrait devenir la marque déposée de Schmid & Hanson" (*La Vérité sur l'Affaire Harry Quebert*, 448); the English translation notably removes the name of the fictional publishing house: "if they are the first ones to bring out a book on this, Nola Kellergan could become a registered trademark for them" (*The Truth About the Harry Quebert Affair*, 322).

13. Gisèle Sapiro, "French Literature in the World System of Translation," in *French Global: A New Approach to Literary History*, eds. Christie McDonald and Susan Rubin Suleiman (New York: Columbia University Press, 2010), 311–313.

14. Leïla Slimani, *Chanson douce* (Paris: Gallimard, 2012); *The Perfect Nanny*, trans. Sam Taylor (New York: Penguin, 2018).

15. Dan Sinykin, *Big Fiction: How Conglomeration Changed the Publishing Industry and American Literature* (New York: Columbia University Press, 2010), 10. Restricting his study to U.S. literature only (in the case of literary genre fiction, books by such authors as Cormac McCarthy, Joan Didion, Toni Morrison, and E. L. Doctorow), is what Sinykin calls the "largest lacuna" in his book (13).

16. My review of the English translation of Slimani's novel originally appeared in the *Los Angeles Review of Books* on February 2, 2018.

17. Slimani, *The Perfect Nanny*, 2, and *Chanson douce*, 14. See Wendy Ruderman and Marc Santora, "Two Siblings Killed in New York; Nanny Arrested," *New York Times* (25 October 2012): https://www.nytimes.com/2012/10/26/nyregion/fatal-stabbings-on-upper-west-side-nanny-is-arrested.html.

18. Michael Daly, "Killer Nanny Case: What the Krims Didn't Know About Yoselyn Ortega," *The Daily Beast* (26 June 2013): https://www.thedailybeast.com/killer-nanny-case-what-the-krims-didnt-know-about-yoselyn-ortega.

19. Slimani, *The Perfect Nanny*, 214.

20. Slimani, *Chanson douce*, 213.

21. Slimani, *The Perfect Nanny*, 213.

22. Slimani, *The Perfect Nanny*, 227. Photographs of the flowers and drawings outside the New York apartment building widely circulated online in the wake of the murders; see, for example, the photo and caption accompanying this *New York Times* article: https://www.nytimes.com/2012/10/27/nyregion/2-children-slain-at-home-in-city-nanny-arrested.html.

23. References to these photographic images can be found in *Chanson douce* and *The Perfect Nanny* (214–215 in both editions). The New York family's personal blog, accessed in 2018, is no longer available online.

24. Olivia Harrison and Teresa Villa-Ignacio, "Introduction: Translating the Maghreb," *Expressions maghrébines* 15, no. 1 (Summer 2016): 3.

25. This despite several of his crime novels translated into English, including *The*

Absolute Perfection of Crime (2003) and *Beyond Suspicion* (2009), both translated by Linda Coverdale and published by the New Press.

26. Tanguy Viel, *La disparition de Jim Sullivan* (Paris: Éditions de Minuit, 2013), 10; *The Disappearance of Jim Sullivan*, trans. Clayton McKee (Dallas: Deep Vellum/Dalkey Archive Press, 2021), 4.

27. Viel, *The Disappearance of Jim Sullivan*, 4.

28. Viel, *La disparition de Jim Sullivan*, 10.

29. Viel, *The Disappearance of Jim Sullivan*, 12–13; *La disparition de Jim Sullivan*, 18.

30. Viel, *The Disappearance of Jim Sullivan*, 13; *La disparition de Jim Sullivan*, 19.

31. Catherine Cusset, *L'autre qu'on adorait* (Paris: Gallimard, 2016) and *Le problème avec Jane* (Paris: Gallimard, 1999), translated as *The Story of Jane* (New York: Simon & Schuster, 2001). Catherine Cusset was a professor of eighteenth-century French literature at Yale from 1991 to 2002.

32. Louis-Philippe Dalembert, *Milwaukee Blues* (Paris: Sabine Wespieser, 2021); *Milwaukee Blues*, trans. Marjolijn de Jager (Tucson: Schaffner Press, 2023).

33. Russell Williams, "The Franco-American Novel," in *Contemporary Fiction in French*, eds. Anna-Louise Milne and Russell Williams (Cambridge and New York: Cambridge University Press, 2021), 91, 108.

34. In a very different context—a discussion of hipster coffee houses—the critic Kyle Chayka makes a similar point, calling this a "phenomenon of sameness"; see "The Tyranny of the Algorithm: Why Every Coffee Shop Looks the Same," *The Guardian* (16 January 2024): https://www.theguardian.com/news/2024/jan/16/the-tyranny-of-the-algorithm-why-every-coffee-shop-looks-the-same.

Index

Note: Page numbers in *italics* indicate illustrative material.

ABC (TV network), 66
active listening, 145, 198n73
Adair, Gilbert, 139
Adorno, Theodor, 13, 63
Agamben, Giorgio, 131–32, 137–38, 140
Albin Michel (publisher), 30
Allen, Esther, 57
All That Fall (Beckett), 68, 69–70
L'amant (Duras), 152
Les Amants d'Avignon (Triolet), 28
L'Âme d'une reine (Bates-Batcheller), 37
American Friends of France, 35, 36
American publishing. *See* publishing industry, U.S.
L'amour (Duras), 184n94
Anderson, Christopher, 65
Andrews, Chris, 196n40
L'anomalie (*The Anomaly*) (Le Tellier), 150–53, 156, 159
Appleton-Century-Crofts (publisher), 2, 107
Aragon, Louis, 27

Aristotle, *Metaphysics*, 137
Art et magie de la cuisine (TV series), 83–84, *84*, 85
An Attempt at Exhausting a Place in Paris (Perec), 148
L'avenir est dans les oeufs (Ionesco), 87
awards, literary, 25, 27, 38, 130, 151, 152, 156, 159, 168n6

Bachi, Salim, 200n1
Bachmann, Ingeborg, 62
Bakewell, Sarah, 171n31
Baldwin, James, *Giovanni's Room*, 172n39
Balzac, Honoré de, 6, 104; *Peau de chagrin*, 108
Barrès, Philippe, 32
Barthes, Roland, 8–9, 111, 125, 157
Bates-Batcheller, Tryphosa, 23; *L'Âme d'une reine*, 37; *La France au soleil et à l'ombre*, 37
Baudrillard, Jean, 16

Bazin, André, 181n40
Beach, Sylvia, 13
Beauvoir, Simone de, 14, 16; *L'Invitée*, 27
Beck, Simone, 84
Becker, Daniel Levin, 134
Beckett, Samuel: as innovator of theater of the absurd, 12; screenplay work, 62, 69–71, 73, 74–77; works: *All That Fall*, 68, 69–70; *. . . but the clouds . . .*, 75; *En attendant Godot*, 108; *Film*, 62, 70–71, 72, 73, 74–75, 76, 181n40; *Ghost Trio*, 75; *Nacht und Träume*, 75; *Not I*, 75; *Oh Joe*, 75; *Quad I* and *Quad II*, 75; *What Where*, 75
Bedient, Calvin, 140
Bello, Antoine, 200n1
Bellon, Loley, 92
Bellos, David, 130, 138–39, 193n5, 193n6
Benamou, Michel: *Mise en train: Première année de français* (with Ionesco), 108–11, 188n28; *Pour une nouvelle pédagogie du texte littéraire*, 109
Benda, Paul, 28
Benjamin, Walter, 122
Bens, Jacques, 131
Berkeley, Bishop, 70
Berlant, Lauren, 87–88
Berne Convention (1885), 6
Bespaloff, Rachel, *De l'Iliade*, 32
Bishop, Tom, 114, 121, 190–91n69, 192n98
Blanchot, Maurice, 26–27, 111
Blatt, Jessica, 144
Bober, Robert, 132, 142, 143, 146–47
Bogle, Donald, 88
Bon, Antoine, 32, 175n38
Borchardt, Georges, 1, 112
Bourdieu, Pierre, 12
Bourdon, Jérôme, 67
Bourgeade, Pierre, 3, 168n8
Bourget, Paul, 157
Bowen, Catherine Drinker, 176n66

Brancky, Anne, 97
Brée, Germaine, 108
Brentano, August, 33
Brentano's Books (publisher), 21, 24, 30, 32, 33–42, 48, 59
Breton, André, 17, 31, 32, 34, 44, 51
Brieux, Eugène, 34
Brodovitch, Alexey, 43
Brodsky, Joseph, 138
Brook, Peter, 92
Brouillon pour un dictionnaire des amantes (Wittig and Zeig), 173n53
Bruller, Jean (Vercors), 27–28
Buñuel, Luis, 74
Butor, Michel, 16, 192n96; *Mobile*, 127, 172n53
. . . but the clouds . . . (Beckett), 75
Buurma, Rachel Sagner, 127

Camarades de combat (Conrad), 37–38
camera, as protagonist, 70, 71, 72–73, 74, 96, 97
La Caméra explore le temps (TV series), 67
Camus, Albert, 26; *Le malentendu*, 108; *The Stranger*, 10
Canoës (Kerangal), 127
La cantatrice chauve (Ionesco), 78, 110, 188n30
Cantier, Jacques, 26, 27
Capote, Truman, *In Cold Blood*, 157
Carlu, Jean, 41
Carroll, Jordan S., 10
Carver, Raymond, 170n29
Casanova, Pascale, 4, 168n11
Cassidy, Marsha, 85
CBS (TV network), 65, 66
Céline, Louis-Ferdinand, 16, 27
censorship, 26
Cestre, Charles, 30
Les Chaises (Ionesco), 67, 77
Chanson Douce (*The Perfect Nanny*) (Slimani), 159–61

Chateaubriand, François-René de, *Voyage en Amérique*, 6
Chayka, Kyle, 202n34
Child, Julia, 84–85
Les choses (Perec), 130, 133, 193n6
Cixous, Hélène, 16
Claridge, Laura, 10
Cloonan, William, *Frères ennemis*, 7
Coates, Ta-Nehisi, *Between the World and Me*, 6
Le Coeur sur la Main/The Heart on the Sleeve (Dorval), 41
La colère (Ionesco), 79–81, *81*
colleges and universities, as novel setting, 127, 162–63
college textbook publishing: combined linguistic and literary pedagogies, as outmoded, 126–27; combined linguistic and literary pedagogies, Benamou and Ionesco collaboration, 108–11, 188n28; combined linguistic and literary pedagogies, Robbe-Grillet and Lenard collaboration, 117–23; foreign language pedagogy, Lenard as expert, 106, *107*; and New Novel pedagogy, 114–16; rapid growth of, 105; teaching editions of French novels, 107–8, 113–14
Combray (Proust), 108
commercialism: and international success of French literature, 123, 127, 151–52, 158–59, 164; intersection with experimentalism, overview, 12–14; and television, 63–64, 67, 82, 97
Conrad, Florence, 23–24; *Camarades de combat*, 37–38
Consuelo de Saint Exupéry. *See* Saint Exupéry, Consuelo de
Conversions (Mathews), 133
cooking show genre, 83–85
Cossu-Beaumont, Laurence, 10
Cottenet, Cécile, 10

Coverdale, Linda, 202n25
Crespin, Vitalis, 30, 32
Crèvecoeur, J. Hector St. John de, *Letters from an American Farmer*, 6
La Croix païenne: contes d'Irlande (Mackay), 38
Cusset, Catherine: *L'autre qu'on adorait*, 163; *Le problème avec Jane*, 163
Cusset, François, 8–9, 102, 163, 170n24, 170n25

Dalembert, Louis-Philippe, 192n96; *Milwaukee Blues*, 127, 163
Damrosch, David, 9, 170n25
Debû-Bridel, Jacques, 28
Dekobra, Maurice, 32
Deleuze, Gilles, 71, 72
Dell (publisher), 107, 108
Démocratie en Amérique (Tocqueville), 6
Denoël (publisher), 26, 27, 30
Derrida, Jacques, 8–9, 170n24
Désert (Le Clézio), 126
Destination America (documentary film), 146
Dib, Mohammed, *L.A. Trip*, 172n53
Dicker, Joël, *La Vérité sur l'Affaire Harry Quebert (The Truth About the Harry Quebert Affair)*, 156–59
Dick Powell Show (TV series), 65, 66
Dick Powell's Zane Grey Theatre (TV series), 66
Dis-moi pour qui j'existe? (Waberi), 127, 163
La disparition (Perec), 12, 117, 131, 133, 139, 190n54, 199n78
La disparition de Jim Sullivan (Viel), 161–63
Djebar, Assia, 192n96; *Le roman maghrébin francophone entre les langues, entre les cultures*, 172–73n53
Djinn: Un trou rouge entre les pavés disjoints (Robbe-Grillet), 105, 122–26

domestic life, 80–81, 82, 85–86, 98–99
d'Oncin, Paule, *Plympton House*, 60–61
Dorval, Marcelle, *Le Coeur sur la Main/ The Heart on the Sleeve*, 41
Dos Passos, John, 6
Dreiser, Theodore, *An American Tragedy*, 157
Drieu la Rochelle, Pierre, 26
Duchamp, Marcel, 34, 44
Dumas, Alexandre, 6
Duras, Marguerite: and French television culture, 68; literary prizes, 27, 152; as New Novelist, 103; screenplay work, 62, 90–100; **works**: *L'amant*, 152; *L'amour*, 184n94; *La Femme du Gange*, 184n94; *Hiroshima mon amour*, 2, 91; *Les impudents*, 27; *India Song*, 184n94; *Moderato Cantabile*, 2; *Sans merveille*, 184n100; *Le square*, 2, 108; *Ten-Thirty on a Summer Night*, 2; *Le Vice-Consul*, 184n94. See also *The Ravishing of Lol Stein*

École des Beaux-Arts, Paris, 43
Éditions de la Maison Française (publisher), 30, 32, 40, 176n67
Éditions de Minuit (publisher), 27–28, 103, 105, 161
Éditions Didier (publisher), 30, 32
Éditions du Sorbier (publisher), 144
Edwards, Blake, 65
Einstein-Auproux, Nina, 53
Ellis Island (*Récits d'Ellis Island*) (Perec): content overview, 142–43; interview dynamics, 145–46; Mathews's translation of, 134, 141–42, 144, 145–46, 150; potentiality in, 142, 145, 146–47, 149; print editions, 144–45; research and field work for, 130, 147–49
Elsky, Julia, 77, 188n30
Emmerich, Karen, 194n12
Emre, Merve, 12–13, 42, 171–72n39
En attendant Godot (Beckett), 108

Ernaux, Annie, *La place*, 126
Ernst, Max, 44
Evergreen Review (journal), 64–65
Evergreen Theater, Inc., 64–65. See also screenplays
existentialism, 10, 171n31

fait divers (news story) genre, 157, 159
Falk, Peter, 66
Faulkner, William, 6
La Femme du Gange (Duras), 184n94
53 Days (Perec), 152, 193n2
Film (Beckett), 62, 70–71, 72, 73, 74–75, 76, 181n40
Flaubert, Gustave, 125
Floyd, George, 163
La folle de Chaillot (Giraudoux), 108
foreign language pedagogy: Benamou and Ionesco collaboration, 108–11, 188n28; Lenard as expert, 106, *107*; outmoded nature of literature combined with, 126–27; Robbe-Grillet and Lenard collaboration, 117–23
Foucault, Michel, 9, 170n23
Four Star Playhouse (TV series), 65
Four Star Productions (TV production company), 65
France: German occupation of, 26, 35–40, 43; television in, 63–64, 67–68, 83–84. See also publishing industry, French
France, été 1940 (Morize), 174n28
La France au soleil et à l'ombre (Bates-Batcheller), 37
France de ce monde (Lanux), 174n28
La France que j'aime (Mackay), 39
Franco-American cultural exchange, overview, 5–10
Frank's Return (Robbe-Grillet), 70, 71–73, 74
The French Chef (TV series), 85
French global disciplinary approach, 8

French literary experimentalist movements, 11–12
French publishing. *See* publishing industry, French
French theory, 8–9, 102, 170n24
Frick, Grace, 173n53
Fry, Varian, 22, 56–57, 59

Gallimard (publisher), 21, 26, 27, 51, 54, 55, 103
Galvin, Rachel, 139, 140
La garde montante (Lebel and Perrier), 40–41
Gardner, Colin, 73, 181n44
Gaulle, Charles de, 25, 68
gaze, the: male, 56, 86; and self-perception, 70–71, 72–74; and spectatorship, 73–74, 97, 98; watching without seeing, 94–97
gender: and domestic life, 85–87; masculine literary tradition, 4, 25, 31, 52–53; and racist stereotypes, 87–88. *See also* women writers
Genet, Jean, 62, 63
Germany: occupation of France, 26, 35–40, 43; television in, 75
Gershwin, George, 6
Ghost Trio (Beckett), 75
Gide, André, 31
Giovanni's Room (Baldwin), 172n39
Giraudoux, Jean, *La folle de Chaillot*, 108
Glass, Loren, 10, 64, 102, 114
Godard, Jean-Luc, 67
Les gommes (Robbe-Grillet), 103, 112, 113
Grasset (publisher), 26
Grey, Zane, 66
Groffsky, Maxine, 136
Grove Press (publisher): Evergreen Theater, Inc., 64–65 (*see also* screenplays); scholarship on, 10; translation publications, 1, 2, 112–14, 126, 130, 168n6, 193n6
Guérin, Jeanyves, 124

"The Hard-Boiled Egg" (Ionesco), 78, 82–83, 85, 86–89
Hardouin, Maria le, 27
Harper and Row (publisher), 106
Harrison, Olivia, 161
Heffernan, Laura, 127
Helmle, Eugen, 139
Hench, John, 24, 28, 29, 39–40, 59, 174n31
Herren, Graley, 73
Hidalgo, Miguel, 44, 177n78
Higgins, Lynn, 69
Higonnet, Margaret, 38
Hiroshima mon amour (Duras), 2, 91
Hitchcock, Alfred, 65
Holt, Rinehart and Winston (publisher), 103
Howard, Richard, 193n6
Hughes, Margaret, 24; *Les lauriers sont coupés*, 35–36, 40
Hugo, Victor, 157; *Poésies choisies*, 34
Hunter, Adriana, 151
Huyssen, Andreas, 13, 152, 180n26

Les impudents (Duras), 27
In Cold Blood (Capote), 157
India Song (Duras), 184n94
intimate potentialities, 131–32, 137, 138–41, 142, 145, 146–47, 149
invisible cinema, 68
L'Invitée (Beauvoir), 27
Ionesco, Eugène: college textbook collaborations, 108–11; as innovator of theater of the absurd, 12; screenplay work, 62, 77–83, 85, 86–89; **works**: *L'avenir est dans les oeufs*, 87; *La cantatrice chauve*, 78, 110, 188n30; *Les Chaises*, 67, 77; *La colère*, 79–81, 81; "The Hard-Boiled Egg," 78, 82–83, 85, 86–89; *La leçon*, 110; *Mise en train: Première année de français* (with Benamou), 108–11, 188n28; *Rhinocéros*, 77, 78

J'ai faim! . . . Journal d'un Français en France depuis l'armistice (Le François), 36
La jalousie (Robbe-Grillet), 103, 112, 114, 124
James, Alison, 139, 140, 197n46
Jarlot, Gérard, 184n100
Jay, Martin, 97
Jeannelle, Jean-Louis, 68
Jefferson, Thomas, 5
Je marche sous un ciel de traîne (Kerangal), 127
Jong, Erica, *Fear of Flying*, 172n39
Jordan, Fred, 63
Journal of Small Things (Mackay), 38–39
Joyce, James, 13

Kaplan, Alice, 10
Keaton, Buster, 70
Kerangal, Maylis de: *Canoës*, 127; *Je marche sous un ciel de traîne*, 127
Kérillis, Henri de, 32
Kershaw, Angela, 25
Kincheloe, Joe, 145
Knopf (publisher), 10, 147, 193n6
Knopf, Blanche, 10
Koyré, Alexandre, 32

Lacan, Jacques, 1, 8–9
Lafayette, Marquis de, 5
Lalou, Étienne, 183n90
Lane, Helen, 193n6
Langeais, Catherine, 83–84, 85
L'anglais sans peine (*English Without Toil*), 110
language learning. *See* foreign language pedagogy
language translation. *See* translation
Lanux, Pierre de, *France de ce monde*, 174n28
Last Year at Marienbad (Robbe-Grillet), 66, 69, 72, 78, 113, 181n40
L.A. Trip (Dib), 172n53

Les lauriers sont coupés (Hughes), 35–36, 40
L'autre qu'on adorait (Cusset), 163
Lazareff, Pierre, 32, 34
Leak, Andrew, 193n6
Lebel, Claude, *La garde montante* (with Perrier), 40–41
Le Clézio, J. M. G., *Désert*, 126
La leçon (Ionesco), 110
Le François, Louis, *J'ai faim! . . . Journal d'un Français en France depuis l'armistice*, 36
Le Lionnais, François, 12, 131
Lenard, Yvone: career success, 106–7; collaboration with Robbe-Grillet, 103, 116–23, 126 (see also *Le rendez-vous*); *Parole et pensée*, 106, 107, 109
Lescure, Pierre de, 27–28
Le Tellier, Hervé, 132, 139; *L'anomalie* (*The Anomaly*), 150–53, 156, 159
Letters from an American Farmer (Crèvecoeur), 6
Lettres d'Amérique (Sarraute), 173n53
Lévi-Strauss, Claude, 31
Life: A User's Manual (*La vie mode d'emploi*) (Perec), 126, 129–30, 134, 135, 193n6
"Lift Machinery" (Perec), 134
Lindon, Jérôme, 103, 115
Lish, Gordon, 170n29
listening practices, 145, 198n73
The Little Prince (Saint Exupéry), 52, 54, 57, 178n107
London, One November (Mackay), 38
Losey, Joseph, 92
loss, and archival discovery, 100–101
Loyer, Emmanuelle, 32, 176n67
Lynes, Carlos Jr., 108
Lyotard, Jean-François, 9

Mabanckou, Alain, 192n96
Mackay, Helen, 24, 38–39; *La Croix païenne: contes d'Irlande*, 38; *La*

France que j'aime, 39; *Journal of Small Things*, 38–39; *London, One November*, 38; *Patte Blanche*, 38; *Sainte terre de France*, 39, 41
Macmillan (publisher), 107, 108
Magny, Claude-Edmonde, *L'Âge du roman américain*, 7
Le malentendu (Camus), 108
Malle, Louis, 67
Margolies, Joseph, 40
Maritain, Jacques, 17, 31, 32
Mascolo, Dionys, 94
Mathews, Harry: friendship with Perec, 136–37, 138–41; on Perec's legacy, 149–50; translation collaboration with Perec, overview, 133–34; translation collaboration with Perec, intimate potentialities, 137, 138–41; translation collaboration with Perec, wordplay, 134–36; **works**: *Conversions*, 133; *The Orchard*, 197n60; *The Sinking of the Odradek Stadium*, 134; *Tlooth*, 134–35
Mathy, Jean-Philippe, 17
Maupassant, Guy de, 157
Mauriac, François, *Thérèse Desqueyroux*, 108
Maurois, André, 17, 31, 32, 34
McCarren, Felicia, 200n1
McDonald, Christie, 8
McGrath, Laura, 10
McGurl, Mark, 10, 104, 127, 192n96
Melville, Herman, "Bartleby, the Scrivener", 137–38, 196n41
Mémoires de la rose (Consuelo de Saint Exupéry), 52
Mendès, Pierre, 32
Message aux Français (Romains), 174n28
Mille regrets (Triolet), 27
Milligan, Jennifer, 25
Milosz, Czeslaw, 138
Milwaukee Blues (Dalembert), 127, 163
Le miroir qui revient (Robbe-Grillet), 112
Mise en train: Première année de français (Benamou and Ionesco), 108–11, 188n28
Mitrani, Michel, 70, 184n100
Mobile (Butor), 127, 172n53
Moderato Cantabile (Duras), 2
Modern Language Association, 109, 110
Molho, Isaac, 30, 32
Molière, *Tartuffe*, 108
Monk, Ian, 139
Monnier, Adrienne, 13
Morand, Paul, 16
Morize, André, *France, été 1940*, 174n28
Morrissette, Bruce, 111–13
Mostel, Zero, 181n49
Moukhine, Tatiana, 92
Moura, Jean-Marc, 200n1

Nacht und Träume (Beckett), 75
Nadeau, Maurice, 133
NBC (TV network), 66
Némirovsky, Irène, 24
Nettelbeck, Colin, 31
New Directions (publisher), 144
New Novel (*nouveau roman*) movement: and Americanization, 14; decline of, 128, 192n98; emergence and mission, 12, 103–4; and language-learning manuals, 103, 104; and pedagogy, 114–16; and television industry, 69; and visual perception, 97
New Press (publisher), 144, 202n25
news story (*fait divers*) genre, 157, 159
New Wave (*nouvelle vague*) movement, 67, 69, 70, 74
New York City: descriptions of, 4, 16–17; French exiles in, 31–32; popularity of French literature in, 29–30
New York publishing. See publishing industry, U.S.
New York Times (newspaper), 30
Nicholas, Nancy, 147–48
Nishikawa, Kinohi, 10
Nizan, Paul, 25

Norton Anthology of English Literature, 107

Not I (Schneider play and Beckett screenplay), 75

Office of War Information (OWI), 40–41
Oh Joe (Beckett), 75
Oliver, Raymond, 83–84
Ollivier, Albert, 67
Oppède (Consuelo de Saint Exupéry): critical reception, 55–56; editions, 21–22, 48, 53–55, 59; Fry's copy of and response to, 22, 23, 56–57, 58, 59; images, 48, 49, 50, 55; plot overview, 44–47; setting, 43–44; women centered in, 48, 51, 52, 53
Oppède group, 43–44, 52–53
The Orchard (Mathews), 197n60
ORTF *(Office de Radiodiffusion-Télévision française)*, 64
Other Press (publisher), 151
Oulipo group: and combined linguistic and literary pedagogies, 117; establishment and mission, 11–12, 131, 190n54; potentiality in, 138, 140, 146; translation within constraints of, 139
Overseas Editions, Inc., 29

Pagès, Jean, 38
Pantheon Press (publisher), 31
Paraf, Yvonne (Mme Desvignes), 28
Parole et pensée (Lenard), 106, *107*, 109
La part du diable (Rougemont), 34
Patte Blanche (Mackay), 38
Paulhan, Jean, 28
PBS (TV network), 146
Peau de chagrin (Balzac), 108
pedagogy. *See* college textbook publishing
Peignot, Charles, 60
Penguin (publisher), 156
perception and self-perception, 70–74, 96, 97

Perec, Georges: death of, 141; friendship with Mathews, 136–37, 138–41; influence on Le Tellier, 152; legacy of, 149–50, 153; mentioned, 14; as Oulipo member, 11; translation collaboration with Mathews, overview, 133–34; translation collaboration with Mathews, intimate potentialities, 137, 138–41; translation collaboration with Mathews, wordplay, 134–36; **works**: *An Attempt at Exhausting a Place in Paris*, 148; *Les choses*, 130, 133, 193n6; *La disparition*, 12, 117, 131, 133, 139, 190n54, 199n78; *53 Days*, 152, 193n2; "Lift Machinery," 134; "Rorschash," 134; "Still Life/Style Leaf," 134, 137; "Ulcérations," 152, 199–200n90; *La vie mode d'emploi (Life: A User's Manual)*, 126, 129–30, 134, 135, 193n6; *W ou le souvenir d'enfance*, 130, 142, 199n78
The Perfect Nanny (Chanson Douce) (Slimani), 159–61
Perrier, Françoise, *La garde montante* (with Lebel), 40–41
Perse, Saint-John, 16, 32
Pétain, Maréchal, 37–38
phenomenology, 97
Piatier, Jacqueline, 3, 124
Pinget, Robert, 67–68, 103, 115
Pinter, Harold, 62
La place (Ernaux), 126
Plon (publisher), 27, 30
Plympton House (d'Oncin), 60–61
Poésies choisies (Hugo), 34
P.O.L. (publisher), 144
Polan, Dana, 84
postmodernism, 13, 97, 180n26
poststructuralism, 9
potentiality, 131–32, 137–41, 142, 145, 146–47, 149, 152–53
Pound, Ezra, 13
Pour une nouvelle pédagogie du texte littéraire (Benamou), 109

Powell, Dick, 65–66
Le premier accroc coûte deux cent francs (Triolet), 25, 28
prizes, literary, 25, 27, 38, 130, 151, 152, 156, 159, 168n6
Le problème avec Jane (Cusset), 163
Projet pour une révolution à New York (Robbe-Grillet), 3–4, 15, 168nn9–10
Proust, Marcel, *Combray*, 108
public-private boundaries, 73–75, 80–81, 98–99
publishing industry, French: center of, shifted from France to New York, 30–31; challenges of wartime, 22–23, 26–28; misogyny in, 25–27. See also *specific publishers*
publishing industry, U.S.: cross-cultural mediation in, 35–42, 59; French literary experimentation fostered in, 33; New York as replacement for French publishing, 30–31; wartime mission, 28–29, 39–40, 41. See also college textbook publishing; *specific publishers*

Quad I and *Quad II* (Beckett), 75
Quebec, French book market in, 174n29
Queneau, Raymond, 131

radical listening, 145, 198n73
Rainey, Lawrence, 13
Ramsay, Raylene, 192n98
Random House (publisher), 21, 54, 56, 59
The Ravishing of Lol Stein (Duras): critical reception, 1, 89–90; manuscript chronology, 92–94; plot overview, 91–92; *Prix de Mai* for, 2, 168n6; screenplay lost script, 99–100; screenplay-novel comparative analysis, 94–99; screenplay origins, 62, 90, 91
Rebatet, Lucien, 27
Récits d'Ellis Island. See *Ellis Island*

Rémy-Labaudt, Yliane, 53
Le rendez-vous (Robbe-Grillet and Lenard): overview, 102–3, 104–5; drafting process, 118–21; objective, 117; plot overview, 118; precedent for, 107–11; rendezvous in, 121–22; reprinted as *Djinn*, 105, 122–26
La reprise (Robbe-Grillet), 126
Resnais, Alain, 66, 69–70, 78, 90–91
Rhinocéros (Ionesco), 77, 78
Rimbaud, Arthur, *Oeuvres complètes*, 34
Robbe-Grillet, Alain: and Americanization, 14; college textbook collaborations, 102–3, 116–23; and French television culture, 68; as New Novel leader, 12, 103–4; pedagogical interests, 114–16; scholarship on, 111–12, 125; screenplay work, 62, 69, 71–73, 74, 113; **works**: *Djinn: Un trou rouge entre les pavés disjoints*, 105, 122–26; *Frank's Return*, 70, 71–73, 74; *Les gommes*, 103, 112, 113; *La jalousie*, 103, 112, 114, 124; *Last Year at Marienbad*, 66, 69, 72, 78, 113, 181n40; *Le miroir qui revient*, 112; *Pour un nouveau roman*, 104; *Projet pour une révolution à New York*, 3–4, 15, 168nn9–10; *La reprise*, 126; *Romanesques*, 126; *Souvenirs du triangle d'or*, 124; *Topologie d'une cité fantôme*, 124; *Le voyeur*, 97, 103, 112, 113–14
Rolin, Dominique, 27
Rollinat, Madeleine, 53
Romains, Jules, *Message aux Français*, 174n28
Romanesques (Robbe-Grillet), 126
Le roman maghrébin francophone entre les langues, entre les cultures (Djebar), 172–73n53
Roosevelt, Eleanor, 37
Roosevelt, Franklin D., 29, 37
"Rorschash" (Perec), 134

Ross, Kristin, 14–15
Rosset, Barney: mentioned, 1, 10, 91; television projects, 62, 63, 64–65, 75, 91; translation projects, 112–13, 126
Rougemont, Denis de, 31, 32; *La part du diable*, 34
Rourke, Constance, 176n66
RTF (*Radiodiffusion-Télévision française*), 64, 67, 82, 83–84
Russ, Joanna, 23, 55–56, 57–59

Sainte terre de France (Mackay), 39, 41
Saint Exupéry, Antoine de, 31, 32, 39, 51; *The Little Prince*, 52, 54, 57, 178n107
Saint Exupéry, Consuelo de: artistic projects, 51; background, 23; relationship with Antoine, 51, 52; wartime refuge, 43–44; works: *Mémoires de la rose*, 52. See also *Oppède*
Sanger, Margaret: *What Every Boy and Girl Should Know*, 34; *Woman and the New Race*, 34
Sans merveille (Duras), 184n100
Sapiro, Gisèle, 6, 9–10, 158–59
Sarraute, Nathalie, 16, 103; *Lettres d'Amérique*, 173n53
Sartre, Jean-Paul, 16, 104
Schiffrin, Jacques, 31
Schlanger, Judith, 90, 100
Schneider, Alan, 69; *Not I*, 75
Schoenfeld, Eric, 188n32
screenplays: gaze and perception in, 70–75, 94–95, 96, 97; novels originating as, 62, 90, 91, 94–99; social critique in, 78–83, 85, 86–89, 98–99
Seaver, Richard, 1, 10, 78, 182n69
Seem, Mark, 170n23
self-perception and perception, 70–74, 96, 97
Seligmann, Kurt, 34
Senghor, Léopold Sédar, 16
Serreau, Geneviève, 133
Serres, Adrienne, 53

Sévigné, Marie de Rabutin-Chantal, marquise de, *Lettres*, 26
Shaw, George Bernard, 34
Simenon, Georges, 16
Simon, Claude, 103, 115
The Sinking of the Odradek Stadium (Mathews), 134
Sinykin, Dan, 10, 159, 201n15
Situationist movement, 97
Slimani, Leïla, *Chanson Douce* (*The Perfect Nanny*), 159–61
Souvenirs du triangle d'or (Robbe-Grillet), 124
spectatorship, 73–74, 97, 98
Spelling, Aaron, 65
Spigel, Lynn, 66, 75
Spivak, Gayatri, 140
Le square (Duras), 2, 108
Steinbeck, John, *The Moon Is Down*, 28
Steinberg, Saul, 129
"Still Life/Style Leaf" (Perec), 134, 137
The Stranger (Camus), 10
Suleiman, Susan Rubin, 8, 25, 97, 125, 168n10
Sullivan, Hannah, 11
Surrealism, 74, 84, 97

Tati, Jacques, 14
television industry: avant-garde style emulated in, 66–67, 68; camera as protagonist, 70, 71, 72–73, 74, 96, 97; and commercialism, 63–64, 67, 82, 97; cooking show genre, 83–85; and domestic life, 80–81, 82, 85–86, 98–99; in France, 63–64, 67–68, 83–84; telefilm series genre, 65–66. See also screenplays
Tenger, Robert, 24, 34, 38, 39–42, 53–54, 59
Ten-Thirty on a Summer Night (Duras), 2
textbooks. *See* college textbook publishing
Thackway, Melissa, 183–84n92
theater of the absurd, overview, 12
The Moon Is Down (Steinbeck), 28

Thérèse Desqueyroux (Mauriac), 108
Thomas, Edith, 25, 27; *Contes d'Auxois*, 28
Tlooth (Mathews), 134–35
Tocqueville, Alexis de, *Démocratie en Amérique*, 6
Topologie d'une cité fantôme (Robbe-Grillet), 124
Torre, Mónica de la, 144
Tran Huy, Minh, 157
translation: "born translated" phenomenon, 7, 63; dishonest, 54–55, 59; increased demand for, 6; potentialities of, 137–41, 152–53; wordplay, 134–36. See also foreign language pedagogy
Triolet, Elsa: *Les Amants d'Avignon*, 28; *Le Cheval blanc*, 27; *Mille regrets*, 27; *Le premier accroc coûte deux cent francs*, 25, 28
Truffaut, François, 67
The Truth About the Harry Quebert Affair (La Vérité sur l'Affaire Harry Quebert) (Dicker), 156–59
Turner, Patricia, 87

"Ulcérations" (Perec), 152, 199–200n90
Un chien andalou (short film), 74
universities and colleges, as novel setting, 127, 162–63. See also college textbook publishing
U.S. publishing. See publishing industry, U.S.

Valet, Henriette, 25
Vallier, Jean, 92
Vangelisti, Paul, 172n53
Vercors (Jean Bruller), 27–28
La Vérité sur l'Affaire Harry Quebert (The Truth About the Harry Quebert Affair) (Dicker), 156–59
Verne, Jules, 6
Le Vice-Consul (Duras), 184n94
Victor, Serge, 44

Viel, Tanguy: *The Absolute Perfection of Crime*, 201–2n25; *Beyond Suspicion*, 201–2n25; *La disparition de Jim Sullivan*, 161–63
La vie mode d'emploi (*Life: A User's Manual*) (Perec), 126, 129–30, 134, 135, 193n6
Villa-Ignacio, Teresa, 161
violence: and perception, 72–73, 74; race-based, 163
Violet, Jeanne, 53
Voyage en Amérique (Chateaubriand), 6
Le voyeur (Robbe-Grillet), 97, 103, 112, 113–14

Waberi, Abdourahman A., 192n96, 200n11; *Dis-moi pour qui j'existe?*, 127, 163
Walkowitz, Rebecca, 7, 63
Ware, John, 147–48
What Where (Beckett), 75
Williams, Russell, 163–64
Wittig, Monique, *Brouillon pour un dictionnaire des amantes* (with Zeig), 173n53
women: and domestic life, 85–87; racist stereotypes of black, 87–88
women writers: characteristics of wartime, 23–24; as cross-cultural mediators, 35–39, 40, 41–42, 47–48, 59; suppression of, 23, 25–27, 55–59; underground efforts, 28. See also *specific writers*
Woodford, Charles, 106
Woods, Katherine, 30, 54, 174n28
W ou le souvenir d'enfance (Perec), 130, 142, 199n78
W. W. Norton (publisher), 29

Yourcenar, Marguerite, 173n53

Zehrfuss, Bernard, 44
Zeig, Sande, *Brouillon pour un dictionnaire des amantes* (with Wittig), 173n53

Francisco E. Robles, *Coalition Literature: Aesthetics on the Move in Midcentury US Multiethnic Writing*

Myka Tucker-Abramson, *Cartographies of Empire: The Road Novel and American Hegemony*

Michael Shane Boyle, *The Arts of Logistics: Artistic Production in Supply Chain Capitalism*

Adam Kelly, *New Sincerity: American Fiction in the Neoliberal Age*

Adrienne Brown, *The Residential Is Racial: A Perceptual History of Mass Homeownership*

Patrick Whitmarsh, *Writing Our Extinction: Anthropocene Fiction and Vertical Science*

Rebecca B. Clark, *American Graphic: Disgust and Data in Contemporary Literature*

Palmer Rampell, *Genres of Privacy in Postwar America*

Joseph Darda, *The Strange Career of Racial Liberalism*

Jordan S. Carroll, *Reading the Obscene: Transgressive Editors and the Class Politics of US Literature*

Michael Dango, *Crisis Style: The Aesthetics of Repair*

Mary Esteve, *Incremental Realism: Postwar American Fiction, Happiness, and Welfare-State Liberalism*

Dorothy J. Hale, *The Novel and the New Ethics*

Christine Hong, *A Violent Peace: Race, U.S. Militarism, and Cultures of Democratization in Cold War Asia and the Pacific*

Sarah Brouillette, *UNESCO and the Fate of the Literary*

Sophie Seita, *Provisional Avant-Gardes: Little Magazine Communities from Dada to Digital*

Guy Davidson, *Categorically Famous: Literary Celebrity and Sexual Liberation in 1960s America*

Joseph Jonghyun Jeon, *Vicious Circuits: Korea's IMF Cinema and the End of the American Century*

Lytle Shaw, *Narrowcast: Poetry and Audio Research*

Stephen Schryer, *Maximum Feasible Participation: American Literature and the War on Poverty*

Margaret Ronda, *Remainders: American Poetry at Nature's End*

Jasper Bernes, *The Work of Art in the Age of Deindustrialization*

Annie McClanahan, *Dead Pledges: Debt, Crisis, and Twenty-First-Century Culture*

Amy Hungerford, *Making Literature Now*

J. D. Connor, *The Studios After the Studios: Neoclassical Hollywood (1970–2010)*

Michael Trask, *Camp Sites: Sex, Politics, and Academic Style in Postwar America*

Loren Glass, *Counterculture Colophon: Grove Press, the* Evergreen Review, *and the Incorporation of the Avant-Garde*

Michael Szalay, *Hip Figures: A Literary History of the Democratic Party*

Jared Gardner, *Projections: Comics and the History of Twenty-First-Century Storytelling*

For a complete listing of titles in this series, visit the Stanford University Press website, www.sup.org.

The authorized representative in the EU for product safety and compliance is:
Mare Nostrum Group
B.V Doelen 72
4831 GR Breda
The Netherlands

www.ingramcontent.com/pod-product-compliance
Lightning Source LLC
Chambersburg PA
CBHW022015220426
43663CB00007B/1091